Praise for *Out from the Shadow of Men*

"Some books are important. Some books you can't put down. Out from the Shadow of Men is both. Laila El-Sissi has given us a groundbreaking memoir of two young sisters growing up in Egypt whose courage, devotion to each other, and struggle for their own autonomous lives will make you fall in love with them and remember their story forever."

—Ellen Bass, author of *The Courage to Heal*

"Out from the Shadow of Men is a powerful story of a courageous young Egyptian girl who defies all odds of culture, religion, and power to change her destiny. Laila El-Sissi's story is captivating and meaningful, and her writing is superb."

—Geraldine Solon, best-selling author of Love Letters

"Out from the Shadow of Men takes readers into the mind and heart of a young woman battling against the odds within an oppressive family to gain her freedom and live the life of her dreams. Laila El-Sissi has given us a memoir written in a voice that's unforgettable: it is the voice of a girl discovering her womanhood as she struggles to understand the conflict between her desires and the rules of her environment."

—David Paul, coauthor, Souls in the Hands of a Tender God

"From the first time that Laila began to read her story to us at a Fremont-area writers' open-mic night in 2013, I thought immediately that what I was hearing were the polished words of a published writer. Only when she was finished reading did we find out that this was her first book. Wow! Laila has the talent, drive, desire, and capability to go a long way in the publishing world. Her story captivated all of us that evening and should do the same to many readers worldwide."

— Robert A. Garfinkle, President, California Writers Club

"This poignant memoir chronicles one young woman's agonizing struggle to reconcile her family's wishes, the values of her patriarchal culture, and the tenets of Islam with her burgeoning desire for personal freedom. The author's journey highlights the many ways in which self-realization commands a steep price but ultimately is a triumph worth fighting for."

—Sidney Mobell, Honored by the Smithsonian Institute, National Museum   ıral History

In powerful details, Laila addresses the conflict between deeply rooted culture, and the archaic understanding of religion against modernity. This conflict is the culprit of the present turmoil in the Middle East.

Out from the Shadow of Men addresses women's treatment not only in Egypt, but in many parts of the world.

The book is a page turner. I recommend this book to teenagers and young adults. It will open their eyes to the mistreatment of women in different parts of the world.

Amal Mulaomerovic, Milpitas High School, California

OUT FROM THE SHADOW OF MEN

BY

LAILA EL-SISSI

Dearest ████ with much Love and Gratitude Laila Love

5-11-15

OUT FROM THE SHADOW OF MEN

ISBN: 978-0-9903354-1-2 (paperback)
ISBN: 978-0-9903354-2-9 (hardback)
ISBN: 978-0-9903354-3-6 (digital)

Cover Designer: Laila El-Sissi & H.A.
Editor: Annie Tucker
Interior Formatting: Debbi Stocco

Published by: Laila R El-Sissi

I dedicate this book to Rawyia, my sister, without whom I would not be where I am today; to my brother, Hady, for his support and love; and to my mother, who taught me the true meaning of love.

ACKNOWLEDGEMENT

I would like to thank Vicky Santos for putting me on the first step of writing, Ellen Bass for providing the safe environment I needed to write my memoir, Anis Mulaomerovic my coworker for his unending help and patience, and all my friends for their assistance and backing. And last but not least, thank you to my sons Omar and Shareef for their love, support, and encouragement.

CONTENTS

Part 1: *Childhood*

Part II: *Beautiful Brides*

Part III: *Promises*

PART IV: *Safe Shelter*

Part V: *New Beginnings*

Hymn to Isis
the Egyptian Goddess

For I am the first and the last
I am the venerated and the despised
I am the prostitute and the saint
I am the wife and the virgin
I am the mother and the daughter
I am the arms of my mother
I am barren and my children are many
I am the married woman and the spinster
I am the woman who gives birth and she
who never procreated
I am the consolation for the pain of birth
I am the wife and the husband
And it was my man who created me
I am the mother of my father
I am the sister of my husband
And he is my rejected son
Always respect me
For I am the shameful and the magnificent one

- 3RD OR 4TH CENTURY BCE, DISCOVERED
IN NAG HAMMADI, EGYPT

PART 1: CHILDHOOD

CHAPTER 1

Mama looked subdued when she walked out of her bedroom. She struggled to maintain the lifeless smile she adopted after arguing with our father. Papa must have added a new rule to his forbidden list. We children counted on Mama to bend the rules, and she never failed our expectations. Mama owned the throne of our hearts.

Later that morning, Mama took us to San Stefano beach—me; my older sister, Rawyia; and my younger siblings, Hala, Hady, and Samir. Summertime had begun. It was June 1962, I was fifteen, and I had just started my vacation.

A blazing disk overhead scorched the golden sand and radiated its warmth deep beneath the cold waters. Towering white puffs patterned a clear blue sky, the air so gentle, the leaves on the trees barely moved. Lazy morning waves speckled the mass of liquid sapphire. Seaweed traced the shoreline, waiting for our feet to crush it while we covered our noses. I smiled. This was a wondrous day, and nothing would spoil my joy.

Vacationers flocked to Alexandria beaches at the end of the

school year to escape the desert heat. Egyptians, as well as tourists from neighboring countries, called Alexandria the Bride of the Mediterranean Sea. They descended upon our beaches, covering the sand with a mosaic of colorful parasols. Looking at Alexandria from the sea at night, one could see the city lights, a strand of pearls dazzling our "bride's" décolletage. The city of Alexandria came alive in the beautiful summer.

Today, my thirteen-year-old brother, Hady, helped the beach guard anchor our parasol close to the shore. The young man proceeded with a smile that extended from east to west, brightening his sunburned face. He knew Mama would tip him generously.

"Not so close to the water," Mama demanded as he set up the parasol.

This puzzled me, since our mother preferred to stay close to the wet sand. She said the sea foaming around her ankles soothed her aching legs. Mama believed the salty water had magical curative power and that the gentle folding of the waves at her feet relaxed her. She said it healed her from the inside out. Yet today, she motioned us to a spot farther away from the water.

On the beach, vendors carried bamboo baskets filled with the daily catch of clams known to locals as *om el khouloul*. Alexandrians found them barnacled in clumps on rocks or holding on to green algae. Those clams were my mother's favorite snack. She ate them with a squeeze of lime. But today, she declined the vendor's repeated attempt to get her to buy the clams. Something was wrong.

A feeling of alarm crept up inside me. I brushed it off. I was excited to be at the beach. I refused to let Mama's uncharacteristic action affect my first day of summer. Still I noticed, and so did Rawyia, one year older than I and born with the courage I lacked.

"Why, Mama?" Rawyia asked. "Why so far from the water?"

Mama ignored her. She clamped her lips in the intense way she did when she spoke to our father, ordering the beach guard to continue. Furrows appeared on her forehead. Rawyia and I looked at Mama in disbelief, but Mama avoided eye contact with us. Her behavior was mystifying and alarming.

As soon as the parasol was anchored, she started to undress. She seemed eager to be out of her clothes; she already wore her bathing suit underneath. Rawyia unzipped her capri pants.

"Keep your clothes on, Rawyia," Mama said, her voice sounding unfamiliar.

My apprehension turned into fear. By then, I was sure Mama was keeping something serious from us and that our father was behind her unusual demeanor. Papa must have upset her earlier. She always announced his new rules without hesitation, she shared his concerns, but she rarely enforced his strict orders. Such rigid demands were his, not hers.

"Your father . . ." Mama sank her plump frame into the beach chair and looked away. "Your father said no more swimming for you and Rawyia." She affirmed her unyielding demand with a harsh, staccato punctuation.

I crouched on the sand next to Mama and motioned Rawyia over. Mama had a soft spot in her heart for Rawyia and me, and I was the one who reached that spot in difficult times. I knew Mama would give in when I reached for her emotional comfort with an embrace.

"Mama, look at me," Rawyia said, with her hands on her hips. "Is this Papa's new order?" She did not wait for Mama to reply and grabbed me by the hand. "We are going swimming," she said.

I freed my hand from Rawyia's grip and showered Mama with kisses and hugs. I tried to restore the smile she normally wore at the beach. But Mama anchored her gaze on me as if she were about to throw a spear. I pulled back. I had never seen her show so much support for Papa's rules.

13

"No swimming today," Mama pressed. "Tomorrow or any day. I cannot help. It's your father's new order."

The air turned cold. My heart shivered. Rawyia collapsed onto the sand. I tried to keep my feelings under control. Still, I failed to hold back the tears. Mama's statement hit me in the gut like a tsunami, wiping out my hopes and joy for the summer.

"I won't abide, Mama," I said. "Papa cannot take away from me the only fun I have during my vacation."

"Laila, my dear," Mama answered in a gentle voice. "You have no choice but to accept your father's orders today, tomorrow, or any day."

"Why?" Rawyia reached out to turn Mama's face toward her. "Why did you bring us here, then?"

The look on Mama's face softened with a smile. Our mother struggled between her love for us and the fear of God's punishment if she disobeyed our father. Like a good Muslim woman, Mama tried to obey her husband's orders.

"Okay, my dears." She shook her head in despair. "Go enjoy your day."

Rawyia and I rejoiced. We knew Mama's love for us would win out in the end.

Mama wore a light cotton dress over her large frame to help her tolerate the intense summer heat. Next to her sat a straw bag filled with sandwiches she had prepared for us that day. She covered her head with a round straw hat and shielded her eyes with white-framed oval sunglasses. She melted in her chair, reached for the newspaper in her beach bag, and opened it to her favorite page: the daily horoscope.

The midday sun spilled enough heat deep beneath the cool morning waves to give the water the comfortable temperature that Alexandrians and visitors enjoyed in the summer.

Rawyia and I took off our capri pants and cotton T-shirts and tossed them onto Mama's lap.

We ran to join our siblings in the water. Rawyia dove into

an incoming wave like a fish. Her long chestnut hair glistened. She already had a tan from the June sun. My olive complexion got even darker in the summer. I had to wear my hair in braids to keep my tight curls under control. Coupled with my bony figure, they considered me to be an ugly duckling. My physical appearance was not appreciated in Egypt at that time. I shook my head in admiration of my sister's beauty.

Rawyia swam until I could no longer see her. I remained close to the shore in my orange bikini. Water splashed from the waves and crashed against my legs. I was afraid of drowning. I feared the sea and its unpredictable mood swings.

Mama enjoyed the seaside, especially the time she spent with us at the beach. She could sit for hours, losing herself while admiring the waves. I asked her once why she never got bored sitting all day, waiting for us.

"The cool breeze, the warm sun, and the gentle murmur of the wave help me forget your father's tyranny," she confided.

This day, Mama kept her gaze fixed on the horizon. But she never missed waving to me when I called to her from the shoreline.

After lunch, I stayed close to Mama but kept a sharp eye out for the young man I had met the previous summer at the seaside of Alexandria. I wanted him to see me in my new orange bikini with the sunflower print, a suit Mama had bought for me this year.

The summer before, when we had met the first time, I'd had a blue bikini, which I had inherited from Rawyia. This orange bikini was the first one bought just for me. Orange was the summer mode of the sixties. And I was ready to be noticed as I made my way through adolescence.

The previous year, in my hand-me-down blue bikini, I paraded with Rawyia along the shore, away from Mama's watchful eyes. Then I noticed something I had never expected: boys looked at me and not just at Rawyia. My tall, thin frame was winning attention. The surprise pleased me and filled me with confidence.

One of the young men approached us. The sunlight struck his naked chest, bathing it in radiance. His honey-colored eyes glistened with intelligence under his dense lashes. I admired the young man's tall and muscular body. Rawyia gave him a smile. He ignored her.

"What's your name?" he asked me with an irresistible smile and a warm huskiness in his voice.

I could not believe he had addressed me. He must have made a mistake. His flirtatiousness paralyzed and enchanted me.

"My sister's name is Rawyia," I said, my voice quavering.

"No, I am asking you," he said, almost touching my chest with his finger.

"Me?" I had a sinful desire to be touched by him and to touch him, too. I felt no shame or guilt for liking him. His attention pleased my ego.

"Yes, you."

I turned to Rawyia.

"Her name is Laila," Rawyia said, her eyes widening in what I assumed was disbelief that I was the center of his attention.

"Laila, I like you." The young man winked, eyeing me from head to toe, running his tongue over his lips, turning them moist and inviting.

I thought he must be lying, but when I saw the look of amazement on Rawyia's face, happiness lifted me off the ground. I could fly. I drank in his compliment, savoring every word and storing away his look at my body. He introduced himself as Ghassan. He was from Lebanon, and he was a student. After he told me that, I stopped listening and just sipped at the sweet taste of his compliments.

As a young girl, I had learned from my family that beauty was to have a plump body and fair skin. I had neither. No one ever admired anything in me, let alone my body. The whole family reminded me with piteous comments and stares that my skinny frame was unattractive. Ghassan proved them wrong.

Ghassan extended his hand. Without thinking, I gave him mine. He squeezed gently, sending a wave of pleasant feeling throughout my whole body. Then he pulled me closer and warmed my cheek with his breath. I almost passed out.

"Let's go!" Rawyia grabbed my hand and turned me around. I checked to make sure Mama and our siblings were not looking for us.

Ghassan called my name from behind us. I freed my hand from Rawyia's grasp and walked back to where he stood. He handed me a folded piece of paper. I slipped it into the left side of my swimsuit top, and then we ran back to Mama. I didn't have to look to know he'd given me his phone number.

When we got home, Mama cracked an egg into a tall glass of milk. She added a generous portion of melted butter and four sugar cubes. She stirred the mixture to a smooth, creamy texture. Twice a day, for as long as I could remember, Mama had ambushed me before mealtime with this fattening potion.

"Drink it, my dear," she would chide, eyeing my slender figure, so different from Rawyia's plump, curvy body.

Egyptian suitors found Rawyia so attractive. By comparison, I had a brittle, reed-like figure, unappealing to menfolk, or so I had thought. On that day, however, with Ghassan's flattering attention fresh in my mind, I found the courage to refuse the glass filled with Mama's concoction.

"No, Mama," I said, hardly believing my own words. "I don't need the fattening drink."

"I will never force you," she said. "I love you the way you are." I heard honesty and love in Mama's voice. She smiled and drank it herself, though she certainly didn't need it.

To my family, I was flawed. Papa, I knew, favored Rawyia's looks over mine. Our father wanted to believe that Rawyia had inherited her beauty from him. However, I began to see myself through different eyes—the eyes of someone who could find me attractive, maybe even irresistible.

In contrast, my olive skin and black eyes, inherited from my mother's side of the family, Papa considered treasons, against his wishes, and unfortunate traits that needed improvement— not that I had any say in the matter or any control over the shape of my body. But to Ghassan, I was beautiful. Life suddenly had meaning, and I had a goal.

Ghassan had promised to meet me on the first day of this summer vacation. I had believed him. Through the whole winter, I'd woven our reunion in my imagination. I'd lived the details of meeting him again at the beach. I'd longed for his eyes and sweet words. Now, I did not see him.

"Mama," I asked on the way home, "will you be taking us to the beach tomorrow?"

"Only if God is willing," she said, sounding empty and unsure.

"Mama," I said, "would you go against God's will for us?"

She looked at me with eyes full of love and smiled. I smiled back and hugged her hard.

CHAPTER 2

That evening, while the sun prepared to set, we followed the daily mealtime routine. Around the dining table, we settled into the seats our father had assigned. With Rawyia to my right, I sat as rigid and brittle as an old piece of wood. Hala, our fourteen-year-old sister, who always chewed her fingernails, sank into her chair to my left. Hady and Samir, the two youngest, laughing discreetly, scrambled to get the seat closest to Mama. Facing us was our older brother, Reda, and our cousin Ahmed. Ahmed's mother had died giving birth to him. When his father, Papa's stepbrother, had passed away two years later, Ahmed had come to live with us. Our parents treated him like a son.

Silence shrouded the room, except for the occasional sound of Rawyia's exasperated breath. She was annoyed by Ahmed's spiteful stares. Rawyia maintained an unyielding animosity toward Reda and Ahmed. She rejected their control and the privileges our parents gave them.

We waited for our father before we could serve food onto our plates. All of us had learned to accept the rules. No other family functioned like ours.

Rawyia and I read books about freedom of speech and expression, yet Papa forbade the use of those words in our home. Our father controlled every move we made, every breath we took.

Moist, heavy air fogged the mirror of our mahogany buffet. A lazy breeze tinkled the crystals hanging from the three-tiered chandelier, announcing yet another silent mealtime with Papa. The signs of summer permeated the atmosphere.

Mama stood at the door in a loose, light cotton dress. Our father's deliberate footsteps echoed down the hall from his bedroom. Mama confirmed with a hand signal that Father was approaching. We all stood.

Papa entered the dining room like a general who had come to review his troops. He concealed the fatherly warmth we craved behind his austere facade. We had been trained to accept our father's stern appearance. It was his way to enforce obedience and respect.

He stopped, his hands behind his back, and drew his short frame to its greatest height. His upper lip twitched, and his chest rose and fell behind his starched white-collared shirt, still with its morning creases. My father's hawk-like eyes darted left and right, before fastening on my face. I shivered.

The three female servants scrambled to perform their last-minute tasks before he would sit down. They polished the wood of his armchair. The older maid, *Om* Zoubeida, kept a sharp eye out for flies and buzzing mosquitoes that might trigger our father's anger.

Mama followed the routine. She served Papa the best helping first. Her sad eyes revealed a dejection I had not seen before. An ominous feeling filled me. I rested my hands on the back of my chair and hoped dinnertime would be short and Papa would not announce new rules. I could not wait to escape into my fantasy world with Ghassan.

The gentle heat of the Alexandria sun still warmed my skin.

I dreamed of the next day, when I would plunge again into the lapis lazuli waters of the Mediterranean. While I dreamed, I could neither escape nor ignore the frown on Papa's face. My heart expanded with joy, then constricted with anxiety as I recognized Papa's tense look. It was the kind of tension that preceded serious announcements. I turned my gaze to Mama, standing behind him, but she avoided my eyes and moved to her place at the table opposite Papa. Papa sat down, and we all followed.

We grew up with our father's detachment and unfriendly demeanor. But that evening, something in his behavior seemed different. His aloofness lasted longer than usual. An ominous feeling warned me that Papa would impose new rules for our beach excursions. I took a deep breath and waited for his lips to move.

Two male servants stood behind Reda and Ahmed, ready to take their orders. For the simple event of having been born boys, our brothers and Ahmed enjoyed a privileged treatment, almost as special as Papa's.

My aunt Akeela and her adult daughter, Fareeda, sat on the sofa in the glass-covered balcony adjoining the dining room. They always ate their meals together there and never joined us in the dining room.

We waited to hear our father say *Bismillah*—"in the name of God"—so we could eat. Mama cleared her throat, a gesture she used to break the silence and prompt my father to eat so we could begin our meal. Nothing happened. The air felt stifling and hard to breathe. Loula and Calipso, our puppy and our black-and-white cat, stopped playing with Rawyia's and my feet.

I looked at Papa, alarmed at how he clenched his facial muscles. My heart raced beneath my ribs, and sweat broke out on my forehead. We had not started eating dinner yet when Papa gave my sister and me a most challenging look.

"Next Thursday, you and your sister"—he pointed at Rawyia, then me—"will be betrothed." He cleared his throat and took a sip of water. "Your wedding day will be decided later." Papa blinked with every word of his announcement.

His voice sounded like the hissing of a cobra, and his tone felt as sharp as a bee's sting. My alarm was realized. When Rawyia's hand squeezed my leg under the table, I knew what I had heard was real and not a dream. My father's face looked as if carved from stone—not a trace of emotion, grave or spiteful, except for his blazing eyes. Those eyes were the only thing that told me my father was still a man and not entirely devoid of human feeling. Now they burned into me, yielding no sign of fatherly love.

Betrothed? How? And to whom? Those words kept ringing in my ears. Although I saw my father's lips continue to move, I could only hear his pronouncement tolling again and again in my head: "Next Thursday, you and your sister will be betrothed."

Rawyia and I sank deep in our seats, unable to do more than stare up at him. After a moment, we glanced at Mama. She lowered her head and left the room.

"Five years ago"—Papa's voice echoed again, crushing our already-shattered world—"I promised Laila to Farook and Rawyia to Gamal. I honored my word with the recitation of *Al Fatiha*, the opening words of our holy book."

Panic tightened in the pit of my stomach. I tried to make eye contact with Rawyia to get some idea of what all this meant, but I could not connect with her. She had an intense look on her face. I sank deeper into fear.

Across the table, Ahmed smirked. Reda nodded, as if pleased with the announcement. The whole room seemed to shimmer and waver. A rush of emotions consumed me. The announcement left an acid taste in my throat. I wanted to scream and tell my father, *you cannot decide for me whom I will marry. You cannot force me to marry someone I have never seen or heard of before.* But the determination in his eyes paralyzed my thoughts and my voice.

My dreams of education and summer on the beach with Ghassan vanished in a second, and a dark cloud of despair enveloped me. My entire future had been shaped. My father expected me to accept it. Sick to my stomach, I sobbed and ran to the bathroom. Rawyia trailed me. Mama joined us. Papa followed her.

"Minak Lillah ya, Kamel!*"* Mama said, giving Papa a look of blame. "May God be your judge, Kamel!"

"I'm all right," I said, but my head ached and my heart pounded. My ears rang, and my pulse seemed to repeat my father's word in cadence: *betrothed, betrothed.*

Mama stroked my brow. I reached for her hands. A strange new sound reached my ears. Papa's face was red, and his eyes glistened. He reached inside his pocket for his handkerchief and blew his nose. In my mind, I saw love in his teary eyes. It hurt me to see my father cry.

This was the second time I had seen his tears. The first time he wept was when Rawyia and I had a tonsillectomy. I was five years old, and Rawyia was six. After the surgery, Papa stood weeping at the recovery-room door. He could not bear to see us in pain. I loved my father and trusted that he would never do anything to hurt me, but today, he had betrayed me. I wanted to ask why, but I knew better than to question his word. So, hungry for an answer, I looked at Mama.

"Your father loves you. Trust his decision, my love." Mama saw the disappointment and mistrust in my eyes and shook her head. She had no choice but to support my father's decision. "Many parents choose husbands for their daughters," she said. "Girls live a happy marriage."

Mama's words sounded empty and void of conviction.

"How do you know, Mama?"

"This is our culture," she stressed. "You have to live by its rules."

Mama had no better answer. She always used culture and religion to legitimize our father's control.

"I promise you, Mama," I said, shooting my father with eyes full of anger, "I will not follow this culture with my children. They will have the freedom to choose whom they marry."

Mama shook her head with a wry smile. I knew she did not believe me.

For a moment, I thought of standing up to my father. But I feared that behind his show of sadness, rage brewed, and it frightened me. Without uttering another word, Papa turned and headed toward his room.

The sudden loss of my dreams and aspirations gave me enough courage to voice my anger for the first time.

"I hate you, Papa!" I yelled. Mama covered my mouth with her hand.

"Accept your fate, my dear," she pleaded. "It is the will of God."

"Mama, don't blame God for Papa's decision." I held Mama's hands and faced her with a desolate look. Even though I felt her pain and torment, I could not give her the compassion she expected.

"It has been as hard on me to accept your father's order as it is on you," she said, wrapping her arms around me. Mama was always honest with me. In this case, I knew she told me the truth. I loved her dearly.

"Laila and I," Rawyia spoke up, "will challenge our fate."

CHAPTER 3

Following the betrothal declaration, Rawyia and I retreated to our bedroom. We used a key to lock the door of our sanctuary.

I paced while my eyes filled with tears. I hated myself for having walked out of the dining room without protesting. *Why couldn't I say no to my father? Why didn't I object? Why does Papa not enforce marriage on my brothers?*

Rawyia shook her head. "Stop crying," she snapped. "We need to understand what our betrothal really means, why Papa did not accept a simple engagement."

What did Rawyia mean? While I had no prior knowledge of betrothal, I had learned from my classmates that boys and girls got engaged before marriage. Mama, *Tante* Akeela, and Fareeda never spoke to us about betrothal. I composed myself to help Rawyia focus. She always found solutions to our problems with the older boys. Rawyia was capable of finding us a way out.

"Papa would insist on *Katb el-Kitab*," she said, "the legally binding betrothal contract. Knowing Papa's paranoia about sex and virginity, I assume he would consider the fiancé a stranger.

Perhaps it would be only a temporary arrangement." She was pacing, too.

I nodded and followed her with wide eyes, perplexed and mystified but yet impressed with Rawyia's legal information. I was not concerned with how she acquired her facts.

"We both know," Rawyia said, "that no strangers, including the men Papa chose, would be allowed to come near us before a wedding." I had never seen my sister so absorbed and serious.

I had dreams and hopes, including finishing school and seeing Ghassan again. No longer nodding, I covered my ears with both hands. This betrothal scared me.

"I read in Eve's magazine *Hawaa*," Rawyia said, ignoring my anguish, "that a betrothal is certified by a legal document for marriage."

The word "marriage" shook me to the core.

"Do you mean we would be legally married?" I asked.

"Yes. Betrothal is a much stronger commitment than an engagement and very messy if the couple divorces."

The impact of what it meant to be betrothed hit me. In one week's time, I would be legally married. My throat dried. The space around me shrank and turned dark. I wanted to scream.

Because Papa's orders were sacred, the more Rawyia explained, the more worried I became.

Our room shared a wall with our parents' bedroom. This gave Papa ample opportunities to overhear our conversations. Rawyia's voice got louder and louder as she delved deeper into the legal facts.

I had been eight when Papa had moved us to this apartment. It hadn't taken me long to recognize the disadvantages of our bedroom being right next to our parents'. Papa gave us the illusion of privacy inside our walls, but it became clear what this arrangement meant for Rawyia and me. We also shared a balcony and a bathroom with our parents. The bathroom had a small window that faced the cement wall of the neighboring building. Papa insisted we keep it shut all the time. On the side opposite the balcony, the two bedrooms opened to a sort of vestibule that opened onto the rest of the apartment. Our father locked the glass door separating the vestibule from the rest of the apartment at night. He kept the key on the night table by his bed.

Rawyia and I came to perceive our new room as a "golden cage." Rawyia soon discovered, however, that our room had a key.

"This is good," she said. "No one can walk in uninvited."

I didn't understand why she wanted our bedroom door locked, because she often complained about the constant confinement we lived in. Other times, she insisted on locking the door. Her behavior confused me, but I never complained.

Her preoccupation with doors started when she was six years old. She sneaked into our parents' bedroom, where Papa kept his architect blueprints rolled up on his desk.

Rawyia climbed up, knelt on Papa's chair, and opened one sheet of the parchment papers. She then took Papa's blue pencil and drew squares in different spots on the paper. I was standing next to her when Papa materialized behind us, a scowl on his face.

Rawyia froze, still on her knees, the pencil clenched in her fingers, her lips parted in a big O shape. She locked her eyes on Papa's furious stare.

I took a few steps back, until I felt the wall behind me. Papa approached Rawyia and took a quick glimpse at the parchment sheet. Before he could verbalize the anger shooting from his eyes, I heard Rawyia's trembling voice. "I drew some doors for people, Papa."

Papa ignored Rawyia's message and motioned us out of the room.

I nodded, confirming Rawyia's desire to keep our bedroom door locked.

"We can leave the room," she said, turning the key in the door lock several times. "During the day, whenever we want to."

The night of our betrothals' announcement, Mama knocked at our door, the three gentle taps we had agreed upon. Rawyia unlocked it.

Mama hauled her stout frame into our room. Sweat plastered her blue nylon nightgown to her back. She plopped herself down on the chair facing the dresser's mirror and fanned her face.

"Open the shutters."

I threw the four wooden shutters wide open and stood there for a moment, watching the big orange disk merge into the horizon and fade in the sky, and worried my dreams would soon vanish into the dark future my father had planned. My heart interrupted the silence but Rawyia didn't speak. She paced.

As I stood at the window, I wished Mama had expressed disagreement with Papa's decision. I wanted to wipe out the look of despondency in her eyes. Although I empathized with her predicament and knew her limitations, I blamed her and wished I had a stronger mother.

The cool evening breeze floated in, drying the perspiration on Mama's body. She maintained her silence. A while passed, and finally I couldn't take it anymore.

"Mama, who is the man Papa has chosen for me? Have I ever met him?"

"Well, my dear, he is a nice man." She let out a sigh. Her words sounded rehearsed. "He's worked with your father for years."

Rawyia stopped pacing and bit her lower lip hard. She was in her scheming mood. I was familiar with her nervous demeanor—many times before, when she'd plotted against Ahmed and Reda, she'd exhibited this behavior.

"Has he ever seen me?" I asked.

"No," Mama said. "Farook is college educated."

College education was a trump card. Egyptian men used it to win marriage proposals of their choice. Mama wanted to impress me. She failed.

"My brother-in-law," Mama continued, "chose him to run his company's finances because he is trustworthy." She searched my face for any sign of approval, but she found only tears welling up in my eyes. She continued, "Farook is wealthy, too," then turned to Rawyia, who looked away as Mama told her, "I'm sure he will treat Laila like a queen."

"Queen? Who wants to be a queen?" My voice choked. "I want to be a student, Mama."

Farook must be old, I thought. *Om* Zoubeida, our maid, had told Mama that if she had married an older man, he would have treated her like a queen.

"How old is he, Mama?" I asked.

"My dear Laila," Mama said, forcing a smile, "he is in his prime. Farook is young."

Mama's words were meant to reassure me, but she said them with difficulty, and her pleading eyes didn't move me.

"How about mine, Mama?" Rawyia interrupted us. "Who was chosen for me?"

"Gamal is your cousin," Mama said with a relieved look on her face. "He is Sameha's son."

Mama had never before talked about her sister. Sameha had never visited us, either.

"You had a sister, Mama?" Rawyia asked. "And we never met her? Why?"

"Twenty years ago, my sister cursed your father during an argument." Mama looked straight into my eyes.

I gave her a cold stare, utterly disappointed in her submissive personality.

Mama took a handkerchief from her sleeve and wiped her eyes, but I had no sympathy. "They fought constantly back then, and your father ordered me to cut ties with her."

Rawyia and I said nothing.

"He threatened to divorce me," Mama continued, "if I ever talked to my sister again."

Mixed emotions filled me as I listened to Mama's confession. I wanted to console her, but the loss of my aunt, whom I'd never met, along with my father's demands was disheartening.

"Sameha," Mama whispered, "passed away a few months ago." Tears dripped from her eyes.

My disappointment melted into sympathy. I stood and took Mama in my arms.

"Shortly after her death," Mama blew her nose, "Gamal called your father and asked to marry you. It was my sister's deathbed wish. She hoped this would bring our families back together again."

The cruelty of our parents shocked me. I cried, mourning the death of my aunt, a woman I hardly knew.

"You are as bad as Papa," I said, my anger rising again.

"Your father demanded it."

I couldn't believe my mother's blind obedience to Papa's orders. "You agreed to ostracize our aunt from our lives because Papa asked you to?"

"Yes." She lowered her head.

Rawyia stood and faced Mama. Her chest rose and fell with each breath. She, too, seemed irritated with Mama.

"Your father doesn't like Gamal," Mama said. "But he believes this marriage will put an end to your rebellion." Mama took Rawyia's hand, a conciliatory gesture.

Now I was not sure and felt confused. Was it Mama's fault that Papa had so much control over her and us? Or was it God's fault that He had bestowed Papa with such power? Was the loving God I knew capable of discriminating? I couldn't find answers.

Rawyia pulled her hand out of Mama's. She returned to her place next to me on our bed. I couldn't imagine a man getting between my sister and me. I wanted Rawyia to know that no one would ever force me to stay away from her, so I hugged her and kissed her on the cheek. She squeezed me back, hard.

Our parents had raised us to believe and abide by God's words, but as I had grown older, I had begun struggling to accept that God favored boys over girls.

"You will burn in hell if you question the will of God," my aunt Akeela and *Om* Zoubeida had said. Even the nuns at school had warned me. I did not want to upset God. In fact, I feared Him as much as I feared Papa.

"Why did you give your consent before asking Rawyia and me?" I asked.

"A woman must obey her husband." Mama avoided eye contact with us. "It is a command from God."

I could not understand why God demanded that women obey men, and why the same demand didn't apply to men.

"What would happen if you stopped obeying?" I wanted to pressure Mama into defiance of Papa and solidarity with us.

"Your father has the right to physically punish me or even divorce me," she stated with conviction. "God ordered men to beat up women if they become disobedient."

"Why, Mama? What's wrong with women? Why did God give men such a privilege? Why didn't He order women to beat men?"

Mama gave me a wry grin.

"Why did God create us if He despises us so much?"

Mama rubbed her right knee in a slow, circular motion, something she resorted to when she was thinking or felt unable to answer.

She knew me well. I was neither a risk-taker nor a fighter, like Rawyia. Still, I would not stop until I got a satisfactory answer.

"God allowed beating women with a twig that small." She pointed to the length of her palm. "God never meant anyone to harm women, physically or otherwise."

I refused Mama's explanation. While I could not change her religious belief, I promised myself never to allow any man to abuse me.

Rawyia wrung her hands and tapped her right foot. "This is not the time to question God's discrimination. We cannot exchange our God with another one, who loves women."

Mama took a deep breath, then invited Rawyia and me into her arms. "Gamal will be a good husband for you, Rawyia. He is a marine officer. He has traveled abroad and has seen how different societies treat women. I am sure you will enjoy some freedom with him."

Rawyia pulled back. Mama's reassurance did not resonate well with my sister.

"How about mine, Mama?" I asked my voice cracking. "Who chose Farook?"

"Farook approached your father at work and asked for your hand. He is a distant cousin to my brother-in-law." She patted me on the back, but I pushed her hand away. "Your father could not turn him down."

"Why not?" I lashed out. "Does Papa care more about a stranger's feelings than about his own daughter's happiness? I hate him."

"I told your father that you, Laila, are not a rebel, that you are good in school, that you don't need this yet." She sighed. "'It's too late,' he told me. 'I gave my word.'"

"I hate Papa," I said, my chin quivering.

"It is the will of God. Accept your fate." Mama took a deep breath.

"Mama, how much of God's will do I have to accept?" I sobbed, my tears flowing freely. "I will fight this marriage till I die, and I won't need anyone's help."

Rawyia left the room and returned with a small towel soaked in cold water. She wiped my face. "Crying won't change Papa's decision," she said matter-of-factly. Then she disappeared under the eiderdown. Mama joined her.

Exhausted, I crawled between them, incapacitated and feeling coerced into cooperating with my executioner.

Before I closed my eyes, I asked Mama, "How old is this man?"

"Thirty-nine, my dear, though he looks young for his age." Mama turned her face away.

I pulled the eiderdown over my head, longing for a divine power to help me forget what had happened. Reaching for the pleasant reveries of Ghassan, I fell into a deep sleep.

CHAPTER 4

Before the sunlight traced the horizon, the sound of running water on the other side of the wall woke me up. My father always got up first for ablution. Mama would follow him for the dawn prayer. *Tante* Akeela, our father's sister, and her daughter, Fareeda, would join them.

Fareeda had taught us children how to pray, but our parents never enforced the religious practice on us. My father believed that protecting our virginity was more important than practicing the five pillars of Islam.

The aroma of the brioches *Tante* Akeela baked every Sunday before the morning prayers permeated our room—irresistible and comforting. I wanted to jump out of bed and grab one right out of the oven, but then I remembered the betrothal announcement.

The light of dawn now spilled through the shutters' cracks. I welcomed the sun's invasion and wondered if it carried hopes.

Everything in the room occupied a spot in my heart, and in my mind: the double bed I shared with Rawyia, the green-velvet vanity chair, and the dresser's mirror we took turns using while we experimented with different makeup on our faces, away from our father's eyes; the cherubs that hugged the white medallion in the ceiling, which I counted every morning while I waited for Rawyia to wake up; the Philips record player on Rawyia's night table that allowed us to listen to the romantic lyrics of our favorite singer, Abdel Halim Hafez, but only when our father and brother weren't at home. I pulled the covers back over my heart—broken and crushed.

Rawyia walked into the room and stood at the foot of our bed, still in her pink nylon nightgown, with her hair falling straight and sleek. I rubbed my eyes and sat up.

My sister slid back into bed. "Look, La, you can make him do anything you want." She snapped her fingers and winked.

"Who are you talking about?" I wasn't in the mood for Rawyia's playful antics.

"Your husband, silly," she whispered.

"He's not my husband yet." I pushed her away.

"Well, next Thursday he will be," she teased.

I groaned into my pillow.

The rest of the day, Rawyia and I camped in our room, refusing to open the door to anyone, including Mama. We paced restlessly for hours like two animals in a golden cage awaiting their demise.

In the evening, when hunger rumbled in our stomachs, Rawyia snuck out and brought us some pita bread, a few slices of *kashkawan* cheese, and a plate of watermelon slices. She checked the hallway, making sure Reda and Ahmed were nowhere in sight, relocked the door behind her, and joined me in bed. Rawyia worried that Reda or Ahmed eavesdropped on us when Papa was not home.

"From now on," Rawyia said, "we have to be especially careful."

"I know," I said, although I didn't understand what she meant. I was used to her plotting and her mistrust and hatred of Reda and Ahmed.

Rawyia shivered, dug her teeth deep into her lower lip, and then made a fist with her right hand, as if to punch someone. "La, Ahmed is the reason I want to get married and leave this house."

Her hand shook, and the veins popped out on the surface of her fist. I had never seen Rawyia so agitated. But I nodded to comfort her and show my solidarity.

"Ahmed and Reda are monsters." She eyed the door. "The sooner we both get away from here, the better it will be for us."

"Are you afraid of them?" I asked, baffled and alarmed.

"No, but they are only trouble for us."

Rawyia was bold and challenging. I was malleable and feared all the males in our family.

CHAPTER 5

Papa and Mama had another daughter, Hala, only one year younger than I. Hala was never on Papa's radar. He treated her differently and didn't worry about her as much as he did about Rawyia and me. Hala looked different from us and didn't have to be concerned about boys being attracted to her. She was short and chubby and had a severe acne problem—not pleasing to boys, in my father's eyes. Her room shared a wall with our brothers' rooms, as well as to *Tante* Akeela's and Fareeda's rooms, all situated on the other side of the locked glass door of our sheltered environment.

While Rawyia spend most of her days fighting with Ahmed and Reda, I had time for my sister. Hala suffered from chronic stomach pain. Her acne problem kept her withdrawn in her room most of the time. I was ten when I asked Papa to take her to a dermatologist. He refused. My father believed Hala's acne would clear up on its own. Mama and I pleaded with him until he hired a Greek nurse who came every other day and gave Hala a cleansing facial. With time and repeated treatments, Hala's face cleared up, and she seemed more outgoing and happy.

Hala and I developed a special relationship. I played the older sister who gave her advice, something I could not do with Rawyia. Sometimes I included Hala in my daily activities, studying with her and helping apply her acne medication every day. I enjoyed my place with Hala and Rawyia, and I needed both of them, though in different ways.

Hala often expressed her dismay at Rawyia's behavior. "Laila, Rawyia is disobedient and failed in school. She will get you in trouble. Don't listen to her."

While I suspected Hala felt jealous of the closeness I had with Rawyia, I appreciated her advice.

Hala performed religiously the five required prayers with Aunt Akeela. When she turned twelve and felt grown up, she tried to talk me into praying.

"I am not going to pray," I said, "to a God who doesn't like girls."

She shook her head and never mentioned the subject again.

Rawyia, on the other hand, preferred to stay away from Hala. She interpreted Hala's closeness to me as Hala's rejection of her, even though she stood by Rawyia after every fight that broke out between her and the boys.

I envied Hala for escaping Papa's, Reda's, and Ahmed's attention. However, I did not envy her acne.

Whenever Rawyia and I broke our father's strict rules, Reda threatened to kill us. I took him at his word and really believed he might get angry enough to take our lives, so I kept my distance from him, worried that Rawyia's rebelliousness might push him to that breaking point.

"La," Rawyia confided, "I want to tell you so much about them, especially Ahmed, but now is not the right time."

I didn't like the mystery masking Rawyia's words; I wanted to know what she kept from me and why she took Reda's threats so lightly. She always underestimated my composure, mistaking my cautious and shy personality for immaturity.

"Rawyia, you can trust me. Tell me now. I cannot wait for the right time."

Rawyia paced, shaking her head. My heart clenched in anticipation. She pushed her prescription glasses higher up on her nose and sat down.

"Papa or even Mama," she whispered, "would not believe me if I told them what Ahmed has done to me." She covered her face with both hands. "I want to forget, and I want you to help me."

I could barely hear her. Words came out of her mouth muffled. Tears gathered in her eyes, and I panicked, unable to stand seeing her cry.

"Okay, Rawyia. I will wait only if you promise to stay out of trouble."

"Don't worry about me, La. Ahmed and Reda don't scare me, but I don't understand why our parents trust Ahmed."

I believed Rawyia, having seen her fight with them with defiance. She endured weekly beatings from them but never shed a tear. Everyone else in the family believed Rawyia deserved the beating she received.

"La," she told me once, "I will not shed a single tear to validate their abuse."

I admired Rawyia's audacity.

CHAPTER 6

Next to Mama, I trusted Rawyia the most. I knew she would forever stand by me. No one understood me the way Rawyia did. She felt my pain, my happiness, and my needs, even while I slept. With Rawyia in my life, I felt secure and at peace.

Rawyia always woke up when she heard me get out of bed to go to the bathroom in the middle of the night. She knew I feared darkness. Half asleep, she would lean on the frame of the bathroom door, wait, and go back to bed without complaining.

One night, I awoke to a strange sensation, something I had never experienced before: a mild cramp, followed by a wet feeling in my panties. Reaching down furtively, worried that Papa would somehow sense my discomfort and burst into our bedroom, I felt inside my culotte. When I pulled my hand out, I saw, by the dim light that crept into our room, blood on my fingers.

"Rawyia." I choked back a scream and whispered, "Help me. I have blood in my culotte."

She laughed. "La, calm down," she said with the confidence

of an experienced adult. "What you have in your culotte is the 'X.'"

The menstrual period, as we called it, was the "X."

Rawyia got up and retrieved one of her small white cotton serviettes and a fresh culotte. She then showed me how to insert the serviette in my culotte. "You must change it three times a day, depending on how heavy the flow of blood is."

I nodded and smiled, feeling grown-up, just like her.

"Don't be so happy, La. The 'X' isn't fun. You'll know that soon."

But I didn't care. I wanted to be an adult just like Rawyia. We slipped back in bed and hugged.

Rawyia taught me what I needed to know when Papa forbade the mention of the word "menstruation" in our home. Our father did not allow anyone to discuss with us any subject that had to do with our private parts. He wanted to preserve our ignorance—and, he thought, our innocence—as long as possible. In that moment, I felt grateful to have Rawyia as a sister.

By then, my body had been betraying me for some time. My breasts developed early and became a visible shame. Using one of Mama's silk scarves, which our father forbade her to wear because of its vibrant colors, I tied my breasts flat every morning before leaving for school. For as long as I could, I wanted to escape the look of disgust in my father's eyes every time he glanced at Rawyia's womanly figure.

When Rawyia discovered what I had been doing to my breasts, she scolded me. "Don't you ever be ashamed of your body."

I wanted to believe Rawyia but could not. Our father pinned a badge of shame on our chests like the scarlet letter of Hester Prynne, just because we were born girls. Guilt grew inside me like a parasite, consuming my innocence and self-worth.

Rawyia and I learned from a young age that in Islam, a girl's body is *awrah*—containing parts not to be exposed to strangers: arms, neck, cleavage, legs, and feet. Our father waited until we started menstruation and demanded we cover our *awrah*. My mother defied the rules away from our father's eyes. Many times, we heard her lie to him. It did not matter if she ingrained unhealthy examples in our young minds; she simply wanted us happy. That was Mama's way of expressing her love and support. We appreciated her efforts and loved her more for them.

I admired Rawyia's fighting spirit. Still, I never had the desire to join in her insubordination. My parents considered me the obedient daughter. Rawyia believed I lacked courage.

She often fought my fights. When I cried, her eyes teared up and her chin quivered. Then she would dry my tears and say, "I will always be here for you, but I want you to learn to speak for yourself."

Rawyia wanted me strong and independent. Feeling pressured to become someone I could not be, I nodded to express my willingness to change.

"The men in this house are controlling. If you let them scare you, you will be their slave forever."

So, to keep my distance from Ahmed and Reda, I stayed in my own world, focused on my aspirations for the future, and dreamed of the day when I would find a peaceful life away from home.

Sometimes I tried to express courage like Rawyia. I would wear glasses just like her and even tried to look like her. In fact, I admired Rawyia so much that I lied about my eyesight, telling my father I couldn't see a sewing needle on the carpet.

He took me to an optometrist. During my vision test, I pretended not to see one row of letters. A few days later, I wore glasses just like Rawyia. I couldn't imagine my life without her.

How had Rawyia been born with so much confidence? Soon, I learned she had help.

During one of our late-night talks, Rawyia let it slip that she read the magazine *Hawaa*, one that Papa forbade Mama to buy.

Our father knew it contained articles written by liberal women who would plant rebellious ideas in our minds.

"We're not supposed to read that," I said.

"Just go ahead—read it. It will introduce you to writings by women who do not accept men's superiority."

"Who are these women?" I asked, tantalized.

"Nabawiyya Moussa and Huda Shaarawi, born in the late 1800s. They fought for women's liberation." Rawyia spoke with excitement about the dead women as if they were her best friends. "Nawal El Saadawi is another one. She is still active in fighting for women's independence."

Her thrill was contagious. She had won my full attention.

"When you read about their struggle for freedom, you will know I am not crazy." She pointed at herself with pride. "Other women think like me."

"How did you get this magazine?"

"Kareema." She smiled. "Maids are good for more than cleaning. She bought it for me. I made her swear not to tell anyone, not even you."

We treated Kareema like a sister, allowing her to come into our room anytime she wanted. Kareema also acted as a spy for Rawyia and me. She warned us when Papa, Reda, or Ahmed came home. We trusted her.

I felt stupid and a bit hurt that Rawyia had kept this magazine secret from me. Although I rejected her patronization, I suppressed my feelings to avoid confrontation. Mama did the same with my father.

"Okay, then. Let me read the magazine. I want to learn to be more like you." I moved closer to Rawyia.

"I don't want you to be like me," Rawyia cautioned. "I am only thirteen, but I have already seen so much ugliness from the people I trusted." Her voice changed, and she sounded bitter. "I don't want you to go through the same experiences, La." She hugged me. "How I wish I could replace your head with a more mature one!"

"That could happen," I said with sarcasm. "Just let me read what you've been reading." I was ready to grow up.

"It's not the magazine itself, La." She grinned. "It's Amina Al-Said."

"Who's she?" By then, I was impatient. I wanted to start reading.

"She's the woman who opened my eyes." Rawyia said. "She taught me how to fight for my God-given rights."

"Rights? I didn't know we had rights."

Rawyia ignored my surprise. "Amina Al-Said has a column where she advises women to stand up for their liberty. It's because of her that Papa doesn't want us to read *Hawaa*."

I asked Rawyia to show me where she kept the magazines. She lifted the edge of the mattress and smiled as she pulled out a small stack of magazines.

"Here." Rawyia tossed the magazines onto my lap. "I hope you learn something I haven't already taught you." She smirked, and took them back to tease me.

"Rawyia," I said, rejecting her playfulness, "if you benefited from reading these, you should not have kept them from me."

"I am showing you now." She handed me the magazines.

I held the copies tightly against my chest. Glancing around the room for a safe spot to hide them, I searched for a secret place of my own to satisfy my new independence and then wedged the magazines tightly into the gap between the wall and the armoire.

A few nights later, Rawyia woke up in the middle of the night to find me reading a copy of *Hawaa* under the covers with a flashlight.

"You're still awake?" she said, her eyes half-shut. "It's very late."

I pushed back the covers and shined the flashlight on Rawyia's face. "Yes, I'm reading *Hawaa*."

Rawyia blinked. "Put the magazine aside and let me show

you something." She pulled a pack of Cleopatra cigarettes from her bra. Rawyia's bra was her secret place, even when she slept. "Do you want to try one?"

"You smoke?" I gasped. Smoking, of course, was one of Papa's many taboos. "Since when?"

"I just started," she said nonchalantly. She was only fourteen.

"What does it taste like?" I wanted Rawyia to tell me that cigarettes tasted bad.

"You have to try it yourself. Try it only in the bathroom when the guards aren't at home."

We called Reda and Ahmed "guards" behind their backs.

"Make sure the window is wide open," Rawyia advised.

"Okay!" I always wanted to do what Rawyia did.

"You hold the cigarette between these two fingers, your pointer and the middle one." She placed her two fingers over her lips. "Then you suck hard. When you get enough smoke in your mouth . . ." She removed her fingers. "Try to release it slowly through your nose."

We rehearsed for hours with an unlit cigarette. At the first opportunity, when we were certain Ahmed and Reda were out of the house, we sneaked into the bathroom. Rawyia helped me light up. I put the cigarette to my lips and sucked hard, as she'd said. Immediately, I broke into a coughing fit.

"You're not ready yet," Rawyia laughed. "We'll try again another day."

My smoking sessions in the bathroom always ended in failure, but I nagged her to give me another chance.

"Okay, La. The idea is not to cough and choke. Skip the nose step and release from your mouth."

"Don't give up on me," I pleaded.

She never did—not on smoking or anything else.

One summer day when she was fifteen, Rawyia lit up on our balcony. Papa caught her. He locked her up in a four-by-six-foot pantry that had no windows. A small mesh screen at the top of the wooden door provided ventilation. Papa gave Rawyia a blanket, a pillow, a tall glass of water, and bread and cheese. He forbade her to talk to anyone. When my father came home for lunch, he escorted Rawyia to the bathroom.

I prepared some foods Rawyia particularly liked—chocolate, green olives, sharp cheese, and French baguettes—and hid them in the bathroom. During each bathroom break, Rawyia took her time eating before Papa escorted her back to her cell. I couldn't stand seeing her locked up.

Most of the other members of our household—all my younger siblings, plus *Tante* Akeela and Fareeda—felt sorry for Rawyia. They joined me in helping her.

"I need empowerment, La," Rawyia said. "I have to stay strong to survive the cruel treatment of the men in this house."

While I believed Rawyia deserved to be disciplined, since she had done something she was not supposed to do, I rejected the way Papa had punished her.

I placed a chair in front of the pantry door and read to Rawyia articles from *Hawaa,* especially the ones written by Amina Al-Said, the feminist and founder of the magazine. The other members of the family took turns guarding the foyer and the window.

At night during Rawyia's incarceration period, I tossed and turned, unable to sleep without my sister in the bed beside me. So I took my blanket and pillow out into the hallway outside the door to her cell. Rawyia warned me I would be punished for doing so, but that didn't stop me. I enjoyed the role of the responsible sister, which Rawyia had never seen before and now counted on during her ordeal.

In the gray moments before dawn, Rawyia roused me. I sneaked back into our bedroom before Papa got up for his early-morning prayers. For her sake, I had the courage to face even my father's anger. I feared no one.

By Friday, Rawyia had already spent one week in the pantry.

My father performed a two-hour prayer in the mosque before he set her free.

Rawyia walked out with her head held up high in an attempted show of defiance, looking at our father with eyes spewing hatred and contempt. She went straight to our bedroom. I followed her and locked the door. We sat quietly on our bed, facing each other.

Something had died in her. Her eyes lacked the luster of bravado and the zest for fighting. Her silence reflected defeat and humiliation. I took Rawyia's hands and rubbed them gently, wanting my sister to be the person I was used to. As she stared into empty space, I hugged her, but her body seemed lifeless. Next, I kissed her on the forehead and her cheeks, trying to revive her rebellious spirit. I could not.

When she saw my tears rolling down my face, she took me in her arms and wiped my tears dry. "Don't be sad, La," she whispered. "I will get over this soon."

I needed Rawyia strong and hugged her tight. She was my mentor, my best friend, and my rock.

"Don't you know, La?" she said the morning after my father's marriage declaration. Her voice echoed excitement. "Marriage will be our ticket to the outside world." Rawyia sat down on the bed and crossed her legs. She looked out the window and winked with mischief. "Finally, the doors of this prison will open. We will do everything we were deprived of doing: ride on public transportation, dress the way we please, wear makeup, talk to boys, and socialize with our friends. We will no longer be under Papa's, Reda's, and Ahmed's control—and no more school."

I excelled in school and dreamed of becoming a journalist, even though I knew my father would never support such ambition. The life Rawyia described sounded exhilarating, but I did not share her excitement about leaving school. Would Farook be so open?

Rawyia had just finished her first year of high school and had failed all her exams. She hated school and often told me that our lives would be no different with an education and that even if we had college degrees, we would remain slaves to men if we stayed in Egypt.

Still, I believed in the importance of education. I doubted my future husband would fulfill my ambitions. When I voiced this concern to Rawyia, she raised her hands. "Don't you know? You just give Farook sex, and he will do whatever you want."

My mouth fell open as Mama stepped into our room. She frowned at Rawyia and looked away, shaking her head with contempt.

"Mama," I said, taking her hand, "would I be allowed to attend high school?"

"Why, yes, my dear. Why not?"

"Come on, Mama," Rawyia interrupted. "The nuns don't allow married girls in school."

I looked at Mama in dismay.

"You could study at home. I'm sure your husband wouldn't mind."

"Is it up to my husband? Have you discussed it with Farook already?"

"No," Mama said.

"You're naive, La. A man who marries a girl young enough to be his daughter is not looking for intellect."

Mama was quiet.

A cloud of sadness settled over me. I didn't know if I should be angry with our father or blame my passive mother. My only solace became the hope that my future husband might allow me to pursue my dreams of becoming a journalist and that Rawyia and I might find a way to escape our fate.

CHAPTER 7

When my siblings and I were growing up, our mother trained us to accept an invisible power called fate. With time, we discovered that fate had as much power as our father. We learned to fear it and live by its rule. Although I had doubts and questions, I kept them to myself.

I was seven years old when Papa burst into the family room and ordered all of us children to follow him out to the balcony. Papa marched, and we followed like ducklings in a row, scrambling, none of us wishing to feel Papa's hand sweeping up stragglers. My father stood in the middle. The seven of us arranged ourselves around him.

Rawyia and I exchanged fearful glances. Hala moved closer to me and rocked her body back and forth, a habit she had developed whenever she became anxious. I squeezed her sweaty hand until she stopped.

When Mama joined us, he asked her to leave. Mama raised her gaze to the sky, as she always did following her arguments with him. She engaged her lips in pantomimic conversation with God. Once, I asked her what she was saying, and she answered, "I ask the Almighty to give me patience."

Our mother, like most Muslim women, endured a dysfunctional marriage. She believed God would reward her in the afterlife if she accepted her husband's mistreatment—and her fate.

When Mama disappeared from our view, we turned our attentive gaze to Papa like obedient soldiers standing before their general.

"What color is the sky?" Papa asked, darting his gaze between Rawyia and me.

"Blue!" we answered in chorus, eager to please him. I shouted it out at the top of my lungs, thrilled that I might please my father the most.

Papa favored us with a slight grin. "Correct." He looked at each of us in turn. "But you must know . . ." He pointed his finger at Rawyia. "If I tell you the sky is black, you will agree with me. You must say it is black. 'Yes, Papa, it is black.'" He smiled a different smile that filled me with dread. "Now tell me, what color is the sky?"

I exchanged a worried glance with Rawyia. She shook her head.

"Black," we all mumbled, our enthusiasm gone.

Papa nodded. He smiled in satisfaction and went inside. Puzzled why Papa said it was black, I looked at the blue sky. Silently, I promised myself that when I grew older, I would challenge my father. But I couldn't keep my promise, even later, when he made the betrothal announcement. I obeyed my father just like my mother did.

I didn't understand the divine power bestowed on my father, or why our mother was excluded from that privilege. When I was eleven, I became aware of our father's dominance and aloofness toward my mother, even more toward us children. My friends in school hugged and kissed their fathers when they picked them up from school, although Mama always insisted that our father was like all fathers.

Later, I approached my aunt Akeela about it.

She sat Rawyia and me down. "You don't understand," she said softly, a wistful, sad look on her face. "Kamel, your father, was four when we lost our mother." *Tante* Akeela drifted away for seconds that seemed like hours. She sighed. "Our father died a year later." Our aunt shifted her gaze to the window. "Our maternal uncle volunteered to raise us." A pool of tears gathered in her eyes, but she composed herself quickly and frowned. "Our uncle also took control of the wealth that we inherited from our mother."

Rawyia and I never knew anything about our father's childhood. It saddened me to know that Papa was orphaned at such a young age. I wanted to hear more from *Tante* Akeela to help me understand my father's behavior toward us.

"Did your uncle treat you well?" I asked with compassion.

"Sadly, in our uncle's house, we suffered both physical and verbal abuse." Sorrow dripped from her every word. "The physical abuse your father endured from his uncle's wife created the person that he was to become." She fell into her memories again.

"Aunt Akeela," I urged, "continue, please."

"Your father sees his uncle's wife not only in your mother, but in all women."

I did not understand what Aunt Akeela meant but remained attentive and refrained from interrupting her.

"Our uncle's wife," she whispered, "kept us in the maids' quarters of the big house. She gave us one meal a day and a daily beating session with a bamboo stick."

By then, I did not want to hear more. My aunt saw pain in my facial expression.

"May God the Almighty punish our aunt for her cruelty. We were orphans," Aunt Akeela whispered, and wiped her eyes, ending her confession.

Even though it hurt me to hear that Papa suffered from abuse as a child, I refused to accept that his controlling and domineering ways were exclusively the manifestation of the upbringing he endured.

"Papa must have another reason for protecting us and for worrying so much about our virginity," I said, expecting to hear more from Aunt Akeela. I always suspected a mystery shrouded my aunt's celibate life and the absence of her daughter's father. "And you, Aunt Akeela? What happened to you?"

"May God burn him in hell," she mumbled, and bowed her head.

Aunt Akeela loved my father. She was not talking about Papa.

"Who are you talking about?"

"No one for you to worry about," *Tante* Akeela said with a tone of finality.

Papa never spoke of his early years. He trained as an architect and joined his brother-in-law's construction company. Over time, he earned the respect of his employees and built a good reputation for himself in the industry.

In fact, my father became one of Alexandria's highly respected architects. Among other works, his firm designed numerous important buildings at the Universities of Alexandria and Cairo, including a new medical complex for the University of Alexandria, as well as a set of chalets at Montazah Palace that were used as guesthouses for visiting heads of state during meetings of the Arab League.

Papa's skill and hard work allowed our family to live very comfortably, and we attended the best schools. Papa took great pride in his achievements. He relished the respect and power he commanded in our community.

We had no doubt about Papa's authority at the workplace, for we knew how he controlled us at home. He fretted about the fact that Rawyia and I would soon reach puberty. Our proximity to boys in the neighborhood only increased his anxiety.

My father believed boys and girls of our age should not mingle. It didn't matter that the neighbor's boys were children with whom we'd grown up. They were boys, and we were girls.

I was eight when Papa's budding concern about Rawyia's and my honor played a role in his decision to move from our small apartment in Alexandria's Zizinia district to Roshdy. The rich and socially famous lived in Roshdy, where the streets were wide and clean—lined with eucalyptus, sycamore, ficus, and acacia trees. We had outgrown our old living quarters in Zizinia. Papa believed that Roshdy better fit our social status. In reality, he wanted to move away from our neighbors, *Tante* Howayda and *Tante* Nareeman, each of whom had five sons and no daughters.

Papa spent a month preparing the new apartment, where Rawyia and I, in particular, would be protected from any outside temptations. Rather than one of the luxurious villas, Papa chose to move us into a fourth-floor apartment in one of Roshdy's relatively few multifamily buildings. Mama told us living on the fourth floor gave our father peace of mind during the hours he spent at work and that a villa would have been too close to the street. We girls might be tempted to sneak out and meet boys. Up on the fourth floor, Papa believed, we were safe and our virginity would be protected.

My father worried that if Rawyia or I did something that brought shame to the family, it would destroy him socially. To preserve his immaculate reputation, Papa took every precaution. Rawyia and I would be shielded from men.

Every door had a lock. Papa had keys for all of them. He had enclosed the front balcony in glass to keep us from standing at the railing, where boys might see us as they passed along the busy street below.

Even the family telephone, a black model standard in those days, had a lock on the rotary dial to make it impossible for us to use.

Unlike Rawyia, I looked forward to moving, especially when Mama told us we would be close to San Stefano, our favorite beach.

On the day of our move, Papa's private chauffeur picked us up. We drove to Roshdy, past high-end boutiques and well-manicured villas adorned with roses, bougainvillea, and water fountains. To me, it all looked elegant.

Our car pulled into the underground parking. I ran inside the building and dashed up the stairs. Mama and the other kids took their time riding the elevator.

Papa met me at the door to our new home. "Follow me. I'll show you where you and your sister will sleep."

I trailed Papa down a long, narrow softly lit hallway. On the right, midway down, stood the kitchen. *Tante* Akeela and *Om* Zoubeida had arrived ahead of us and were preparing dinner. They had opened the windows on this humid July day. The breeze carried the familiar aroma of sautéed garlic mashed with coriander. The paste would be mixed with *mouloukhiya*, a traditional green soup made from Jew's mallow leaves. *Mouloukhiya* was the number-one dish in Egyptian cuisine.

I caught up with Papa in a small, square vestibule set off from the rest of the apartment by a glass door. He opened a wooden door off the vestibule.

"This will be your room and Rawyia's." Papa backed up and pointed to another room, adjacent to our bedroom. "You and your sister will share this bathroom with your mother and me." He turned to face a large refrigerator standing next to the glass door. "Everything you will need during the night is here."

Inside the refrigerator, I found bottles of water, pita bread, feta cheese, fruits, and several small red ceramic containers packed to the rim with Mama's homemade yogurt prepared specially for our father. Papa believed the yogurt would make him live longer and more healthfully.

With this arrangement, Papa ensured his constant surveillance over Rawyia and me. The enthusiasm and excitement I initially felt dissipated and left me consumed with anxiety.

In his struggle to apply the appropriate forms of discipline, Papa trusted the Quran as his guidance, which, according to our father's interpretation, meant enforcing the strictest control over our behavior as Rawyia and I grew up.

"God created women from one of man's ribs, as proof of men's superiority. It's a command for women's obedience." To explain his beliefs, he said it often to force Mama into complete submissiveness and to ensure she didn't allow us too much freedom.

"Men came from women's womb," Mama said one day. "How come that makes men superior to women?" On rare occasions, Mama demonstrated courage and challenged our father, but he smashed her down with a fearsome stare. This courage of hers didn't happen often.

Papa's obsession with his daughters' purity did not make him any different from most other Egyptian fathers. Rigid rules overshadowed the softer side of his personality.

Our father provided us with all the comforts money could offer. Most Egyptians would have envied our home, located in a fashionable and safe neighborhood. There was plenty of space in our apartment, even for our large household, which totaled fourteen people. Despite all of that, Rawyia and I felt as if we lived in a prison, with Papa playing the part of the warden. He carried his many keys on a large iron ring, which he never once left at home.

Papa took every opportunity to remind us of his supreme power, especially as we grew older and Rawyia began to show her independent nature more and more.

One day, when I had turned ten and Rawyia was eleven, Papa took the two of us along with him to a construction site in the small Nile Delta city of Kafr el-Dawwar, where he was working on a project. We never enjoyed spending time with our father, but we welcomed the chance to get out of our apartment.

Papa had given the chauffeur the day off and drove us himself. Rawyia took the passenger seat next to Papa. I took the backseat, from which I was able to watch the *fellahin*, peasant girls my age, walk along the bank of the canal, a branch of the Nile River. Two goats and a cow walked by the girls' side. There was no male companion in view to protect them. I envied the *fellahin* for the freedom they enjoyed and wondered if they were Muslims. To avoid one of his moral and religious sermons, I didn't ask Papa.

As we approached the site, Papa took off his sunglasses and smiled at us. "Watch my dogs run up to greet me."

Rawyia and I peered through the window as three German shepherds and eight mutts raced behind our car.

"They are loyal to me and only me." Papa's face shone with glee.

He got out of the car and held a piece of raw meat up in the air. The dogs circled him, wagging their tails and drooling. My father patted their heads and whistled. He threw the meat onto the ground, not far from where he stood. The three dogs dove into the meat. The rest followed Papa to the car. Papa took more raw meat from the package in the car and threw a generous portion to each dog. He stood nearby, admiring them with a smile. Rawyia and I pressed our backs against the cold steel of the car.

"Have I told you the story of my two employees who came to my office to discuss a project while my dogs were there?" Papa asked, without looking our way.

Rawyia and I nodded. We had heard the tale many times, but Papa told it to us anyway, laughing as if it were a joke.

"Two workers came into my office to discuss some details of an electrical wiring project. As the conversation grew more heated, the employees raised their voices. The dogs leaped at them, thinking the men were fighting with me."

Papa laughed uncontrollably. When he could laugh no

more, he continued. Rawyia and I stood silently. It was a rare moment to see him so happy.

"I controlled my dogs with a single order," Papa explained with pride. "They were protecting me because they love me. They are my best friends." Papa continued to watch his dogs devour their meal. I stood quietly next to Rawyia, feeling jealous of the animals. Papa showed them more sensitivity than he showed us.

I had never seen that glow of excitement in my father's eyes before. While I liked his happy face and wished Papa would keep it forever, for us, I knew that could happen only if we gave him the unconditional submission he cherished in his dogs.

Deep in my heart, I knew that one day, when I grew older, I would enjoy my freedom, but, unlike with his pets, my father would not be happy to see me free.

CHAPTER 8

Our father's attempts to control us extended outside the apartment. We rode an all-girls school bus and never used public transportation. My father even forbade us to ride with his male chauffeur unless he, Mama, Reda, or Ahmed rode with us. It went without saying that our father considered interaction with boys outside the immediate family a taboo. However, he did trust Ahmed and Reda and charged them with the preservation of our virginity when he was not home.

At a very young age, I wished to have been born a boy so I could enjoy the privileges and free life of our brothers. One time, I asked God why He hated girls so much and why He gave boys the right to control us. I saw God as another male to fear, but I knew I couldn't hate him as I wanted to, so I asked fate, whom I blamed, to help me accept the reality. But I did not want to hold Mama responsible for the suppression and suffocation we grew up learning to accept as she had done. Mama was as much a victim as we were, and I loved her unconditionally.

Papa worked hard to prevent any contact between his

daughters and male strangers, but once, he made an exception. He hired a sixty-year-old man to tutor us at home in the Arabic language. *Ostaz* Shafeek had a shiny bald head and a swollen belly. He often held a handkerchief in his hand to wipe the sweat that beaded his brow.

Shafeek never used the elevator, preferring to climb the stairs to our apartment. As a result, he suffered from shortness of breath. Rawyia once asked him why he didn't use the elevator. He said with a smile that he didn't want the stairs to feel lonely.

Funny and kind, Shafeek treated us with gentleness, but we always got bored during the hour of Arabic tutoring. When we lost our focus and yawned, Mr. Shafeek squeezed our hands gently to restore our attention.

One day, Papa walked in and caught Shafeek in the act of squeezing our hands. Papa fired him on the spot and hired a female teacher in his place.

Rawyia understood the connection between our father's action and our future education. "Are you planning to put us in an all-girls university?" she asked Papa a few days later, not knowing then that no such place existed in Egypt. Even if one had existed, it would have had male professors.

"It's too early for you to think about college," Papa answered her with a sneer.

Despite Papa's precautions, he could not imprison our hearts. My first taste of love was through the window of our school bus. I was thirteen. Every morning, a boy waited in the street for his ride as we passed by.

At first, the boy and I exchanged quick glances, then a nod and a smile each time we saw each other. One day, the boy waved to me. These stolen moments on my way to school satisfied my romantic curiosity. Papa never knew. I considered it my own act of rebellion.

Like us, Mama could not escape our father's domination.

Papa gave our mother a strict curfew and forbade her to visit Hameeda, Mama's only surviving sister. Our aunt lived a liberal lifestyle Papa considered disgraceful. Yet despite Papa's restrictions, Mama always spoke of Papa with pride and respect.

She often repeated an Arabic proverb: "The shadow of a man is better than the shade of a wall." Our father provided the security our mother needed. As children, we accepted the power of fate and the supreme control of our father—and of all males in the family. Mama wanted us to believe that without the shadow of a man, our lives would be difficult to lead on our own. Rawyia and I did not believe her, but we still loved our mother dearly.

From the rebellious way Rawyia reacted to our father's, Reda's, and Ahmed's control, I knew she would not seek the shadow of men for protection. I, too, never accepted this proverb and refused to believe that the shadow of a man would be better than what I could provide for myself. Mama lived in utter subordination to Papa's control. She obeyed my father's tyrannical orders without question simply because he gave her the security she couldn't provide for herself. But I wanted to have a different kind of life, a life based on mutual respect and appreciation.

Mama's retelling of this proverb both disappointed and surprised me. I didn't understand how she could think this way when she suffered from an unhappy life with our father. Why couldn't Mama instill independence in me and teach me to rely on myself and not on men? Despite myself, I resented Mama for wanting me to be just like her—submissive and accepting of men's superiority. I wanted out from the shadow of men.

On many occasions, Mama would break the rules for us, but almost never for herself. Against Papa's strict orders and without his knowledge, Mama would violate restrictions on the long list of forbidden acts she thought too constraining. She bought us bikinis and allowed us to wear makeup, the most sinful thing of all on our father's list.

"Lipstick and eyeliner are for unchaste women," Papa often told Rawyia and me.

Like all girls our age, however, Rawyia and I applied makeup on our faces in the privacy of our bedroom and away from our father's eyes—and with Mama's approval.

While I appreciated Mama's support, her passive behavior confused me. I wanted her to challenge our father's rules in the open, and in his presence, but we were happy with whatever support Mama gave us. We always found excuses for her submissiveness and thus kept our love for her unshaken and strong.

Growing up, we often heard Mama arguing with Papa behind their closed door, mostly about Rawyia and me.

"Give them freedom," Mama pleaded with Papa again and again.

Unlike our father, Mama opened her mind to wise and flexible changes, without deviating from what she believed was an order from God.

"No mention of swimsuits in the Quran," Mama told us when she bought them for us. Our mother found excuses when she needed them. But our father hated change. Mama's advice vaporized before reaching our father's ears.

"I overcame the death of my parents," he said. "I endured the cruelty of my uncle's wife, took care of my three sisters, and became a skilled professional. I have plenty of experience to help me make the right choices in raising my children," he repeated often.

"Rawyia and Laila are not your uncle's wife or your sisters," Mama snapped back. "Show them your love with action. Get close to the girls and listen to what they want." She raised her voice to assert herself. "You cannot lead the life of a desert nomad when you live in a big city and your daughters attend a French Catholic school."

My father did not allow Mama or anyone else to tell him

how to raise us. He believed he had enough experience in life to back the decisions he made.

"Talking to your father is like blowing into a punctured balloon," Mama once confided to us out of frustration.

Papa also assumed he had backing from Allah. Our father believed himself second in command to God. As children, we believed it, too. Who were we to question God's words?

Papa often quoted verses from the Quran, such as Chapter 17, *Surat al-Israa*, 23–24:

> *Thy Lord hath decreed that ye worship none but Him and that*
> *ye be kind to parents. Whether one or both of them attain old*
> *age in thy life, say not to them a word of contempt, nor repel*
> *them, but address them in terms of honor. And out of kindness,*
> *lower to them the wing of humility, and say, "My Lord! Bestow*
> *on them thy Mercy even as they cherished me in childhood."*

Like most men of his time, Papa used the banner of Islamic teaching to control the women in his life. Our lives became like putty in his hands. He shaped it the way it pleased him.

Papa knew the right interpretation of the verses. Although one said that no girl should be forced to marry a man she doesn't want, my father chose to twist the scriptures to his liking—a privilege, I thought, of being second in command.

Rawyia and I believed our culture reflected the teaching of the Quran. So when our father made the marriage announcement, we searched the Quran for what Islam taught about marriage and how girls ought to be treated. We discovered we had the right to refuse to marry and to choose whom to marry. These findings awakened the rebellious little girl inside me, which I suppressed as a child out of fear of my father.

CHAPTER 9

I believed education would be the weapon that could free me from the domination of the men in my family. As a child, I often heard my mother say education gave a woman the courage to stand up for her rights.

Our mother didn't have the courage to oppose Papa, nor to go against the culture she grew up in. In her heart of hearts, she wanted us to live a life different from hers. When we asked why she allowed our father to control both her and us, Mama would say, "If I'd had an education, I would have left your father and worked to support myself."

The first time she said something to this effect, I was eight. Mama's comment confused me. It terrified me to think she might actually leave us.

"I'm glad you're not educated, Mama," I said. But I soon grew to love school and to understand the power that knowledge gave me.

A week before the announcement of my betrothal, I graduated from junior high. As the big day dawned, my main concern was my grades, which would be announced during the graduation ceremony. Only Papa attended. My mother stayed at home with my younger siblings.

Papa always expected the best of me. Less-than-perfect end-of-year grades triggered his anger. Not that Papa planned a higher education for me. It was simply to exercise his power and control. Even though I knew I had done well on my final exam, my heart raced as my classmates and I sat in the auditorium, waiting for our names to be called.

That day, the school allowed us to wear what we wanted. My classmates giggled as they compared the length of their skirts, the plunge of their décolletage, and the height of their heels. I felt self-conscious about my dress, made to my father's specifications with long sleeves, a round collar, and a skirt that covered my knees.

Around my neck, I wore a chain with a pendant engraved with the Arabic characters for Allah. Waiting nervously, I clutched the pendant and remembered my mother's advice. "To relieve your anxiety, recite the first verse of the Quran," she had said.

As I mouthed the words, *Bismillah al-Rahman al-Rahim*— "In the name of God, the Most Gracious, the Most Merciful"—I began to feel calmer. Then I heard *Mère* Bernadette's voice echoing through the room as she called my name.

"Baraa! Baraa Kamel!"

Baraa, "innocent," was my given name. My father chose it. I never liked it and always preferred my nickname, Laila. Mama told me I was the only one in Egypt with that name. She accepted it, but she did not understand that telling a fourteen-year-old girl that no one else in the world had the name Baraa would be more a trauma than something that would make the girl proud.

I glanced around to see the effect of my formal name on the other students. Relieved when they did not laugh, I took a deep breath and walked to *Mère* Bernadette's podium.

"Congratulations, Baraa, you came up with the highest grades, as usual." *Mère* Bernadette paused and studied me. "I have always been curious about your name; is there a story behind it?"

When I turned ten, I had asked Mama why they'd registered me in school as Baraa. She had told me that someday, when I was older, she would explain. That day had still not come.

"I don't know," I said to *Mère* Bernadette. "My father named me."

"Will you be coming back next year, Laila?" She smiled warmly.

"Yes." I was sure my father would be happy with my grades and would encourage me to continue my education.

Mère Bernadette handed me the certificate. Placing it over my chest, I walked back to my seat. I couldn't wait for the ceremony to end. Although I looked forward to hearing my mother's praise, my father's approval meant more to me. His praises came in droplets. Nothing satisfied his expectations.

The ceremony ended. My father picked me up in his black Citroën. To my surprise, he showed no interest in my grades and remained oddly quiet. No words melted his frozen tongue. His facial muscles clenched, and his gaze focused on the road. Every now and then, I glanced at his face, searching for an expression to calm my racing heartbeats. His silent message was loud and clear: I would not continue.

When we got home, I ran to Mama and melted in her embrace. She bathed my face with warm kisses. I felt safe and forgot about Papa's cold demeanor.

"*Mabrook*," she exclaimed. "Congratulations, my dear daughter. You are now ready to start a new life." Her face was glowing with happiness.

I pulled back and looked her in the eyes. A jolt traveled through my body, a warning that something serious was waiting to happen.

"Which new life are you talking about?"

"The life every girl looks forward to." She turned to walk away.

"Wait, Mama. I told you before I want to continue my education."

Her smile died. The sparkle in her eyes disappeared, and she wrung her hands.

"What's wrong?" I demanded.

"N-n-nothing." She headed down the hall, leaving me to stand alone in the foyer, lost in my fearful thoughts and uncertainties.

In another week, Mama's meaning would become perfectly clear. My life had been determined without my consent.

School wasn't important to Rawyia. She received the news of her betrothal with open arms. To Rawyia, the announcement could not have come at a better time. My sister had been waiting for the day when she could free herself from the tyranny of our father, Reda, and Ahmed. That day had arrived. Once Rawyia left our parents' home, Papa could no longer dominate her life. And Rawyia's cleverness would ensure that she bent her future husband to her wishes.

"Dear sister, whatever kind of men our husbands turn out to be, they couldn't be worse than Papa." Rawyia tried to plant some courage in me. "La," she said as she lay on her back while I sat next to her, "marriage is our only opportunity to get out of here. Don't you want to be free?"

I agreed, but with some hesitation.

Rawyia got up, walked partway around our bed, and threw her arms open. "Everything outside is waiting for us to discover. We will go to the Arabic movies. We will wear what we like, and we will even try alcohol!" She clasped her hands behind her back, stepped slowly toward me, and spoke softly. "We will even try the sinful one—sex."

I listened raptly, as if Rawyia were a teacher giving me instructions for a final exam. "Are you planning to have sex with

Gamal before your wedding day?" I asked. Unlike Rawyia, I was not ready for sex or alcohol and wanted to be free for different reasons. I knew marriage would rob me of my dreams of becoming a journalist.

"You are so naive." Rawyia shook her head, laughing. "You need to use the brain God has given you, not the one Papa has designed for you."

"I don't want to think like you, Rawyia. I have my own plans for the future."

Rawyia frowned. I clenched my teeth and paced nervously while she explained that only a legal divorce could break a betrothal contract. I knew Rawyia had enough courage to engage in sex before moving to her matrimonial home.

"Are you telling me that you will have sex with Gamal?"

"According to our custom," she said, "if an engaged girl loses her virginity to her fiancé, she becomes morally corrupted and her family will dishonor her. But if she loses her virginity to her betrothed, the moral consequences are not as severe."

Rawyia's show of savoir-faire did not impress me. Having sex with Farook or any man was not in my plans.

"That piece of paper, my dear sister," Rawyia said, holding one hand out as if she held the betrothal document, "will be the ticket to our liberation. Once we sign that betrothal contract in a few days, Papa will relinquish his control over us to our future husbands. We could give them sex. In return, they would give us some freedom."

It shocked me that Rawyia was ready and able to exchange sex for her freedom.

Rawyia spoke with such an air of authority that it didn't occur to me to ask her how she had become such an expert on sexual behavior. The magazine could not have taught her to use sex as a means to get what she wanted from men. I kept my doubts to myself as I needed Rawyia by my side, since I lacked the courage needed to fight the betrothal.

The one complication in Rawyia's plan was that the betrothal contract did not mean we would immediately be free to leave Papa's house. We still had to wait for our parents to furnish our matrimonial homes. The waiting period depended on the parents' financial status. The preparation could take from two to five years. If the parents could afford it, girls wouldn't have to wait long. We knew our parents had money, but neither of them had talked to us about when exactly we would be married and living in our husbands' homes.

Rawyia leaned forward. "Listen, La."

I took a step closer. "I'm listening."

She looked me straight in the eye. "Personally, I'm not worried about myself. I'm happy about this arrangement for many reasons, but I'm concerned about you. You aren't ready to leave the house, let alone get married." She paused, then continued, "First, I have to find out from Mama everything we can about Farook. I want to make sure he won't be your next jailer."

Although I doubted Rawyia could force Farook or even Gamal to submit to our wishes, I felt more secure when listening to her. Rawyia's words transported me to an uncertain world. I wanted to stay in the present and to enjoy my life as a girl, to go to school, to continue my basketball training, and to spend time with Ghassan.

"Are you afraid of marriage?" Rawyia took me in her arms.

"I don't know."

"Then why are you crying?"

"I will miss my friends at school."

"This is not the time to cry for your schoolmates. We face an unhappy future. The most important thing is whatever is outside this room." Rawyia let go of me and gestured toward the balcony. "It will be better than what is in here." She banged her fist on the mattress and then faced me with a mischievous smile. "Don't you want to have the freedom to see Ghassan?" Rawyia said, eyeing me with a smile.

Those words were like magic. They transported me to a state of joy and happiness.

"Yes," I said, not thinking about how marrying Farook would help me see Ghassan. "That is all I want."

Rawyia laughed and guided me to sit down. Standing before me, she cupped my face in her hands and spoke softly. "La, I want to have a serious talk with you about your emotions."

I was alarmed, not wanting to hear anything that would spoil my happy feeling.

"You need to stop believing in love."

I frowned and pulled back.

"What do you think Ghassan wants from you? You think he loves you?"

I nodded with defiance. She took my hand, pulled me to my feet, and dragged me toward the dresser.

"Look, La," she said, pointing to my figure in the mirror. "This is what Ghassan wants from you—nothing more. The sooner you realize that, the easier it will be for me. I don't want to spend the rest of my life consoling and nursing you over failed relationships with men."

I didn't want to believe Rawyia's cruel and dry words. "I don't expect you to watch over me for the rest of your life. I am not rejecting our father's control to have you take his place." My answer surprised me as much as it did Rawyia. She raised her eyebrows in disbelief. I ignored the look on her face and continued. "I don't intend to forget about Ghassan now or in the future."

Ghassan was the only person who made me feel beautiful, and I had no intention of forgetting him—neither for Rawyia nor for my future husband.

"I know that you have been my loving guide for many years," I said, "but it is time for you to understand that I will choose whom to love."

"I'm not telling you not to see him. I'm just trying to give you some sisterly advice. You are too emotional and romantic. That can lead to trouble, especially if you're married to another man."

Rawyia was right, but I didn't care. I shrugged and walked away.

CHAPTER 10

Though Rawyia and I fought against Papa's measures, we knew the importance of virginity in our culture and our future. Most Egyptian men were interested only in marrying virgins, a fact Egyptian girls learned at an early age from their parents, their families, their friends, and the culture in general.

In the privacy of our room, *Om* Zoubeida told us stories about how seriously virginity was taken in her home, Asyout, in Upper Egypt. *Om* Zoubeida had worked for Mama since long before Rawyia and I were born, and she had gotten married while living with our family. Her devotion and kindness had won my parents' trust. We had grown up treating her as a member of our family. In return, she considered us children an extension of her own family. Rawyia and I treated *Om* Zoubeida as our confidante.

One night, Rawyia and I snuggled in bed while *Om* Zoubeida sat on the rug and described how, on the wedding night, the groom took his bride to the bedroom while both families stood outside the door, waiting to see proof of the bride's virginity.

A few minutes later, the groom appeared, waving a piece of white cloth soiled with blood to demonstrate his bride's purity, like a flag in the hand of a conqueror.

Om Zoubeida laughed. I trembled with fear and placed my hands over my private parts. She stood and moved my hands. "That will never happen to you or to your sisters," she said. "It's only in the villages."

I was only nine years old at the time and asked how the blood got on the cloth. *Om* Zoubeida explained that the groom or a designated woman covered one finger with a white fabric. The bride, who was prepared ahead of time for the procedure, lay down in a ready position for the finger to penetrate her. "They poke the bride's hymen, and the bloody cloth becomes the proof of her virginity." *Om* Zoubeida's voice dropped to a whisper. "After that, the cow is ready to impregnate."

I felt nauseated listening to the gory details of the procedure and was appalled at *Om* Zoubeida's laughter.

A devout woman who always covered her head with a black veil, *Om* Zoubeida took charge of our religious education, but when Rawyia and I asked her why men didn't follow the Prophet Mohamed's advice to treat women with kindness, mercy, and respect, *Om* Zoubeida did not have an answer, at least not an answer we could understand. She would tell us only that we must thank God and our parents for sparing us circumcision.

One day, we decided we'd had enough of this inscrutable advice.

"What do you mean?" I asked her. "Do girls get circumcised, too?"

"Yes, girls do. I am circumcised," she whispered. Sadness swept across *Om* Zoubeida's face.

"You didn't want to be circumcised?" Rawyia and I asked.

"No, of course not, but I had no choice. All girls in my village had to be circumcised."

"Why?" I shrieked, thinking, *this is unbelievable.*

"It's for the girls' protection. Killing sexual desire guarantees the wife's faithfulness to her husband."

"But then what happens when the girl gets married? Rawyia pressed Om Zoubeida. "Will she be able to get pregnant?"

"Yes, of course."

"So how come we aren't circumcised yet—or are we and we don't even know?" I asked.

This brought the grin back to Om Zoubeida's face. "You'll find out soon,"

"How?" we asked together.

"I can't tell you. You'd better ask your mother." And Om Zoubeida decided to say nothing more.

Rawyia and I waited for the right moment to gather our courage to broach the subject with Mama. Papa forbade any discussion about any part of our bodies. Mama sometimes ignored that rule.

A few days later, Rawyia and I heard our parents arguing. Mama escaped to our room, as she always did. She sat down at the edge of our bed and massaged her right knee in a circular motion.

"Mama, do you enjoy sex with Papa?" Rawyia asked playfully.

The boldness of the question threw Mama off. She looked lost, unsure of how to respond. She collected herself. "Where did you hear about sex?"

Rawyia and I exchanged glances. We could be getting Om Zoubeida and ourselves in trouble.

"Are you circumcised?" Rawyia asked.

Once again, Rawyia's question unnerved Mama. Before Mama could answer, we showered her with kisses to chase away her seriousness. Mama smiled, stopped rubbing her knee, and agreed to respond, but not before she made us take an oath. Rawyia fetched our copy of the Quran, and we placed our right hands on its cover and swore not to tell anyone about the conversation.

Mama kept the book in her hand and assured us that Papa

did not believe in circumcising girls and that she, too, had escaped circumcision.

"Your father didn't have you circumcised, but to protect you from your own sexual desires, he made the decision to betroth you at an early age."

"How do they circumcise girls?" I asked.

Rawyia gave me a smile of approval, but Mama took a deep breath and turned her gaze away.

"When girls are very young," she said, "usually eight to ten years of age, their parents take them to the doctor, or the village barber, to perform *taharah*. *Taharah* literary means 'purification.'" She paused, shaking her head with dismay. "Circumcision is not purification. It is mutilation."

"How do they 'purify' girls?" Rawyia asked, a bit of sarcasm in her voice.

"Do girls know what they plan to do to them?" I asked, my face contorted in empathy.

"Yes, but not in detail," Mama said.

"Oh, Mama!" I covered my face in horror.

"Stop this drama, and don't interrupt!" Rawyia seemed frustrated with my naiveté and show of emotions.

Mama motioned for me to place my head on her lap and ran her fingers through my hair. "Girls are prepared for the procedure from a young age. In fact, they look forward to that day, because it's a family celebration."

"Can the girls refuse?" I asked.

"How can a ten-year-old say no to anything? Can you say no to the rules in this prison?" Rawyia blurted.

I had no answer to that. Frowning, I shook my head. I wanted Rawyia to stop reminding me of our father's control.

"The girls have absolutely no power," Mama continued in a flatter tone, after a short pause. "The child is held down by her parents. If needed, a family member will help to keep her from moving."

"How do they perform this cleaning?" Rawyia asked with irritation.

"With a blade, they chop off a piece of the skin from her private part."

"Which part?" I interrupted, horrified.

"It is just a part from your private area." Mama lowered her gaze to the floor. Naming the private parts was taboo in our home.

"That's why they call it cleaning, right?" Rawyia wrinkled her nose in disgust. "They design a clean hole for the man."

"Most men in the countryside prefer circumcised women. That way, they are sure their wives will never commit adultery." Mama said.

For a few minutes, none of us spoke. Rawyia and I struggled to absorb what we had heard.

Mama broke the silence. "Be thankful you were not circumcised."

"Is this part of our religion, Mama?" I asked.

Mama explained that circumcision was not part of Islam but a custom that had been in practice for thousands of years. "Some Muslim extremists preach that circumcision is part of Islam," she said.

We also learned from Mama that circumcision was practiced during the Pharaohs' dynasties and that it was still believed to be a healthy way to suppress a girl's sexual urges, or *shahwa*.

I wondered why no one cared about suppressing men's *shahwa*, since they were the ones who raped the girls. Mama felt uncomfortable talking about sex with Rawyia and me. She told us just to be thankful and then changed the subject.

For a rare moment, I felt grateful to our father for not subjecting us and Fareeda to such a practice. But Samy, Hady, and the older boys did not escape circumcision. Once they reached five years old, they went under the knife. That was Sunna, Mama told us. In Islam, as in Judaism, boys' circumcision was required.

Tante Akeela and my cousin Fareeda were grateful Papa had taken them into our household. Egyptian society gave no mercy to pretty women like my aunt, who was divorced, with a child. Growing up, we accepted them as members of our family and did not ask why they lived with us. Papa forbade Mama to talk about the issue. When *Tante* Akeela overheard our father's strict orders, she occasionally spoke out and urged him to loosen his grip, but most often, she just gave him a stare and then quietly retreated to her room. Our aunt avoided Papa's enigmatic reminder of her past.

Tante Akeela failed to convince Papa to treat Rawyia and me differently. She recounted to Reda and Ahmed stories about the Prophet Mohamed's kindness toward women, but with them, too, it made little difference. She told Rawyia and me it would take a miracle from God to get the men in this world to treat women like equals.

My aunt's words gave me a deep sense of unease. Still, I refused to accept her resignation and could not believe that God had anything to do with our fathers, Reda's, and Ahmed's control and abuse. But I kept my thoughts to myself.

CHAPTER 11

Reda and Ahmed followed Papa's lead and kept a watchful eye on Rawyia and me. Acting as a proxy for Papa, they invented new ways to spread their reign of terror throughout the household. The five servants were their silent victims, especially the younger maids, Kareema and Tuha.

Our family still lived in Zizinia when *Om* Zoubeida first complained to Mama that Ahmed invaded the female servants' private quarters, and frisked the maids, accusing them of stealing clothes and money from his room. Kareema had just turned thirteen then, and Tuha was only eleven.

Once we moved into the Roshdy apartment, Ahmed's and Reda's behavior escalated. *Om* Zoubeida told Rawyia and me that the boys repeatedly attempted to molest the maids. *Om* Zoubeida tried to stop them, without success. She then informed Mama, but our mother blamed the girls, accusing them of seducing Ahmed and Reda.

In this, my mother followed the norms of Egyptian society, which did not hold men accountable, even if a girl got pregnant and found the courage to name the person who raped her. The fact that Ahmed and Reda molested the maids did not bother Mama, and she never commented on, nor interfered with the boys' sexual activities.

Witnessing such discrimination filled me with anger and intensified my resentment of the patriarchal society in which I grew up. I became determined to fight the rules of this culture, no matter how dear the price.

"If Hatshepsut and Cleopatra ruled Egypt, so can we," I said to Rawyia.

"We live in a different time, La. These kinds of women, like dinosaurs, became extinct."

I shook my head. Rawyia insisted that women lacked the desire to liberate themselves and that they were bound by a patriarchal religion that kept them two steps behind men, but I did not share her pessimistic views about women.

"If women fight hard," I said, "they could regain the power the ancient Egyptian women possessed."

"Remember, La, the ancient Egyptian women lived in a time free of the religion we have now. They worshipped the goddess Isis, a woman."

Rawyia had no hope that women would ever regain their position in our society, and thought her only success would come from manipulating men. She told me Islam was a religion made for men. I disagreed, strongly believing Islam had come to liberate women.

"I agree, La, but Islam came for women living in the desert."

Rawyia always had answers that put doubts in my head. Still, I believed women were capable of ruling the world, as they had in ancient times.

In a society that viewed men as God's gift and women as his biggest mistake, a male child was always more precious. In Reda's case, as the oldest surviving child, having been born after three others who died in infancy, he got the lion's share of my parents' attention. Consequently, my brother grew into a spoiled monster.

Once, when I was nine and Rawyia ten, Reda wanted to go fishing and needed someone to go with him. Samir or Hady usually joined him on those trips, but that day, they had gone shopping with Mama.

With our parents out, my sister and I camped in our bedroom with the door locked. Since we shared our balcony with our parents, we made sure that door was also shut. We did not move or talk, hoping Reda would think we were asleep.

Our precautions were useless. His footsteps came closer with every shallow breath we took. Then the door thundered and Reda's voice roared, "Open the door!"

Reda and I stood motionless. I covered my mouth with my hand, hoping to keep my breathing from reaching Reda's ears.

Reda knocked even harder.

"We will open, but only when Mama comes back!" Rawyia shouted.

"No, now! I need one of you to go fishing with me."

"I will tell Papa," Rawyia threatened.

"If you don't open, I will break the door," Reda bellowed.

Terrified, just wanting the confrontation to end, I told Rawyia I would go with Reda, and opened the door.

Reda grabbed my arm. "You will come with me now."

Rawyia trailing us, I followed him quietly toward the front door. Reda handed me his fishing gear. I looked at my sister, hoping she would come with me, but her eyes spoke a definite *no*.

"La, don't worry. I will tell Papa," she said, but her promise didn't make me feel better. Reda would not be punished.

At first, Reda tried to be nice. I didn't trust his kindness. Though I had never gone fishing with him before, I knew how he treated my brothers when he took them along.

I could think only of the many hours I would have to spend with him. To avoid his rage, I decided to follow his instructions to the letter.

It was almost noon, and the clouds had burned off. Reda wore a straw hat. I had none, and my scalp was melting in the burning sun.

"How long are we staying?" I asked, trying to keep up with his fast walking pace. Reda knew I shouldn't be here. He was not allowed to take me out of the house.

"As long as I please." Reda turned his head and stared at me.

"Okay," I murmured.

When we reached the shore, the sea was raging. Howling waves crashed against the breakwater that paralleled the beach. Reda took his place on one of the gigantic cement blocks that made up the breakwater, while I stood trembling on another, holding his bait in a small basket.

The monstrous waves welled on the horizon and rolled toward me, one after the next. My knees wobbled, and I felt a rush of panic every time one crashed upon my block and showered me in salt water.

"Hand me some bait!" Reda shouted, startling me from my fearful anticipation of the next wave.

I rushed toward him, jumping from my block to his over the intervening gap, ignoring the wall of water racing toward me and being careful not to slip. When I reached him, I handed him one tiny shrimp. Reda took the bait and signaled me to leave.

After I turned and started back, a violent force and a horrifying sound engulfed me. Although I could see and hear nothing, I felt my skinny body being wedged between the rough sides of the blocks. In a second or two, I slipped deep between two blocks, aided by the slimy algae on their sides. I gripped the rim of a block tightly, my lower body dangling in the gap. Before I passed out, I felt my sides burning, and was deafened by the terrifying booming of the waves hitting the blocks around me.

I don't know how long I stayed sandwiched between the cement blocks. When I opened my eyes and looked up, the sun hit me in the face and I felt sand beneath me, hot on my back. Unable to bear the pain from the abrasions on my ribs, I cried out.

My brother stood beside me, looking angry, but I also saw fear in his eyes, the same fear he showed when our father scolded him for his bad grades.

"Stand up!" he shouted over the boom of the waves. "It's getting late, and we need to head home."

I tried to move, but I was in too much pain and began to cry. Reda offered his hand to help me stand, and I grabbed it. As I sat up, I saw blood all over my clothes. I touched my left side, felt dizzy, and almost fainted again.

My cotton dress was glued to my lacerated skin, and blood seeped through the thin yellow fabric. I wanted to scream, but I noticed some onlookers standing not far from my brother, so I held my voice in check. I stood. With a strong grip on my hand, Reda walked us toward the sea. I pulled away, fearful of where he was pulling me.

"Where are we going?" I demanded.

"Just come with me. You need some salty water to wash the blood."

"It's okay," I whispered. "I will wash at home."

"No, you will wash now!"

I wanted our father to see what had happened and punish Reda, but Reda had already thought of that. He grabbed my arm and dragged me closer to the water. Scooping it up with his hands, Reda poured water over my wounds and rubbed the sand off my bare skin. I screamed the whole time. An older woman standing not far from us ordered him to leave me alone. Reda did not answer.

"Let's go." He took my hand and pulled me along.

On the way home, I walked next to him, silently weeping

and holding my dress away from my burning skin. Reda harshly warned me not to tell Mama or Papa about what had happened.

"No, I won't, I promise! I will tell them it was my fault."

"Yes. You must tell them you wandered off on your own to catch crabs from the crevices and fell."

"Are you going to take me fishing again?"

"No," he replied without hesitation.

For a moment, I felt no pain. I even managed to stifle a cry of happiness.

When we got home, Rawyia was the first to see me in my bedraggled state. "What have you done to my sister?" she shouted in horror.

"I fell," I said quickly.

Reda went to his room. Rawyia and I retired to ours and locked the door. I told my sister what happened while she applied Mercurochrome to my wounds. Rawyia was irate but suppressed her anger. She knew my parents would never punish Reda for actions against us. After all, they allowed him to do much worse.

Reda received his share of discipline. Papa could be as harsh with Reda as he was with us girls, and even more so. For Reda, bad grades in school meant a beating with a bamboo stick. Nobody knew what Papa would have done if he had known about Reda's and Ahmed's activities with the servant girls. Well, Mama knew, but she took their side. Mama's inaction reinforced the bias of society that saw girls as the seducers and boys as the victims.

Rawyia often questioned the different treatment Reda and Ahmed received. Why could they go out, visit their friends, and have girlfriends, and she could not? The argument always ended in our brothers' favor. They were boys and could therefore do most anything they wanted.

"Why do boys have such a privilege?" I asked Mama.

"Because boys don't get pregnant, and no one can question

their virginity. We must not question God's creation." Mama used God as a way for us to accept the unfair treatment and stop asking.

But Rawyia kept the pressure on. "Why do girls get punished when boys rape them? Why not punish boys as well?"

"Girls bear the full responsibility for protecting their virginity. This is the way it is in Muslim societies. Boys could sleep with as many girls as they like and still end up with a virgin wife." Mama sounded sarcastic and unconvinced herself.

Rawyia and I continued to refuse these answers, and we never stopped searching for a convincing reason to explain the privileges our society gave to men. Being born girls seemed to be a crime we had not willingly committed, but for which we were blamed and punished nonetheless.

Every night, before she fell asleep, Rawyia prayed Reda and Ahmed would die.

"Do you really mean it, Rawyia?" I asked, surprised at her morbid wish. I resented Ahmed and Reda's cruel actions, and I got angry when they beat my siblings, Hady and Samir, but I did not wish them dead.

Reda and Ahmed forced Hady and Samir to play cards. When Samir or Hady would win, Reda and Ahmed would get angry and punish them with beatings. I mediated between them and did what I could to ease the punishment by pleading with the older boys.

Samir came to me for protection whenever Reda planned his abuse. I never let him down. Sometimes I fought with Reda and Ahmed, exchanging insults until they let Samir go unharmed. Samir, as the youngest, won my full care and attention. He was peaceful and stayed away from confrontations with Reda and Ahmed.

Hady was more like Rawyia and preferred fighting.

"Hady doesn't need our help, La. He is a fighter like me," she said.

Hala somehow escaped Reda and Ahmed's reign of terror. Because Hala was the youngest girl, and because of her acne problems, Reda and Ahmed figured she didn't need any additional torturing. In fact, they treated her nicely.

"She belongs in their camp," Rawyia told me when I tried to include Hala in our private time together. "I don't understand why God keeps Reda and Ahmed alive and makes them grow meaner and more brutal with every day." Rawyia sounded serious.

I did not share Rawyia's passionate hatred, but I did not like them either.

Rawyia fought with Reda and Ahmed constantly, and they did their best to torment her. They followed Rawyia everywhere around the house and barged into our bedroom uninvited whenever Rawyia spent time there alone. Sometimes Ahmed would even walk into our bathroom while Rawyia was taking a shower, pretending he needed to use the toilet, even though there were three other bathrooms in the apartment.

Rawyia pleaded with Mama to stop them from invading her privacy, but her tears did not shake our mother's trust in them. They were boys doing their job of protecting us.

To prevent Reda and Ahmed from barging into our bathroom, we made it a habit to lock the door when either of us was using it. If the other of us wanted to get in, she would knock, using a special code. Rawyia and I also decided, when I turned eleven, always to keep the door to our bedroom locked after what happened one evening.

We were getting ready for bed, when the door handle moved. Rawyia and I stood quietly in our nightgowns, hoping whoever knocked, Ahmed or Reda, would give up and go away.

"Open this door!" Reda said, knocking violently. "Open up or I'll kill you!"

Rawyia and I trembled with fear but did not open the door. Reda banged on the door so hard it knocked Rawyia's portrait off the wall.

Mama heard the noise and came to the scene, standing outside with Reda. "What's going on here?"

But Reda only banged on the door harder. "What are they doing inside? Why do they have the door locked?"

"This is not your room!" Rawyia shouted back.

"Open the door, girls," Mama said.

"Not until Reda leaves."

"Reda, you go to your room now," Mama said.

Rawyia cautiously opened the door. Mama stepped in and shut it behind her. "We have a right to privacy," Rawyia said with indignation.

"Rights! Girls have no rights and no freedom," Mama scoffed. "The protection of your virtue and your safety is your brother's responsibility." We had heard these exact words from Mama before, over and over.

"But, Mama, we are safe in our room. Why is our safety the responsibility of our brother and not ours, or yours and Papa's?" I asked.

"This is our culture. You have to live by its rules."

"No one has the right to control me, not even my brother," Rawyia insisted.

"Mama and Papa have the right to control us, Rawyia," I said.

Rawyia frowned at me.

Mama took me in her arms. "No one should control you, but in this house and in this society, you must abide by the rules, no matter how unfair they seem."

"Who set those rules, Mama?" Rawyia questioned angrily.

Mama heaved a sigh, clearly growing impatient with Rawyia's defiance.

"Did our Prophet Mohamed say brothers are the protectors of their sisters? Does the *Sharia* say that?" I asked. "I want to read the rules of this *Sharia*."

Mama hesitated. We knew that, unlike our father, Mama

did not read the Quran and no one had given her religious instruction. Our mother repeated verses that she had learned merely by recitation.

"I'm not sure," Mama said, "but this is the way my mother raised me. I never argued or questioned the role of any man. This is the way Muslim people treat boys, and women must accept it. A brother who doesn't assume the role of watching over his sisters is not a man in the eyes of the family and the community." She was unyielding.

But we never felt like Ahmed's and Reda's actions were protecting us. The boys were cruel and lorded their freedom over us daily. Like what happened to Rawyia two months shy of her eleventh birthday when she stepped out onto the front balcony. I was behind her, still in the dining room. Papa had not yet come home, and Mama was out running errands. Rawyia came face-to-face with the boy next door, standing on his balcony, twelve feet away.

"Hello," the boy said to Rawyia. He appeared older than she; a light fuzz of hair sprouted unevenly on his face. It seemed to flatter Rawyia that he would speak to her.

"Hello," she replied. "What's your name?"

"Samy." He smiled at Rawyia and ducked back through the door behind him into his family's apartment.

It didn't take long before Rawyia fell in love, and of course she told me all about it. She learned Samy was attending the school of military aviation for one year, training to be a pilot. He would come home for two days at a time, and Rawyia took every opportunity she had to sneak onto the balcony to see Samy. During those brief platonic interludes, Rawyia and Samy exchanged smiles and a few words. Miraculously, they managed to avoid being seen by my parents.

But Rawyia and Samy did not escape the watchful eyes of Reda and Ahmed. One day, Reda caught Rawyia on the balcony, exchanging smiles with Samy. Reda grabbed my sister by the hair and pulled her into the hallway outside our room.

"You're loose!" Reda repeated it and slapped Rawyia's face.

"I'm not loose. I am a virgin!" Rawyia yelled, pulling away. She screamed for help from *Tante* Akeela or Fareeda, but they didn't answer. In their eyes, Reda was performing his brotherly duty, which our parents allowed him to exercise.

Reda slapped my sister again and warned her that the next time he caught her out on the balcony with Samy, he would beat her much harder. He also imposed a new rule: Rawyia and I were forbidden to set foot on any balcony. No one in the family questioned or disputed the rule, and when Rawyia appealed directly to Papa, he supported Reda.

"Girls don't talk to boys," he warned, "even from a distance."

Forbidden love can make it that much sweeter, and Rawyia fashioned her own means of communicating with Samy. I had taken a shower and was drying off, when Rawyia knocked three quick taps, followed by two slow ones, then another, single tap on the bathroom door. I opened the door, feeling proud of myself for remembering the sequence that we had decided upon for that day.

Rawyia stepped inside and locked the door. "I need your help, La," she whispered.

I turned on the faucet, not wanting anyone to hear.

"I need you to stand guard while I talk to Samy. I've come up with a new way," she whispered.

Rawyia showed me a primitive telephone line she had made by connecting the bottom ends of two paper cups with a long piece of nylon fishing line.

Rawyia and I went to the front balcony for a live test with Samy. Rawyia threw one cup toward him. It was too light to reach his balcony. Rawyia ran back inside our apartment and filled the cup with marbles she'd collected from one of our brothers' rooms. Rawyia covered the opening with a handkerchief, tied it shut with some thread, and tossed it. This time,

Samy caught it with both hands and disappeared behind the railing of his balcony.

Rawyia crouched down on the floor of our balcony and instructed me to keep my eyes on the street to alert her if I saw Reda, Ahmed, or Papa approaching our building.

I enjoyed listening to Rawyia's secret conversation and when Rawyia said to Samy, "I miss you, too," I fell in love with their love.

Unfortunately, I got caught up in my reveries and ignored my duties as a watchdog. Suddenly, I heard footsteps behind us. Ahmed materialized from nowhere and swooped down upon us, his teeth digging into his lower lip. Ahmed seized Rawyia's arm, ripped the fishing line from the paper cup, and dragged her into his room, slamming the door behind them. Rawyia's scream sent me running to *Tante* Akeela for help.

Tante Akeela ignored my plea and kept on knitting a sweater. "Let him teach her some morals. Rawyia is a fallen girl. I cannot defend your sister if she has been talking to a boy."

My aunt's toxic words shocked me. I ran back to Ahmed's door. Inside, Rawyia shrieked and screamed. I could hear them scuffling. Fear paralyzed me, and I couldn't stop the warm stream running down my legs.

Rawyia's screams eventually stopped, and she emerged from the room with messed hair and eyes red and half closed with defiance. Her face was flushed, and her cheeks were bruised. Without speaking, she walked past me, and I followed her into our room. She got right into bed and pulled the eiderdown over her. I locked the door, crawled in beside her, wiped her tears, and caressed her face while she lay motionless. After a long while, she fell asleep.

Never again did Rawyia return to the balcony to see Samy.

CHAPTER 12

The summer before our betrothal announcement, I entrusted Rawyia with the piece of paper containing Ghassan's telephone number. One afternoon, when the coast cleared, Rawyia and I pulled the telephone with its long cord out of our parents' bedroom and into ours. The lock Papa had installed across the rotary dial did not stop us.

"Let me show you what I've discovered," Rawyia said with authority. She lifted the receiver, checked the number on the piece of paper, and started tapping the button that closed and opened the line connection—six taps for the number six, four taps for four, and so on—until she had tapped out the complete number. "It's ringing," she said to me excitedly. "Here, take it."

Rawyia handed me the receiver, and for a moment, I lost my composure. When I heard Ghassan's voice on the line, I almost dropped it. *"Alo? Alo?"*

I hardly remember what Ghassan and I said to each other, but I didn't dare stay on the line longer than two or three minutes, for fear that Mama, Reda, or Ahmed would appear and catch me in this forbidden act. Still, Ghassan did have time to ask me if we would see each other on the beach again.

"Yes," I said. "I mean, maybe. I hope so."

One day the previous summer, before we left for the beach, Rawyia had straightened my hair with a hot iron. My hair looked better straight and free of frizz. I counted the minutes. Once we got to the beach, Rawyia and I sneaked into the public restroom, where Rawyia defined my eyes with black liner and loaded my lashes with mascara. Mama pretended she didn't notice.

My knees buckled. I worried someone would see my anxiety.

"Are you okay, Laila? You seem to be off in another world." Mama settled onto her beach chair while my younger siblings dashed off to the surf.

"I'm fine, Mama. Don't worry."

Rawyia and I walked the length of the beach, inspecting every young man with dark skin and a hairy chest. Of course, we kept some distance from them and turned our heads away whenever they returned our gaze. Finally, after we had circled back halfway toward our starting point, I caught sight of Ghassan. He stood knee-deep in the sea about fifty yards from us. The sunlight sparkled on his tanned body. To me, he was a bronze statue.

When Ghassan caught sight of me, he waved, and his voice carried above the crowd and the noisy sea. "Hi, Laila!"

I glanced up the beach to make sure Mama wasn't watching. She had her reading glasses on and looked busy with her newspaper. But not far away from Ghassan, my younger brothers, Samir and Hady, were splashing each other in the water. Although I didn't dare call back to Ghassan, I returned his wave and a smile broke out across my face. Ghassan smiled back but kept his distance, seeming to understand not to approach me as he had the first time we met.

Every time we went to the beach, I looked for Ghassan and

saw him four times every week. My affection grew deeper. At home, when I closed my eyes before sleeping, I saw him again, standing in the shallow water, smiling and calling my name.

I dreamed of kissing him on the lips and chest and even dared to imagine him with me in bed, bathing my lips, breasts, and belly in his kisses. When I started to have a strange sensation that made my private parts throb, I opened my eyes. I could not touch myself, because Mama told us it was a sin.

My encounter with Ghassan, together with Rawyia's efforts at making me pretty, gave my self-confidence a huge boost, but at home, I couldn't wear all the makeup Rawyia applied for the beach days. I used a touch of blush on my cheeks and hoped Papa wouldn't notice and object.

Papa used Mama as his punching bag. He held Mama responsible for everything that went wrong at home. Our father tormented her with his constant complaints, voicing displeasure with the way she managed the household. She took Papa's abuse with silence.

One day, when Papa suspected Rawyia and I had had our hair trimmed, he ordered Mama into their bedroom. We were curious and followed at a safe distance. Reda, Rawyia, and Ahmed led the procession. I followed, holding Hala's hand, with Hady and Samir trailing behind.

Pressing my ear against their bedroom door, I heard Mama's voice. "No, no, Kamel. I would never give them a haircut without your permission."

Papa's words were only a murmur on the other side of the door, but there were other suspicious sounds. Mama's desperate voice grew louder. After what seemed like a long time, the door creaked open and Mama emerged, her face red and her eyes puffy.

"Mama, what's wrong? What happened?" Hady cried. We older children knew our mother would never tell us.

Mama staggered into the salon, clutching her chest. She

opened her mouth, but the only sounds that came out were dry, choking gasps. She seemed unable to breathe.

We guided Mama to a chair by the open window as Samir ran to bring her a glass of cool water. Mama's eyes bulged out of her head, and she ripped open her collar. With one hand wrapped around her blocked throat, Mama gripped the glass of water with the other and poured it in a stream over her heaving chest. I put my head on her shoulder and wept. We all tried to help Mama by embracing her or fanning her body.

Don't worry, my darlings," she said. "It's not your fault."

Growing up, I had seen Mama in this situation many times. As kids, we didn't know the long-term effect of those drilling sessions—as Rawyia and I called them—but we frequently witnessed Mama's suffering when our father released her after what could be hours of interrogation. These sessions did not always trigger Mama's choking attacks, but when one happened, it alarmed us. Our family doctor diagnosed her as having a nervous disorder caused by stress.

Meanwhile, the man to blame for her attacks stayed in his room, unreachable and unrelenting.

PART II: BEAUTIFUL BRIDES

CHAPTER 13

"Get up, beautiful brides," *Om* Zoubeida and Kareema yelled as they clapped and made a ruckus opening the shutters. "Come on, brides!"

I squinted and pulled the pillow over my face. From Rawyia's side of the bed, her breathing deepened with exasperation. "Get out!"

Sharing Rawyia's irritation, I had no desire to wake up or tolerate the maids barging uninvited into our room.

Kareema and *Om* Zoubeida ignored us and let out the traditional ear-piercing ululation of joy called *zaghrouta*. Their voices grew louder and louder, until *Om* Zoubeida happily announced that on Tuesday evening, two days before the betrothals were to take place, our grooms were coming to visit.

Mama walked in with the kind of smile she wore when she had to entertain my father's colleagues and wives for dinner and sat down. With each sip from her small glass, she smiled and made a sound of satisfaction.

She drank black tea several times a day and could not perform any task before she "balanced her head," as she put it.

Balancing Mama's head meant getting her thoughts straight.

Rawyia and I sat up, looked at each other, and then turned to Mama.

"Mama, what's this about?" Rawyia pointed to the two maids.

Mama placed her glass of tea on the night table and started to unbraid my hair. "Your father invited the grooms, and they are coming."

"What for, Mama, to inspect the merchandise?" Rawyia's eyes widened with anger.

"Why, Mama?" I panicked. "I thought the ceremony was set for Thursday."

Mama ordered the maids to leave the room.

"My lady, the *halawa* is ready for waxing." Kareema said before she left.

In the past, when Kareema had cooked this concoction made of water, sugar, and lime, we kids had hung around her in the kitchen to have a taste before she gave it to Mama and Fareeda to remove the hair from their legs and armpits.

Papa appeared at the door with a stern look on his face. "No hair removal, understood?" he ordered, and darted cold stares at Rawyia and me.

I had no courage to retaliate. My eyes spoke the resentment I could not verbalize. Papa's anger scared me, but it did not surprise me. Our father always looked at us with a fury I did not understand.

He walked in and sat on the chair facing us.

"How about nail polish?" Rawyia asked, throwing her shoulders back.

Rawyia showed an eagerness to start exercising some freedom, since she would be legally married in only a few days, but Papa was not yet ready to relinquish his supreme authority.

Our father lectured about the evil of cosmetics and gave Mama an angry glance now and then, the one he used to keep her silent. Surely, I thought, now that we were grown up and about to get married, Mama would say something in our defense. She did not.

"God gave you this color of nail. If *He* wanted it red, *He* would have made it red." Papa held up his pointer finger and rubbed its nail. He faced the mirror. "No lipstick, either. God has chosen this color for the lips." He pointed to his lower lip. "Why do you want to change it? If God wanted this blue, green, or yellow, *He* would have created it that color." He touched the upper lid of his eyes and raised his eyebrows for emphasis. "If God wanted this blue, green, or yellow, *He* would have created it that color."

I placed my mouth close to Mama's ear. "Ask him if I can have a haircut," I whispered, hoping that with our betrothal imminent, we would be allowed at least some things we could not do before.

Mama nodded. "Kamel," she said in a calm voice, "how about a hair trim for Laila?"

"No! God meant for women to have long hair. A woman with short hair is not desirable to her husband."

"God Almighty," Rawyia said. "Tell me, please, were we born only to satisfy men?"

"What are you saying?" Papa snapped, but I knew he had heard her, and I suspected he, too, might be tired of his continuous carping.

"Nothing," Rawyia mumbled, and turned her gaze out toward the balcony.

Disappointed, Rawyia and I kept silent until he finished imposing his restrictions. When he left, Mama followed him, but I called to her and she came back.

"Mama, why are they coming tonight?" I asked.

"To see you and your sister," she said in a dejected voice.

"What for, Mama? Papa already declared our acceptance."

"According to Islam, you both have to see each other before

your betrothal." Mama sounded unconvinced, not quite seeming to agree with this process.

I knew that in Islam, girls were supposed to see who they would marry before the parents could give their consent.

"What if I don't like Farook?" I asked. "Would Papa follow the rules of Islam, which dictate that no girl should be forced to marry a man she doesn't want?"

Mama didn't reply. I felt like the helpless lamb that we sacrificed every year after the Muslims' hajj to Mecca. That Rawyia and I had been selected and were waiting to be paraded to our final destination, in total submission, to the altar of fire.

"What if I refuse to meet Farook, Mama?"

"Don't even try," Mama warned, and walked out. She left me sinking into despair.

But later, Rawyia lifted me up. "I guess it won't be long before you can see Ghassan."

I put on a smile, the one I wore to pretend I approved of what Rawyia told me, though sometimes it wasn't pretense.

"Be serious, Rawyia. From now on, our lives will never be the same. You may be, but I'm not ready for marriage, and I plan to fight it. I will never give in."

"You are full of drama, La. What did you say you wanted to study?"

"Journalism!" I said, in no mood for jokes. "How many times do I need to remind you?"

Rawyia grinned. "Are you sure? Did you ever think of becoming an actress?"

"I honestly don't understand why you are in such a good mood," I snapped.

Mama returned and urged us to cooperate. She wanted to calm the waters and tried to sound cheerful. Her eyes darted back and forth between my wondering gaze and the challenging stare of my sister.

"Your father gave his word of honor," she said. "He sealed your acceptance with *Surat al-Fatihah* from the Quran. There is nothing that you can do to stop this marriage, Laila."

"Did you tell Papa that Laila wants to finish school to become a famous journalist?" Rawyia said.

Mama rubbed her knee.

"What is it, Mama?" I asked. "Is Farook rich? Do we need his money?"

She walked away in a failed effort to hide her glistening eyes.

"Answer me, Mama. Stand by me, please," I begged.

Mama turned back, her eyes swimming in a pool of tears. "Forgive me, my dear. If I could, I would."

I believed Mama. She would not go against our father's orders, especially in a matter as serious as our marriage. Which meant I had no choice but to go along with my parents' wishes: meet my future husband and make them all happy.

"Come on, dears!" my cousin Fareeda cheered as she and *Tante* Akeela rushed into our bedroom. "It's time to get ready. Let's start with a good bath!"

Our bedroom became like a souk, or market. Everyone dashed in, calling out suggestions and giving orders. The maids sang the famous wedding song "*Matzawaeeny Ya Mama Awam Ya Mama.*"

Like every young girl who enjoyed repeating that song, I had dreamed of the day when Mama would beautify my face with makeup, like the lyrics said, and ready me for my wedding. But this day, the words did not fill me with joy; the women's voices were like the shrieking of crows.

Rawyia and I were dazed and speechless, two spectators watching a tribal celebration before the slaughter of tethered animals.

Fareeda and *Tante* Akeela chanted as they escorted me to the bathroom, each holding a large white towel. My mother, *Om* Zoubeida, and Kareema joined the procession. When we were there, they left me alone with Fareeda and my aunt.

Their voices faded away when my bathing ritual began, and cold water trickled over my head. I stood naked in the bathtub, ceding the ownership of my skin to my cousin and my aunt, each of whom brandished a new loofah. Usually, new ones were soaked overnight in water to soften them, but these were as hard and rough as sandpaper.

Fareeda and Akeela jerked me around like a rag doll as they subjected my skin to their abrasive weaponry. They rubbed me as if I were an old piece of leather they were commissioned to smooth and polish. When Fareeda's loofah attacked my face, it burned beyond my tolerance.

"You're hurting me."

"Patience, my dear." She brandished the loofah. "This will lighten your complexion."

"I hate him," I sobbed. "I don't want to marry him."

"No, my dear Laila, don't say that," *Tante* Akeela admonished. "Even Farook can't refuse this marriage. Accept your fate."

"You told me once that fate is God's job, not my father's." I wiped the soap from my eyes.

She didn't respond and continued rubbing my skin with the loofah.

My father excluded Mama from the preparation as a punishment for questioning his decision about my marriage. He commissioned my aunt and her daughter to prepare everything, including buying my outfit. They bought me a light blue satin gown with long sleeves that resembled my school attire.

As they dressed me, I noticed Rawyia had disappeared and wondered where she might be and where she was getting ready. I paced the room, then sat at the edge of our bed and rocked myself to ease the pain developing in my stomach.

At a point, the rocking doing no good, I ran to Mama. She sat alone in the TV room, looking downcast and sad, but when she saw me, she gave me a smile full of love.

"Mama, isn't Rawyia meeting her future husband this evening?"

"No." She turned her gaze to the dying flowers in a crystal vase atop the TV cabinet.

"Did Gamal change his mind?" I knelt in front of her.

"No. He asked to visit on a later day."

"But Rawyia is older, Mama. Shouldn't she be first?"

"It is your father's decision."

We both fell silent. I was sure she was keeping something from me, and she likely knew I wouldn't rest until she told me.

"Mama, do you love me?"

She answered quickly, "Laila! I love you more than life itself."

"Then tell me what you are holding here." I pointed to her chest.

"No, Mama!" Rawyia's voice thundered into the room. She had entered the room quietly and stood behind me. "Let me tell La myself." Rawyia took me back to our room and hugged me. She folded her arms tightly around my waist. "This is your day, La, only yours. Gamal refuses to visit the same day as Farook."

I searched her eyes for an explanation.

"Gamal wants to have his own day to visit and celebrate. We can't blame him."

Somehow, I sensed something in her voice that she was trying to camouflage with a smile.

"Focus on yourself, La, and remember, we plan a different future without Farook and Gamal."

Rawyia's words announced the death of my marriage before it had started. I tried to ignore the ominous feeling, despite knowing Rawyia was keeping something away from me. Tears of uncertainty welled in my eyes. But with her reminder of future plans, I soon got hold of myself.

"I don't want to see tears. Your eyes are already red." Rawyia kissed me on the forehead and examined my face. "What happened to your skin? It is inflamed."

"The loofah."

Rawyia opened the drawer of the nightstand, took out a jar of Nivea cream, and smeared a blob on my face. "This will take care of it. Now wait here. I'll be back." She returned with a small plate holding a few slices of cucumber. "Lie down, La."

Obediently, I lay on the bed.

She placed the cucumber slices on my eyelids. "Good. Stay this way for half an hour. Your eyes will look normal again."

I grabbed Rawyia's hand. For a moment, all the love I needed flowed from her hand to mine and spread throughout my entire body. With her other hand and a tissue, Rawyia stopped my tears before they rolled on the pillow. We were quiet for a while. I could hear her breathing and felt her regret for upsetting me.

Rawyia and Fareeda did their best to make me feel good. They took this opportunity to do the things we were not allowed to do. They defied my father's rules about makeup. They camouflaged the traces of loofah abuse under layers of foundation and powder. They outlined my eyes with black liquid liner and redrew the contour of my brows. They even drew a birthmark on my right cheek, a sign of beauty, they claimed. Rawyia put my hair into a chignon. When I looked in the mirror, I hardly recognized myself. The girl in the mirror looked so funny, she made me smile, even while my tears blurred her vision and muddied her makeup.

With a towel, I cleaned around my eyes. I sat on my bed, waiting to meet Farook. Hala joined me. Samir and Hady walked in and sat quietly next to me. Samir, his eyes glistening with tears, stood and hugged me.

"If I was older," he said, "I would have saved you from this betrothal."

I wiped his tears with my hand. "Don't worry about me, little brother. I can take care of myself."

Rawyia walked in and asked our siblings to leave. "La, remember, this is all temporary."

I was not sure how a legal contract could be temporary, but I nodded in agreement anyway.

CHAPTER 14

At seven o'clock that evening, the doorbell rang. A moment later, I heard my father's voice calling me, and I trudged down the hall to meet my future husband.

I froze outside the salon, where they waited. Then I heard Rawyia's voice behind me. "Go ahead," she urged me.

My hand searched for hers. She reached and squeezed it, then gently patted me on the back. I entered the salon with my head down, my heart beating forcefully. At that moment, I stopped convincing myself it was a nightmare. Reality began to unfold, and I lost track of how and when the ordeal had started and where and when it would end. Going to meet Farook was the start of my fall into a bottomless pit.

Four eyes zoomed in on me, and I stumbled and hit my knee on the marble top of the center table. Farook stifled a sudden cry and involuntarily reached out a hand to help me but froze before he touched me. I quelled my anxiety with a deep breath and rubbed my knee.

Farook was not yet legally my husband, and he knew he could not touch any part of my body, except for shaking my hand in greeting.

The pungent scent of Farook's Old Spice aftershave overwhelmed the fragrance of the fresh rosebuds on the side tables. I struggled to control myself as I faced my two jailers.

Farook extended his hand. A chill ran through me when I raised my head and looked into his face. I gave him a cold stare and then leveled my gaze to his chest, unsure how to behave around him—alone, or in my father's presence.

Farook was a stranger, and I had not been around any men outside my immediate family. I did not have the desire or the comfort to socialize with them. Farook looked almost as old as my father. To escape my surroundings, I thought of Ghassan and relaxed.

"Ahlan, Ahlan!" Farook greeted me, smiling. His clammy hand smothered my fingers.

I pulled back my hand and wiped it on my dress. Looking triumphant, Farook centered himself on the Queen Anne sofa and rested his arm on the gilded wood. A gentle summer breeze drifted in through the windows, but that didn't stop the sweat from dripping off his forehead. The ambient light from the brass floor lamps failed to brighten the gray suit Farook wore, a color I had never liked.

My hands fiddled restlessly. I could not decide where to sit.

My father signaled me to take the seat on the bergère by his side.

"So, you were telling me that the cement budget is running out?" Papa picked up his conversation with Farook.

Farook remained silent. He uncrossed his legs and then crossed them again. I monitored Farook's moves deridingly through the mirror facing us. When Farook stuttered, I tore my inquisitive gaze away from him and looked back down at the floor. The intermittent chirping of sparrows outside filled in the sound in the room when Papa and Farook stopped talking.

"Submit a proposal tomorrow," Papa finally said. "This project is three months late already."

I relaxed when their focus moved from me to center on work, and I drifted away, thinking of Ghassan's sweet words.

Farook's distant voice brought me back to their world. "I will," he said, blinking repeatedly. Like the rest of us, he complied with my father's demands, and that made him even less attractive to me.

I slowly raised my head and looked into the mirror. There was Farook's profile. Dull, straight black hair covered his head, far from the wavy hair of most Egyptians and lacking the golden streaks in Ghassan's hair.

Evidently not realizing I could see every move he made in the mirror, Farook shot a few glances at me, while I helped myself to a full inspection of him. His prominent nose pointed down, covering part of his recently trimmed, wire-like mustache. The gap between his protruding lips gave me a peek at his small yellow teeth. Farook's ears were tiny compared with his big head, and his beady eyes, under bushy brows, were almost invisible. An uncoordinated face, I thought. It repelled me.

Farook's gray suit looked like the one my father wore at construction sites. I set my verdict button to guilty for his cooperation with my father, and guilty again for his unattractive physique. I rested my case.

My love for Ghassan would not have changed even if I had given Farook a favorable score. Never would I spend the rest of my life with Farook.

I knew what I wanted and how to achieve it on my own.

As I plotted my future, I saw Farook give me lingering glances and wondered if he could read my mind. I wanted to scream, to tell him I did not want to marry him.

Sitting next to Papa, I felt like an obedient slave, unable to allow the voice inside me to speak. By the time I lowered my gaze back to the Persian rug under my feet, my eyes swam in tears.

Kareema appeared, carrying a tray with three glasses filled

with sweet red syrup called *sharbat*. I wiped my face with the back of my hand, hoping no one had seen me cry.

Papa and Farook reached for their drinks. I did not. Then Papa asked me to leave the room. Relieved, I rushed out of the salon into the hallway, where Rawyia waited for me.

"You look awful," Rawyia whispered. "What happened? You didn't like him. I can tell. Good, we are together in our endeavor." She followed me back to our room, where I sat on the edge of our bed while she removed the hairpins from my chignon. "You look better with your braids."

I gently pushed her hand away.

"Tell me what's on your mind," she said.

"What's on my mind is me, Rawyia! At fifteen, I'm thinking of divorce when I'm not even married yet."

Rawyia took me in her arms. "By the way, I forgot to tell you. Gamal asked Mama to keep me out of any social activities with Farook after your betrothal."

"Why?" I jerked my head back and searched her eyes.

"It is because of your father-in-law's crimes. Papa asked Gamal to reconsider, and Gamal refused."

"What do you mean? What crimes?"

"Papa didn't like what Gamal decided. He even asked me if I wanted to marry Gamal. I could have asked him to cancel my betrothal, but I like that Papa does not like Gamal. I want a man who listens to me and not to my father."

Rawyia welcomed the animosity between our father and Gamal. She wanted Gamal to be as different from our father as possible, to exercise his rights as a legal husband without Papa's influence.

She felt as exhausted as I did. "Let's sleep now, and we can talk more tomorrow. Maybe I can find a solution for you."

"From now on, my tomorrows will be like my todays—no difference."

In bed, I turned my back to her. She wrapped her arms

around my waist tenderly, but I could not sleep. I jumped out of bed, turned on the light, put my glasses on, and sat down in front of the mirror.

"Am I really ugly, Rawyia? Tell me the truth; don't lie!" I pleaded. "Is this why Papa is rushing me into a marriage to the first man who proposed?"

Rawyia approached me and removed my glasses. "When you take these off, you look much better." She moved to the farthest corner of the room to my right, held up three fingers, and asked, "How many fingers do you see?"

"Three."

"Then you *can* see. Why do you wear these glasses?"

"I wanted to look like you, Rawyia! When you got yours, I told Papa I couldn't see a needle on the carpet. I lied. I thought if I wore glasses, I would look pretty in our father's eyes."

"I suspected as much, but you will weaken your eyesight if you keep wearing them. Besides, you are very pretty, with glasses or without." She sounded honest. "Remember your beach admirer, Ghassan? He liked you without your glasses. Did you forget that Ghassan chose you and not me? Look." She motioned for me to stand next to her in front of the mirror. "You are taller than me and very beautiful. Do you really think that if you were ugly, Ghassan would have given you his phone number?"

"No."

"Then stop this nonsense! Go wash your face and remember that I am getting married, too. You are not alone in this."

We hugged.

CHAPTER 15

Rawyia and I feared eavesdropping on our parents' conversations. We believed our father would see us or know somehow we had listened in on his private conversations with our mother.

That evening, upon leaving the bathroom, I heard loud voices coming from our parents' room. Mama sounded angry. I stepped out into the hallway and inhaled a deep breath while I stood in front of their door, listening. While I knew I could be caught eavesdropping, I had an ominous feeling their argument had something to do with my betrothal, and so I gambled.

"You are not going to tell Laila, and that is an order." Papa's voice reached my ears loud and clear.

My heart raced violently.

"Are you afraid of Farook's father?" Mama's words were a whisper, but I heard them.

I trembled and kept listening.

"Farook is not at all like his father."

"I cannot face Laila. You have to tell her yourself," Mama said. Her voice was firm and loud.

Blood ran slow and heavy in my veins like lava, and I felt my insides melting. I put my hand on the doorknob and stopped when I heard my father's voice.

"No. Laila should not know before her wedding. It's an order, or you will be *talek bil talata*."

The floor sank under my feet. *Talek bil talata* meant divorced three consecutive times. That was an irrevocable divorce. Men in our culture had the divine right to verbally declare a legally valid divorce.

I froze, unwilling to barge in and confront them with what I had heard, too worried Papa would divorce Mama.

A hand covered my mouth, and another grabbed my wrist. Rawyia pulled me back into our room and pushed the door shut. "Since when do you eavesdrop? What did you hear?"

"It's my father-in-law," I said, my voice breaking. "Papa is hiding something from me."

A few minutes later, Mama walked in. She knew me well. Looking at me, she realized something serious had shaken me, and she immediately turned to leave.

"Mama! I need to talk to you."

She sat down on our bed and called for Kareema to prepare a pot of tea. "Laila, my darling, I don't want you to worry about anything." Mama spoke with tenderness. "I know you don't want to get married, and I tried to convince your father, but you know my limitations."

"I believe you, Mama," I said with a pretend smile. "Did you fall in love with Papa before you were married?"

My question caught Mama by surprise. She paused, rubbing her knee.

Kareema appeared with a pot of tea on a tray. Mama placed it on her lap. She filled her cup with the black tea she preferred, added three cubes of sugar, and stirred and stirred and stirred the hot brew.

"The cubes are dissolved, Mama!" Rawyia blurted.

"Yes, I loved him," Mama finally said. "I loved him very much." She took a sip from her tea. "Your father and I both lived in the apartment building his parents owned. Our love was pure and innocent, but he never talked to me. We usually met—by accident, you know—in the stairway. He chased me with his eyes only." Mama's face glowed.

Rawyia and I had heard the story many times.

"Yes, Mama," Rawyia prompted her, "and you could not talk to him but gave him a lot of smiles because he was handsome and the dream of all the girls in the neighborhood, but he chose you to be his wife."

"So, Mama," I said, giving her no time to think, "you and Papa fell in love, right?"

"Yes, of course!"

"Then why are you denying *us* that kind of love?"

"Love will come with time."

"Do you really want me to marry this man, Mama?"

"I don't, my daughter, but it is your father's decision."

I reached for the Quran on the night table and held it between my hands with tenderness and respect. "I want you to swear on this holy book that you will tell me the truth about all of the questions I am about to ask you. And please, Mama, no excuses," I challenged her. "I know you don't go to bed until you've performed your ablutions, so you are cleansed and ready to swear on the Quran."

Mama agreed, but not before she warned us that if our questions were about Farook, she would not answer them.

"Why not?" we both asked in one voice.

"Your father made it clear that if I tell you anything, he will divorce me." Mama sounded serious, and I put the Quran back in its place.

"Okay, Mama, whatever you say."

"Does *Tante* Akeela know anything about Farook's father?" Rawyia asked.

Mama's eyes widened, but she composed herself quickly. "Yes, of course. Your aunt knows everything. Akeela probably knows more than I do."

"Is it all right to ask her?" Rawyia said.

"It depends on what you want to know." Mama shook her head and gave us an irritated look.

"I want to know everything about my future father-in-law," I pleaded with frustration and impatience.

"Your father-in-law?" Mama gave me a surprised look as she stressed every syllable.

Rawyia took over: "Laila heard you talk to Papa about Farook."

"What did you hear?" Mama's hands trembled, and tea spilled onto her dress.

"I can't tell you, Mama, because if I do, you will have no choice but to break your promise to Papa."

Mama lowered her gaze to the ground and shook her head in resignation. Then she lifted her hands and face upward. "Dear God, help them to accept their fate."

"We won't, Mama," we said in chorus.

I waited all night in bed, preparing and arranging in my head the questions I would ask of my aunt, until the call for the *Fajr*, or dawn prayer, from a nearby minaret woke the family. My parents, the maids, my aunt, and my cousin all joined in a community prayer.

My stomach clenched as I wondered what my aunt had to say about my father-in-law. Feeling restless, I sneaked into *Tante* Akeela's room and slipped into her warm bed, expecting her to return to her room, as she always did after dawn prayers. I was not in the habit of visiting her so early.

My aunt walked in, her head loosely wrapped with the white *tarha* she always wore during prayers. She greeted me with a smile.

"Auntie, you don't get along with Mama's family, right?" I asked from her bed.

Tante Akeela gave me a puzzled look but answered with an inviting smile. "Yes, because your mother's sister, Haleema, and her family are not good, abiding Muslims. Why do you ask?"

I wasn't sure what she meant by "good, abiding Muslims," but I ignored her comment to keep us focused on my issue.

"Promise to tell me the truth, no matter what I ask."

"You know how much I love you, my dear. I will tell you anything you want to know." She sat down on the bed beside me, her hands in her lap.

"What do you know about my future father-in-law?" I looked her straight in the eyes, knowing I could trust *Tante* Akeela to be frank with me.

"My dear, Farook has nothing to do with his father," she said, shaking her head and widening her eyes. "Farook is not like him."

Tante Akeela's answer numbed me from head to toe, and a look of anxiety crossed my face.

"Sooner or later," she said, "you will know the truth, so I might as well tell you now."

I nodded. Even though I wanted to listen, I didn't think I would like what she had to say.

"It happened during World War II, when the port of Alexandria fell under the control of the British army and they needed a supply of longshoremen." She guided my head to rest on her lap. I pulled back. "Haytham, your future father-in-law, took a job as manager of the workforce in a large company owned by your mother's brother-in-law, Tharwat. Young Haytham, a hugely built man with shoulders as broad as a wall, possessed a voice that roared like a lion."

"Get to the story," I urged my aunt, wanting her to skip the irrelevant details.

"Haytham's workers accepted his authority, not because Haytham had any special talent, but because they feared him."

"I am not interested in hearing about his voice or his physique, Aunty!"

She ignored my outburst and continued. "Tharwat trusted Haytham not only because they were related but also because Haytham kept the workers in the port under control and productive."

"*Tante* Akeela, please hurry," I pleaded. "I need to know everything before tomorrow."

"Laila, my dear." *Tante* Akeela sighed. "Leave the past alone and look to the future. Farook is a good man. I would not tell you that if I knew otherwise. Accept your fate, and think of the freedom that you are about to experience. I wish I had your luck. If Farook asked to marry Fareeda, I wouldn't hesitate a second to accept."

"Then why don't you offer Fareeda?"

"Your father made the arrangement. He gave his word."

I raised my arms in despair. "Okay, *Tante*, keep going."

Tante Akeela removed the *tarha* from her head. "It was rumored that Haytham had murdered many young men, but the police could find no bodies."

I felt light-headed. Murder? How could my father throw me to such a family?

"Why would Haytham murder people?" I could think of no sane reason for anyone to commit a murder.

"No one knows," *Tante* Akeela answered in a calm voice.

"You promised to tell me the truth," I pressed.

Tante Akeela cracked the bones of each finger and took her time before jolting me with another revelation. "The investigation implicated Haytham, and the police accused him of sexually molesting those boys."

I buried my face in both hands.

Tante gently removed them and held them as she gazed into my eyes. "My dear, the judge declared him innocent of all charges after a lengthy trial."

The room spun as I listened to *Tante* Akeela in disbelief. She asked me not to judge Haytham before she had told me the whole story. I rested my head in her lap again and listened.

"The whole family chose to believe in Haytham's innocence, especially Tharwat. Tharwat did everything in his power to help Haytham, and Tharwat had plenty of power at the time." She seemed proud of this "power."

Numb, I didn't want to hear any more. I tried to stand up but couldn't move.

"Fearing that the allegations against Haytham would cause a big scandal for the family," she said, "Tharwat hired top lawyers to get Haytham's name cleared." *Tante* Akeela drifted away. It seemed as if she were trying to awaken her memories. "The trial went on for several years. The police could not find the bodies. The boys in question had just disappeared."

My aunt sounded as if she was recounting a drama from a movie. I couldn't believe I was part of this gruesome story. I had to be dreaming. Then the sound of her voice told me it wasn't a dream.

"According to the Quran, two witnesses are required to prove guilt, and since there were none, the judge acquitted Haytham." She shrugged.

I moaned like a wounded animal and rocked back with every word. While she talked, I thought of something Mama had told me: Haytham owned the building where Farook and I would be living. The thought of our proximity to him made me panicky.

I had doubts about Haytham's innocence. Gamal had rejected Farook because of his father's reputation. If the police had not found the bodies, then there must be a missing piece in the case. Had *Tante* Akeela kept that from me? And why would Papa have warned Mama and threatened her with divorce if my father-in-law was innocent? But I kept my suspicions to myself. I was sure now I would not spend the rest of my life with Farook.

"How old is my future father-in-law, *Tante*?" I hoped she would tell me something to ease my fear, like perhaps too old to see or to walk.

"I don't know. Haytham must be very old, but I heard he remains strong and is feared by his sons."

"I am afraid of him, too."

"You will be marrying his son," she said. "You and Farook will stay in your apartment, and Haytham and his family in his." *Tante* Akeela tried to convince me Haytham was harmless, but she read on my face how disturbed I was. "Now, let me finish," she said, avoiding eye contact with me. "On the day that Haytham was acquitted, your mother delivered a baby and—"

"I am that baby! My parents gave me the name Innocent to celebrate Haytham's innocence. How could they do that? How could they connect me forever to that man? And why does my father want me to marry Haytham's son?" I felt weak and almost passed out.

Tante Akeela told me my father had felt bad about what Haytham's family had been through and had particularly warm feelings for Farook.

"He worked with your father ever since he graduated from the College of Commerce" she said. "It took several weeks to persuade your father to agree to the nickname Laila for you."

If my parents were sure of Haytham's innocence, why had Mama insisted on giving me another name? My suspicion grew deeper.

"My dear," *Tante* Akeela said, "your name has *Baraka*. It is the word that starts *Surat al-Tauba* in the Quran."

I didn't care about any special blessing.

Tante Akeela reached for the holy book on her dresser, opened it to the tenth chapter, and held it before me, pointing to the first word, *Baraat*.

"It's a special name, a unique name, and you should be proud of it."

I was consumed with rage and disappointment. Shaking my head, I dragged myself out of her room.

When I left *Tante* Akeela's room, I went looking for Mama and found her sitting in the kitchen nook with an untouched, full cup of tea on the table.

I pulled up a chair and sat next to her. She didn't move. Her elbows rested on the table, and her head slumped between her hands.

"You owe me an explanation, Mama."

"What else could you want to know? Your aunt has explained everything."

"She did, but I need to hear from you if my future father-in-law is truly a criminal or not. I want to know what you think." I wanted so much for Mama to corroborate my suspicion. I needed a strong case to back up my rejection of the betrothal.

Mama took me in her arms. "You know that your name is special," she whispered, "just as you are special." She said those words with sorrow in her voice, and I realized she didn't want to answer my question.

I could only give Mama a smile of resignation.

Unable to deal with my heavy load of hatred toward my father and toward my mother's passivity, I promised myself to be assertive and never to yield to a man's control. I was not sure, but I knew I would try to get out of the betrothal.

CHAPTER 16

The surprises and changes that were happening in my life prompted me to think of a way out before the betrothal took place. I sank into a trance, weighing the pros and cons of my escape—either run away or confront my father—until Rawyia's voice filled the air and pulled me out of my reverie.

"La, do you need something to eat or drink? I'll call Kareema to bring you some tea with milk and a sandwich."

"I'm not hungry. I want to run away before my betrothal. You must help me."

"Papa and Reda will kill you." Rawyia's assessment sounded then like the perfect solution.

"Good! I don't want to live."

"Stop this drama," Rawyia said in her big-sister voice.

"I will confront Papa tonight." I got out of bed and paced around the room.

"You know, La, there's nothing we can do now." She opened the window and walked out onto the balcony. "Soon we will be betrothed. No power on this earth can force our father to cancel the ceremony. The invitations have already gone out."

Rawyia's words wiped away my hopes and almost strangled my fighting spirit, but I refused to succumb without a fight.

"Think of all the advantages you will gain from your marriage," Rawyia said. "Look at us both. We are slaves. What could be worse than this?" She poked me in the shoulder. "Consider Farook your savior. That's how I think of Gamal."

I wasn't ready to accept a betrothal. The idea of resigning myself to the situation had not yet settled in my mind. The assertive spirit inside me was still breathing and alive. The air in the room grew lighter.

"Rawyia, I'm sure our father loves us." I looked at her, searching for signs of approval.

She just rolled her eyes.

"Remember how Papa cried the time you and I had our tonsils removed? Maybe if I plead with Papa, he could be that person again."

Rawyia shook her head in disagreement. "You are dreaming," she said, throwing me back into despondency.

"I don't care what you think, Rawyia," I said, now in utter frustration. "I am not yet giving up."

A short time later, Mama entered our room, her head draped in a white prayer veil. Her eyes were red and puffy as she sat down on the edge of our bed. I sat beside her. She pulled the veil over her face.

Through Mama's veil, I saw tears rolling down her cheeks. I wiped them with the veil and stroked her hands. Mama cried even more. I took her in my arms and rocked her gently, like a mother soothing her child.

"Mama, don't be sad for me. I've changed my mind about Farook. I don't mind marrying him," I lied.

Mama squeezed me tight. "I'm sorry, my dear, for being so helpless, for not fighting for you."

"I will try to love him, Mama," I lied again. I wanted her to believe I was okay. Mama's suffering tormented me.

"My prayers will guide you to the right path," Mama murmured, patting me on the back.

"That's what I am counting on, Mama. You have told me many times that mothers' prayers are sacred and your blessing is all that I need from you."

I meant what I said. I hoped Mama's prayers would somehow save me from my fate.

"I pray to God every day," she said. "I am sure your father does as well, to forgive us for our mistakes."

But I was not sure if God would forgive them for forcing me to marry someone I had not chosen.

CHAPTER 17

Souad, our home tutor for the Arabic language and the Quran, told Rawyia and me we had to obey our parents no matter what they did. She warned us, quoting verses twenty-three and twenty-four from the seventeenth chapter of the Quran.

But Souad also told us that the Quran forbade marriage without the girl's consent. Armed with the holy verses and Mama's approval, I faced Papa.

I knocked on my father's bedroom door with that thought running through my head. My father did not invite me in. Mama had followed me for encouragement, stepped forward, opened the door, and signaled me to enter.

Darkness shrouded the room, except for the dawn light seeping through the wooden shutters. Windows closed and sheer curtains drawn, Papa was performing his long morning prayer.

I tiptoed in and waited by the armoire. Papa always performed the ordained prostrations according to Muslim tradition. Sometimes, when time allowed, he followed mandatory prayers with additional prostrations called Sunna.

I sat motionless at the edge of his bed and hoped he would

skip the Sunna. A surge of defiance ran through my veins, and I crossed my legs, something we were not allowed to do in my father's presence.

Every time he bowed for the *ruku* and then went down on his blue prayer rug for prostration or *sujud*, I took a deep breath to empower myself.

Papa stood again and repeated the rituals. I thought he had reached the final phase of his spiritual trip, but he went down, again, onto the two red minarets painted on his rug. He tucked his feet under himself, rocked rhythmically, and spent an additional twenty minutes pleading for God to forgive his sins and to have mercy on his soul in the afterlife. I wanted to ask my father for what sins he asked God's forgiveness, and whether forcing me into an arranged marriage was included in the list he was worried about, but I kept my thoughts to myself.

When Papa finally turned his head to the right and to the left and showered the angels with the salutation *Asalam alaykom wa rahmat Allah*—"peace and blessings be upon you"—my heart raced, for I knew he had finished.

I uncrossed my legs and stood, hesitating, my mind torn between my strong desire to confront Papa and my lack of confidence.

"What are you doing here?" Papa's loud voice startled me.

"I want to talk to you."

"What about?" he snapped. "Your dress?"

"No, I know that it will be delivered soon."

"You will like it," Papa assured me, and remained crouched on his holy rug, facing the balcony.

"I know, Papa," I said in a calm voice. "You have good taste. Thank you."

He nodded. "So, what brings you here?" He sounded annoyed. He stood, gathered his prayer rug, and folded it in half. "If I had any doubts about Farook's compatibility," he said, still facing the balcony, "I would never have accepted him." He padded over to his desk in his stocking feet, still holding on to his prayer rug.

"Would Farook allow me to go to school?" I blurted out. I wanted to tell him how much I despised him for what he had done to my life, but I could not summon the courage to do so.

"I didn't ask him. If you want, you can always study at home." He motioned with his arm, still giving me his back.

"Home?" I shouted back. "You mean Farook won't agree?"

"High school is for loose girls," he said, and faced me with challenging eyes. "School is where girls encourage each other to commit sin." Papa paused. "May God burn him in hell!"

"Burn whom? Whom are you talking about?"

"Qassem Amin," he said with disgust. "He is the reason I am in this position now."

"What do you mean?" I have never heard of this Qassem Amin."

"Qassem is the one who encouraged women to take the man's role in society." He looked at me with a frown. "He told women they were slaves to their husbands and that they should liberate themselves. Since Qassem, women have been asking for their so-called rights."

I wanted to know where this Qassem was located. He sounded different from the men around me, but Papa didn't give that a chance. He blamed Qassem for our impudent behavior.

"We never had any problems when women were confined to raising their children and taking care of their husbands and homes. If it weren't for Qassem Amin, I would not be standing here answering your questions."

I stood, lost in thought, unable to believe that an Egyptian man who called for women's liberation had ever existed.

"Is Qassem Amin alive?"

"No, and he must be burning in hell."

I disagreed but wanted Papa to stay focused on the subject I had come to see him about.

"You don't believe in women's education?" I could not comprehend that an educated man would reject women's education.

"No!"

"If you're against educating women, why didn't you keep us at home?"

Papa's jaw contracted. I knew I had stepped over the line. My chin quivered, but my eyes remained defiantly tearless.

Papa reached for the *Al Ahram* morning newspaper on his desk. "Do you have anything else to talk about?" He opened the newspaper.

"Doesn't the Quran say you have to ask me if I want to marry this man, or any other man?" I felt proud of my courage.

Papa's upper lip twitched. "Yes, what you say is true."

I felt a spark of relief.

But Papa went on. "You are still underage, and I am your legal guardian."

"How can I get married if I am underage?"

"This is not for you to worry about."

"Why did you choose a man whose father had a criminal past?" I was surprised at my words and thought they couldn't be mine, but then, besides Papa, I was the only one in the room.

"Haytham was acquitted," Papa snapped, and disappeared behind the newspaper. I approached him. He lowered the paper. His eyes met mine with an icy stare.

"Do you really believe the judge presiding over Haytham's trial was honest?" My voice quivered some. I was breaking down, my strength leaving me.

Papa turned from me and walked over to his dresser. In the mirror, I could see his pupils were dilated with rage.

Crying, I collapsed on his bed. Papa approached but then stopped. I wished he would take me in his arms and tell me that he'd changed his mind about the betrothal. Instead, he walked away and released a deep breath—guilt or anger, I didn't know. We remained there as I sobbed.

"Why are you in such a hurry to get me married, and to someone I don't want? What have I done to deserve to spend the rest of my life with a man old enough to be my father and whose father was accused of murdering young children?"

"Young children?" Papa snapped. The statement startled him, and he looked concerned. "Who told you that?"

"My aunt."

"Akeela must have told you that it's all rumors," Papa said, expecting me to agree.

"Rumors? Then why is Gamal refusing to socialize with Farook?"

Papa shook his head. "I have made up my mind, and you shall trust my choice. Farook is the one to provide you a good life, not an education."

I gathered every ounce of courage I had remaining. "I will never allow Farook to have me, and I promise you that I will divorce him, even if it takes me the rest of my life."

"You will be the loser." Papa shook his head.

"I have already lost all that is valuable—my future."

CHAPTER 18

The next evening, I heard a commotion in the salon. I opened the door leading to the foyer, and for a moment, I thought I was dreaming. Rawyia sat on the Queen Anne sofa facing the balcony. Our eyes met, but she ignored me. She was smiling and wore a sleeveless off-white chiffon dress I had not seen before. Her legs were crossed in a seductive way, something our father considered indecent.

Next to Rawyia sat a short man with an olive complexion and curly black hair. His smile rivaled hers. Papa occupied the chair facing Rawyia. His eyes squinted, gaze fixed on the closed glass door leading to the balcony.

Between Rawyia and the man with curly hair was an old man wearing a white turban and a light brown caftan. This man pulled a freshly ironed white handkerchief from his pocket and covered the hands of both Rawyia and the man I assumed was Gamal. He recited verses from the Quran while Rawyia and the man with curly hair melted into each other's gazes. When the man finished, he shook my father's hand and congratulated him. "May God bless this union with happiness and healthy children!"

Rawyia betrothed? The space around me spun, and I almost lost my balance. I felt lonesome for having lost my best friend.

Miserably confused, I wanted to run and hide, but when I heard the ululations reverberate through the hallway, my body shivered and I could not move.

Rawyia's gaze caught mine, and she parted her lips as if to say something. Somehow, that released me, and I turned around and walked away.

Why had Rawyia kept her betrothal ceremony from me? Why had it happened so suddenly? Maybe Rawyia herself did not know. Maybe Papa had surprised her as well. I wanted to believe that Rawyia had not betrayed me, so I hung on to the trust and devotion we shared as I headed to our room, where I would wait for her explanation.

Mama caught up with me. "Your father wanted to get rid of Rawyia as quickly as possible. It doesn't matter to him how or when she gets married."

So this was how my father had put an end to Rawyia's courage and defiance. Papa thought a betrothal would keep her from influencing Hala and me with her liberal and nonconforming behavior.

Shortly after I returned to the bedroom, a rattling against the doorjamb startled me from my chagrin.

"La! We're coming in," I heard Rawyia say. Then, as she opened the door, she turned behind her. "Gamal, come in, my darling," she cooed.

With shock, I watched as Rawyia led that man by the hand into our private sanctuary. Rawyia asked Gamal to sit on the dresser chair and, like a child, made herself comfortable on his lap.

"Gamal, my dear, make yourself at home."

Gamal grinned beneath Rawyia's scandalous embrace. Twisting around on his lap, Rawyia turned to meet my gaze in the vanity mirror and winked.

I forced a smile, not knowing what to do or say. Unlike Rawyia, I could not change my timid nature, and Rawyia knew it. A man in our bedroom with my sister all over him not only scared me but made me feel small and uncomfortable.

The space around me shrank, suffocating the freedom I cherished in my bedroom. I expected Papa to barge into the room and blow up with rage.

This was a situation I had not experienced before, and I had no idea how it would end. I sat at the edge of the bed, covered my knees with the eiderdown, and hugged them, rocking myself, anticipating the worst. But when no one came into our room, I relaxed and began enjoying the new and unusual moment, forgetting my anger and disappointment.

Rawyia floated like a ballerina. She stood behind Gamal, dug her chin into his curly black hair, and said in a calm voice, as if she had been introducing me to guys all her life, "Laila, meet my husband. Gamal, meet my favorite sister, Laila. I call her La." Rawyia looked at Gamal with admiration.

I grinned. "Does Papa know Gamal is in here?"

"Papa can't say anything now." Rawyia pulled Gamal up from the chair. They sat down on the edge of the bed. Rawyia pointed her index finger at Gamal's chest. "This is my husband, and he can enter any room in this house. I know my rights."

While I had never seen Rawyia's face glow with such happiness, I doubted her sudden show of romance with a man she hardly knew. I wanted to ask her if the stars sparkling in her eyes were natural. Our cousin Samira swore to us that movie stars used glycerin in their eyes to make them glisten in love scenes.

Yet Rawyia's joy seemed real. She was radiant. I had many questions about the ceremony and the instant love Rawyia exhibited for Gamal, but I didn't have the chance to ask. Gamal stayed glued to her and Rawyia to him.

Our father's voice interrupted, reaching us through the

walls that separated our bedrooms. He seemed to be yelling at Mama. "Go and tell your insolent nephew to respect the sanctity of this house and get out of the girls' room." Papa paused, and then shouted, "This is not a bordello. Who gave your nephew the right to trespass and invade the girls' privacy? Gamal's place is in the salon!"

Rawyia and I listened to Papa in silence. Outrage deepened the furrows on Gamal's forehead. Rawyia tapped the floor nervously, and anger flared from her eyes. I was smiling, curious to see how far she would go with her newly acquired rights. I could not have been more proud of my sister.

Mama walked into our room and shut the door. She fiddled with the purple scarf loosely covering her hair. "Let's all go to the salon. Kareema is coming to clean your room now."

Rawyia took Gamal by the hand and followed Mama. I trailed behind them.

My sister stopped midway between the salon and my parents' room. "I am going out with my husband tonight."

My father, still in his bedroom, did not react. Our father believed that a girl who sat with a gap between her legs was a loose girl, and asking to be raped. Chewing gum was for low-class girls. A girl who wore makeup had a desire to be kissed. A loud girl invited men to fantasize and commit the unthinkable, the mother of all sins, the one orchestrated by the devil himself—sex.

In earlier days, Papa had told Rawyia and me, with nostalgia in his voice, that women wore ankle bracelets with many charms that jingled. The sound alerted men to keep their eyes away from women.

It satisfied us to see the pained look in our father's eyes as he observed Rawyia breaking all the strict rules we had grown up with.

That night, I dozed fitfully in our bed, alone, until Rawyia's footsteps clattered through the hall and startled me.

Papa stayed up late, too. I knew this because before I went to sleep, I saw his bedroom door ajar and a light from his bedside lamp crept into the darkness of the hallway.

When Papa was angry, he sat upright in his chair, one leg folded under his derrière and the other crossed over it, jerking in a rhythmic motion. I envisioned my father sitting like this as Rawyia came through the hall, his arms crossed on his chest and his torso rocking forward and backward in time with his leg.

After jumping out of bed, I opened the door for Rawyia, pointing to my wide-open eyes and then to Papa's room, silently telling her Papa was awake. Rawyia tossed her head and threw her hands in the air. She didn't care.

I signaled for her to button her blouse, but she only opened it farther. Terrified of what might happen next, I scooted back into our room.

Rawyia strode straight into our bedroom, her tousled hair framing an expression of satisfaction, her face red from kissing. She looked like a sultry movie actress with perfect beauty and tragic love, one of those to whom our cousin Samira had furtively introduced us behind our father's back.

"Rawyia," I whispered, "you look just like Faten Hamama."

She sat down on the bed, carelessly patting down her mussed hair, and threw me a sharp glance. "You know, I studied all her love scenes." Rawyia gave me a wicked smile. "I am exercising my newly acquired rights."

"Aren't you concerned about what Gamal might think of you?" I had my suspicion about Rawyia's feelings toward Gamal. Had she actually fallen in love with him, or was she just acting?

Rawyia only smiled again.

Something in Rawyia's gleam made me catch my breath as an almost unthinkable question occurred to me. "Are you planning to have sex before your wedding night?"

"Of course, La. Love is beautiful. Besides, Gamal is my legal husband."

"But what about Papa?"

Rawyia giggled. "I'm not worried about him. Papa knows he has no authority over me now that I belong to Gamal."

That night, I went to bed full of envy and admiration for Rawyia. I wanted so much to be like my sister, to experience love and go out with the man I loved—Ghassan. I craved the life of a teenager and the enjoyment of romance.

Rawyia's adventure with Gamal became a window into my future. I never tired of listening to her descriptions of how she and Gamal kissed and hugged. While I wished to have my sister's courage and cleverness, I was not ready for sex, not even with Ghassan if ever we got the chance to be alone.

Rawyia tested the boundaries, and I learned from her example. Once, she asked me not to imitate anything she did unless she accomplished it successfully.

"Observe how I handle situations," she said, "How I behave with Gamal—what I give him and what I don't."

I didn't want to act with Ghassan the way Rawyia wanted me to, but I nodded.

"Learn from my mistakes." She pointed to herself. "Don't let emotions blind you to the danger you are about to face—and I mean men." Rawyia turned her gaze to the ceiling. "Under this roof, I learned everything about men. Our father trusted Ahmed to protect us." She sneered. "Because of Ahmed, I now not only question, but doubt that God ordered men to guard and protect our chastity."

I was used to Rawyia's incessant complaints and just nodded for support.

Rawyia took a deep breath and held me by the shoulders. "I want you to give me your solemn oath that no matter how many wrong choices I make, how people perceive my actions and misjudgments, you will always remain the person I can come to for support and understanding."

I reached for the Quran on the night table and took it in

my hands. "I swear on this holy book I will always be your loyal sister, no matter what you do."

I would keep my oath.

CHAPTER 19

On the morning of my betrothal ceremony, *Tante* Akeela, Fareeda, and the servants prepared the feast and cleaned the apartment. Wedding songs blasted from the record player.

Delivery boys rushed in and out of the kitchen, placing trays of barbecued kebabs, chickens, veal, and lamb chops on the table. As with any Egyptian celebration, turkeys were a must. They were stuffed with rice, nuts, and raisins mixed with butter and cinnamon. The aroma of three turkeys baking permeated the apartment, overwhelming the fragrance of roses Mama had placed around the area. Mama had also ordered trays of pasta with béchamel—another ceremonial must on any Egyptian table. The feast could not have been complete without dolma, grape leaves stuffed with rice, olive oil, onions, and parsley. There were also numerous salads, my favorites of which were tahini, hummus, and baba ghanoush. The trays of sweets bore a variety of French *gateaux*: mille feuilles, éclairs, and petits -fours. The dessert could not have been complete without Middle Eastern delicacies like *basboussa*, baklava, *konafa*, and *ghorayebah*.

Mama assigned Kareema to guard the trays and keep my brothers from tasting and messing up the arrangement of food.

Everyone sang and danced except Rawyia, Gamal, and me; I had come over to be with Rawyia. That evening, she wanted to go out with Gamal, but Papa refused.

Ali, our chauffeur, rushed through the apartment toward the kitchen, holding two open boxes of whiskey and wine.

"How can Father claim to be religious?" Rawyia questioned with rage, hands on her hips. "Isn't alcohol forbidden in Islam? Our father is not qualified to teach us what haram is and what is not. Going out with my husband is not haram! God ordered us not to drink alcohol, and I'm sure He prohibits serving it as well!"

"Shhh, Rawyia!" Mama looked around. She had no explanation to justify our father's sins, and he had taught us that alcohol was forbidden in Islam.

Her sisters' families were drinkers, though, and Mama wanted them to enjoy the evening. Papa had never liked the women from my mother's side and called them whores, but he disregarded his religious beliefs that evening, apparently seeing no harm in allowing my aunt's family the joy of their drinking.

"So, Mama," Rawyia asked, "how is Papa going to explain this to God when he meets Him in his next prayer?" Now that she had caught a grave mistake that Papa had committed, she would not relent.

"Does God grant exceptions? Will you and Papa go to hell for this?" She stretched her neck toward my parents' room, but Papa could not hear her. The music was loud. "What if we want to have a drink? Does Papa have the right to stop us?" Rawyia tapped the floor with her right foot.

Ahmed and Reda overheard Rawyia's complaints. "As long as you live in this home, you have to abide by its rules," Reda warned, pointing his finger in Rawyia's face.

"I won't. I belong to another man now." Rawyia took Gamal's hands.

To avoid an escalation of the situation, Mama dismissed Reda and Ahmed, asking them to take my siblings, who had followed Mama into the room. She then turned to Gamal. "Would you allow your wife to drink, my dear son?"

"I will give Rawyia the stars if she wished." Gamal put an arm around Rawyia tenderly.

"Thank you, darling," she whispered, as she leaned her head on his shoulder.

Openly defying our father's command, Rawyia and Gamal left the apartment and went to see an Arabic movie.

That afternoon, daylight found its way through the shutters of my bedroom and hit the chandelier. The crystals sparkled and reminded me of the sun's rays as they danced on the clear, turquoise water at Marsa Matrouh Beach. I saw myself with Ghassan, strolling across the white sand. Closing my eyes, I swam in space until I found Ghassan's loving gaze. His smile exposed rows of beautiful white teeth, perfectly arranged between his moist lips. My dreams took me closer to his face, but as my lips were to melt against his, Rawyia burst in and opened the windows.

"Time to get ready!" she said sarcastically.

Rawyia held a white paper package from Hanaux, an exclusive department store. She raised the package above her head and swished it to the left and right, like a kite.

"Get up, La, and see what my darling Gamal has bought me."

A package from Hanaux seemed so strange. Our clothes were either from L'Enfant Chic, a small boutique that specialized in an exclusive line of French clothes for children and teens, or from the hands of Madame Mary, our Greek seamstress.

"Show me what's inside."

"Close your eyes, and don't peek."

I did.

"You can look now."

I opened my eyes and gasped. Rawyia cascaded a black

dress over her body with care and tenderness. My sister looked like a goddess in the princess cut. The back plunged deep, the décolletage so low it would graduate Rawyia to the rank of slut in our father's book.

"Oh, Rawyia! I have never seen *dentelle* so delicately woven."

"They call it guipure, La." Rawyia took pride in correcting and educating me.

"But, Rawyia, your back is naked," I said with serious concern.

Rawyia ignored my comment and moved her attention to the two small packages she removed from the bag. She carefully unfolded the rose tissue paper in one and pulled out a red lacy bra, and from the other she withdrew something matching in color and fabric barely falling within the category of the panties we had grown up wearing.

"Feed your hungry eyes with what we should have been wearing a long time ago, La." Rawyia grinned. She took off her dress and put on the bra and the new panties.

Rawyia looked more beautiful than any movie star our cousin Samira had described to us. Facing the dresser, she sat down, crossed her legs, folded her hands on her knees, and moved her head left and right. She practiced different expressions with every pose, like a model—sweet and innocent, defiant and sultry.

I didn't know how Rawyia's freedom had affected me until I looked in the mirror and saw furrows on my forehead. I was afraid Rawyia's new life would take her away and I would have to fight my battles alone.

Rawyia's finger touched my cheek, bringing me out of my thoughts. She gave me a kiss on my forehead. "La, would you like to wear my dress tonight?"

"You would give me your—"

She took my hands and helped me undress. In seconds, Rawyia's dress clung to my body. We giggled, facing the mirror, and hugged.

We heard knocking at the door and ignored it. Then, seconds later, more taps. Rawyia covered her near-naked body with the pale peach eiderdown and opened the door.

There stood our father, dressed in his dark blue suit and white shirt. His eyes spewed anger. My sister shut the door, but he barged in and slammed our shutters closed. "Why are you dressing with the windows open?"

Rawyia and I stood in silence, like two thieves caught in the act.

Papa glanced at my dress, looked away, and spat with disgust. He turned to Rawyia. "You are a slut," he said in a low and stern voice.

She shrugged and moved toward me, stumbling over the eiderdown. I took a few steps back, until I felt the balcony glass behind me. I kept my eyes fixed on Papa's face. Rawyia sat on the bed and crossed her legs. "May God speed up our liberation from this prison," she mumbled.

I couldn't believe what I'd just heard. Trembling, I stood in the corner and gave her the look Mama gave us when we did something she didn't approve of.

"What kind of life is this?" She glowered at Papa. "No freedom in this house, not even in our bedroom? Is this Karakush's rule?" Rawyia always used that name when she talked about our father. Karakush was a twelfth-century historical figure with an unjust and unreasonable reputation.

Papa took my hand and pulled me out of the room. Shocked at my father's silence, I had no choice but to follow him, my left hand imprisoned in his right.

I glanced back at Rawyia, hoping she would trail us. But she stayed, giving me a nod of courage that I took with me into Papa's bedroom.

Papa shut the door and asked me to sit down. I chose the farthest spot on his bed and wished the floor under my feet would open up and swallow me.

"Laila, you know you have been always my favored child," he said.

I nodded, although he and I both knew he was lying.

"I don't want your sister's vulgar and disrespectful behavior to influence you."

"Rawyia is not vulgar," I snapped.

"Don't interrupt!"

I lowered my head.

"If Rawyia wants to be free and impose her independence on me, she might as well leave the house now."

"What do you mean? What about her wedding?"

Papa stood and faced the balcony. "Gamal and Rawyia won't get anything from me. I didn't accept his dowry." He faced me. His eyes spoke of his determination. "Gamal is free to take Rawyia now, without a wedding ceremony, furniture and trousseau. Rawyia is legally his wife."

"You don't love my sister? What has Rawyia done?"

"Rawyia has made her choice to disobey my rules and challenge my authority; therefore, your sister has no place here." Then Papa softened his tone and told me I had always been the one he had trusted, respected, and relied on to keep the family name clean.

I was not sure what Papa meant, but it pleased me to hear him say it. Still, I worried about my sister. "Does Rawyia know about your decision?"

"No, and I hope you will tell her."

I looked him in the eyes, searching for any sign of love hidden behind the cold stare he gave me. I found none. "It is your job to tell her," I said, turning to go.

"Get ready, and when I ask, you do, understand?"

"Get ready to tell my sister to go, or get ready for the ceremony?" I asked, hoping to hear him change his mind about the decision he had taken against Rawyia and Gamal.

"Both. And take that dress off. You look like a tramp."

Papa's accusation undressed me. I covered my cleavage with both hands and walked out of his room demeaned and confused.

Not knowing how to face Rawyia with my father's decision, I stood at our bedroom door, paralyzed. His words washed over me, and my knees buckled. Would Rawyia really be put out of the house like common trash? How could I bear to tell her that Papa despised her enough to throw her away, that she had never been more than an insult to his good name?

"Why aren't you getting ready, Laila?" Mama's voice startled me. I hadn't heard her come into the hallway. "Laila, what's the matter?"

Mama reached out to me. I felt conflicted between wanting to put my burden into her hands and recoiling from this woman who would willingly go along with Papa's scheme to rid himself of my sister.

"Oh, Mama!" I buried my face in my hands. "Please, I beg you."

"Laila, tell me, what is the matter?" Mama took me in her arms.

"I can't stand the thought of telling Rawyia Papa's decision." I could not hold back my tears.

My words had a strange effect on Mama. She withdrew slightly, and a look of deep concern stole across her face.

"Don't you know? Papa told me he's not giving Rawyia a wedding. He wants Rawyia to move into Gamal's home now, and he won't buy her furniture or a trousseau."

Mama's eyes widened, and it became evident to me that our mother had played no role in this terrible fate. I silently thanked her for that.

Her expression changed again as she collected herself. "Please don't talk to Rawyia about this."

Relieved, I stopped crying.

Back in our room, I found Rawyia pacing like an animal

trapped in a cage. "What did Papa want from you? Tell me."

"Nothing serious." I tried to keep my face from betraying my lie. "Papa wanted me to take off your dress. He said it was too revealing."

Rawyia stepped closer, lifted my chin, and forced me to look in her eyes. I gently pushed her hand and turned away. Rawyia grabbed my hand and jerked me back. "Okay, spit it out. I know it's about me."

"Yes, Rawyia," I said, not able to keep anything from her. "Papa doesn't like your disrespectful behavior."

"I don't care, La." She let go of my hand and shrugged. "All I want is to get out of here."

"How about Gamal? What will he think of you?"

"Gamal doesn't care either."

I didn't believe her.

"My lady, please take your dress." Kareema said from the hallway, where she stood holding my betrothal dress.

The dress looked just like my school uniform: blue, with a wide collar that circled around my neck like a rope and twisted under my chin in a big bow. A belt with a matching ribbon tied in the back.

Rawyia snatched the dress from Kareema and dismissed her. She tossed the dress on the bed with disgust. "Is this what our father came up with for your special night?" Her voice must've been audible throughout the apartment. "Is this a dress or a nun's robe?"

Her confrontational behavior scared me. She sounded relentless, like someone looking for trouble.

"Does our father really expect you to wear it?" She picked it up from the bed and tossed it on the floor.

Mama rushed into the room with Papa behind her. Papa pushed his way to the front and went straight to Rawyia. "Stay away from your sister!"

"Couldn't you find a better dress than this piece of burlap?"

she asked without blinking. Rawyia stood close to Papa's face.

"This is a fine fabric, Rawyia." Mama wanted to ease a tension that was escalating fast.

"What's this bow my sister has to tie in the back?" Rawyia ignored Mama and pointed to the belts attached at each end of the waist. "Laila is not a schoolgirl anymore! Why can't she wear my black dress?"

Rawyia looked at my father with defiant eyes, her wild gesticulations and angry taunts pushing Papa to his breaking point. Papa's facial muscles contracted, and his upper lip twitched—a sign of anger I recognized. Thin little trickles of perspiration crept along my back and my forehead.

Grabbing hold of her sultry black dress, Rawyia made as if to wave it in my father's face. Papa turned pale, raised his hand, and brought it down with a snap across Rawyia's cheek. The blow knocked her down, and she landed on the bed.

She covered her cheek with her hands to hide the reddening spot. Her eyes shot flames at Papa. "This will not stop me," Rawyia hissed. "I will always be there to protect La from you and your tyranny."

I gasped.

Papa proceeded to strike Rawyia again, but Mama took him by the shoulder and guided him out of the room.

Drawn by all the shouting, *Tante* Akeela hurried in and tried to comfort Rawyia, but Rawyia wouldn't listen. She picked up the dress Gamal had bought her, pulled her school bag out from under the bed, and began packing her clothes.

"Where are you going?" I asked Rawyia, alarmed and scared.

She stuffed the bag with her new clothes and her makeup and strode out of the room.

I followed Rawyia as Hala and my younger brothers shut the doors to their rooms to escape the trouble. Mama, Reda, *Tante* Akeela, and Fareeda followed us into the foyer. They tried to stop Rawyia. Papa ran after them.

Reda did not wait for Papa to control the situation. He lunged at Rawyia. Mama stepped between them before Reda could strike.

"Rawyia, go back to your room!" Mama ordered.

Rawyia didn't move.

"*Ne me quitte pas*," I whispered in Rawyia's ear. "Don't leave me."

"Stop whispering!" Reda shouted. "And stop speaking in French!"

"Let me come with you," I whispered in French, ignoring my brother's orders.

"No, La, they will kill you," Rawyia responded in French. "You are not yet married." She grabbed my hand, steered us back to our room, and closed the door behind us. "La, you can't leave this house yet. They wouldn't forgive you for the shame you would bring to the family." She released a breath of frustration. "I will wait for you."

Relief flooded me until she spoke again.

"Laila is not wearing this piece of burlap!" she said, loudly enough for Papa to hear.

It didn't take long for him to come knocking. Rawyia opened the door. He ignored her and stepped straight over to me. "Laila, my dear daughter," he said quietly, "if you don't like your dress, don't wear it."

When Papa left the room, Rawyia gave me a triumphant smile and I hugged her. She went straight to the armoire, pulled out a silver knit top and my tight black jersey skirt, and tossed them on the bed. "Wear these, La," she said with authority.

That night, with my sister by my side, I felt strong and looked forward to the moment when I would stand up to our father like she did.

Still feeling strong, I asked her if she still had Ghassan's phone number.

"Yes, of course. I taped it behind the mirror." She smiled.

"Tomorrow when we go out with our husbands, we will call him."

"How?"

"Don't worry. I'll take care of everything." She patted me on the back. "Now go take a bath and get ready."

We hugged.

I sang my favorite song. "I will meet him tomorrow, the day after and the day after. I will tell him tomorrow . . ." Under the cold shower, I repeated the lyrics loudly. My pleasant tune made me deaf to the world around me.

"Thank God you're happy," Mama yelled. "Is this all for Farook?"

I wanted to tell her the truth about my plans, but, knowing how worried Mama would be, I gave her only a nod and a smile.

Once I had finished my shower, I returned to our room. Rawyia held a little tin box decorated with a red-and-gold geometric design, originally a bonbon container. Inside, I found a variety of lipstick colors, black mascara, a small container of powder, and a tube of Chanel eyeliner.

"Rawyia, where did you get this? How long have you had it?"

"Since last year. You remember Marie Mizrahi, my classmate, the Jewish one? She sold them to me."

"Have you used any yet?" I checked over everything with excitement.

"Not yet. I hid them for the right occasion. I gave Marie my allowance for three days, and all of the bonbons. You see how smart I am? No one knew, not even you." Rawyia smiled, looking proud of herself. "From now on, I want you to use this brain." She pointed to my head. I nodded. "Now, lie down on your back and let me put on your makeup."

I lay down hesitantly, fearing my father would see me with makeup and get angry.

"Don't ever be afraid of anyone," she said, "no matter who that person is. Men act like they follow the teaching of the

Quran, but they don't. We are nothing but possessions to them and have to fight them."

"Even Papa."

"Of course—Papa, too."

"Okay, Rawyia, I will be brave." I meant it. I closed my eyes and puckered my lips.

"I'm afraid it will take you a long time before you act as you say," Rawyia mumbled. "You are a romantic, and that makes you a target for manipulation."

Rawyia held her breath while defining my eyes. I did the same to help her steady hand.

"La, you can breathe," she whispered.

"Can I open my eyes?"

"No, wait till the eyeliner dries. Starting tomorrow, you and I will be semi-free, but the 'semi-' part doesn't matter. We can use this little freedom to achieve what we want." She snapped her fingers.

"What do we want?"

"Well, don't you want to see Ghassan? This is what I mean. Here you are, about to be free, and you don't even know what to do with this precious gift."

I nodded, sensing her annoyance.

"I want you to stand up to Papa and fight back. If you don't like his orders, just say no! And that goes for all men you will meet in your life, including Ghassan."

"Have you ever said no to Gamal?"

"No, I haven't. Gamal hasn't asked me to do anything I don't want to do." She giggled.

"Has Gamal asked you for sex?"

"Men don't ask for sex, La; they just do it."

"You didn't tell Gamal no?"

"Why should I? Gamal is my husband. But Ghassan is not your husband yet, and you should not allow him to kiss you."

"I want him to kiss me." I opened my eyes.

"Then say no after the kiss. Just remember to keep your panties on."

I laughed.

"Look, I'm going to give you some advice you must follow for the rest of your life."

I nodded with excitement.

"Men want only one thing from women: sex. And never trust a man who tells you he loves you. Use men to achieve your goals. If you can pursue your goals on your own, that's even better."

"I hope you don't mean Ghassan—"

"Yes, him too!" she snapped, and then mumbled, "You need more lessons than I thought."

I ignored Rawyia's comment and closed my eyes so she could apply the eyeliner. "I don't know how to handle this freedom."

"Freedom is a long way ahead of us. You and I will stumble over many obstacles before we reach the shore of real independence."

Om Zoubeida walked into our room then, holding two glasses of lemonade on a silver tray. "I thought you might need some refreshment before you go out to meet the guests."

To cheer me up, Om Zoubeida offered to read my fortune in the cards. I could not have asked for anything better. Our maid used cards, Turkish coffee, and tea leaves to interpret the future. I locked the door because Papa did not allow fortune telling in the house. Rawyia went along with us, although her frown told me she really wanted to get on with our makeup session.

"Let's hurry up, before someone comes and asks for you." I sat cross-legged and eagerly faced my fortune-teller.

Om Zoubeida shuffled the cards and called on the Virgin Mary and Jesus the Messiah to help her see the hidden future, which she referred to as el mestekhabi. She handed me two cards: the Jack, which represented Farook, and the queen, for me.

"Now hold the cards close to your lips," *Om* Zoubeida instructed me, "and whisper your questions and wishes."

I whispered so low, neither she nor Rawyia could hear. "Will Farook divorce me? Am I going to marry Ghassan?"

Om Zoubeida slowly arranged the cards, three rows of nine each. She took a deep breath. "My dear, you will cross oceans and will live far away from here."

"With whom?"

"Shall I go on?" She glanced at my sister.

"Yes, of course, keep going," Rawyia replied with annoyance.

Om Zoubeida repeated the arrangement of cards three times, and her brow knit with concern.

"What do the cards say?" I asked her.

Om Zoubeida glanced at Rawyia.

"Make it fast!"

Om Zoubeida turned back to me. "The cards tell me your marriage will not last."

"That's all I needed to hear." I jumped out of bed and kissed her. "The cards have given me hope! You can go now." Even though I knew cards didn't tell the future, it made me happy to hear that my marriage would not last.

"You don't like Farook?" *Om* Zoubeida frowned.

Before I could reply, Rawyia asked our maid to leave the room.

"May God put some sense in your young souls," *Om* Zoubeida said as she closed the door behind her.

While I waited with Rawyia for our father to summon me into the salon, I studied myself in the mirror. For the first time, I dared to wear makeup, not so much because I wanted to as to express rebellion. My five-inch heels made me wobble, and the stack of bouclesboucles or curls, piled on my head made me look older than Rawyia. I didn't like the way I looked or felt: like a clown. The real me—the one with hopes and aspirations, the one in love with Ghassan—had disappeared.

Mama entered the room wearing a look of sorrow and helplessness. We'd often discussed my dreams of becoming a journalist and traveling around the world. I'd promised to take her with me, and I thought it tore Mama apart to see me lose my future.

"May God bless this beauty," she said, approaching me.

"Really, Mama? You like it?" I tinted my question with sarcasm.

"Yes, and Rawyia, you did an excellent job, so good that I'm going to cancel our hairstylist appointment. You are beautiful, Laila." Mama took me in her arms, but her embrace failed to ease my suffering, and she knew it. For a moment, Rawyia, Mama, and I fell into silence.

Suddenly, women entered the room and *zaghareets*, or ululation, penetrated the muteness and exploded in various pitches, like a chorale. We each gave our vocal cords a turn to demonstrate their joy.

Mama untied her tongue and joined the symphony, piercing our ears with her loudest *zaghrouta*. Women charged into our room and took turns congratulating me with hugs and kisses.

When the women were finished and I was left alone in the room, I did not recognize myself in the mirror. Different shapes and shades of red lipstick smeared my face. The curls my sister had piled on my head were deflated and out of shape. I stood numb and wondered when I would wake up from this nightmare.

"How many times have I told you not to wear makeup?" Papa's voice bellowed.

I had no reply except a look of hatred.

My father ignored it and pulled a pin from my curls. "Go wash your face and brush out your hair," he spat out.

Feeling humiliated, I ran to the bathroom. I glanced over my shoulder to see if anyone had witnessed what had just happened and saw Farook standing in the hall. Rawyia trailed behind him. Papa stalked into his room and slammed the door.

"Aren't you Laila's future husband?" Rawyia's voice shook with anger. "Can't you protect your future wife?"

"He's her father. As long as Laila is living with her father, he is the one who disciplines."

I could not hate Farook any more than I already did. The fact that he was unwilling to assume his role as my husband filled me with disgust and disrespect. In that moment, I realized that my fight for divorce would not be as easy as I had thought.

After I cleaned my face, I returned to my room, where I found Mama looking for me. Mama informed me that Papa and Farook had signed the betrothal contract. My life had been planned and sealed, and I had no choice but to accept. I was numb from head to toe.

Farook could not wait to present me, his legal wife, with the *shabka*, a gift of jewelry.

"Let's go into the salon to receive your gift," Mama said to me, her voice quavering, as we sat in my bedroom with Rawyia.

"No. Tell Farook to bring his gift to my room."

Farook did not wait for my mother. He and Haytham burst into our bedroom uninvited. I stood face-to-face with my father-in-law, the man I had heard so much about, the person whose crime would remain attached forever to the name on my birth certificate: Baraa—the innocent.

I looked at his giant-size body and thought of the young men he had murdered, imagining the pain and horror the young men must've gone through. My throat felt dry, and my heart sank deep inside my chest. I wished the floor would suck me in and away from both Farook and his father.

My fearful expression must have been visible to Farook and his father, because they looked stupefied.

Rawyia and my mother quietly departed, leaving me alone with Farook and my father-in-law. Farook extended his hand

and asked me to come closer. Instead, I stepped farther and farther backward with every forward step Farook took.

His father stood behind him, his body filling the door opening and his head almost touching the frame, his belly inflated like that of a pregnant woman about to deliver. Haytham stared at me, his beady, sunken black eyes lifeless and cold. His nose was as big as a Farook's, and it scared me. I shook with fear as Haytham congratulated me without shaking hands and walked out.

Farook pasted a grin over his irritation and began to exercise his authority. "You are my wife now. I expect you to behave accordingly."

"Not until I move out of here!" I asserted.

He removed two small boxes covered in dark blue velvet from his pocket. Inside each box was a wedding band. Farook gathered from my behavior that I would not follow tradition and place the band on his finger, so he picked up the larger one and placed it on his finger.

"Tomorrow you are invited for lunch at my parents' house." He pointed a finger in my face and left the room but returned a few minutes later with my father, who walked straight to where I stood.

Papa handed Farook three small boxes, grabbed my hand, and asked Farook to put the ring on my finger. Farook forced the wedding band onto my uncooperative finger and secured it with a solitaire. I hid my hands behind my back and made a failed attempt to free my finger from the rings.

Farook took the next box and turned to my father, asking for his help without speaking. I surrendered my neck. Farook encircled it with a diamond necklace. The necklace felt like a lasso he would use to control me. He then handcuffed me with a diamond bracelet.

Farook and Papa left me standing in the room, bewildered yet defiant. They walked out with triumph in their eyes, a look full of satisfaction—a look one might see in the eyes of an animal trainer once he had tamed his uncooperative cat.

I must have looked unhappy as I entered the salon, because guests began whispering. One by one, with pitying looks, they patted me on the back.

Mama took me in her arms and kissed me. She spoke of Farook's kindness and tried in vain to persuade me to give Farook a chance. But, I knew that Mama supported my desire for independence and for exercising my right to choose, that I had her silent support for my future plans.

Like a phantom, I walked straight toward the rented portable trellis decorated with fresh roses and melted into one of the two rococo chairs placed under it. I centered myself on the edge of the wide seat, sat straight, and did not feel the back. With both hands, I pulled down my skirt and made it cover my knees. My hands fell lifeless onto the gilded wood. Farook took the chair next to me.

Rawyia was not here. I stood, expecting Farook to prevent me from leaving, but he did not. The guests were busy eating and dancing, the walls echoing the music, along with the sound of voices. No one noticed when I left to find Rawyia. First, I went to our bedroom, but she wasn't there.

Papa had left his bedroom door ajar. Though the light was out, I saw him sitting in his chair, one foot tucked under his derrière and the other crossed over his knee. His elbows rested on his desk, and his fisted hands supported his forehead.

I stuck my head in the doorway.

"She is gone." Papa murmured, and I knew he meant Rawyia.

"Where? What have you done to her?"

A defeated general, his voice broken and eerie, he asked me to call Mama without alerting the guests. I realized that, despite what Papa had said earlier about wanting Rawyia out of the house, her leaving at this moment would be a family scandal.

Feeling panicky, I searched for Mama and found her in the salon, entertaining the guests.

"Papa wants to talk to you," I whispered into her ear. When she saw the anxious look on my face, she managed a joyous smile and excused herself. On the way, I told her about Rawyia's disappearance.

Mama gasped in disbelief. "What a scandal. What a scandal," she said over and over. Mama disappeared into Papa's bedroom while I waited impatiently in mine.

A few minutes later, my mother joined me. The life seemed sucked from her face. She pulled a white handkerchief from her sleeve and repeatedly patted the sweat beading her forehead.

"What a disaster! What a disgrace! What a shame!" She paced the floor as she mumbled.

Tante Akeela remained with the guests throughout the long evening until they left quietly, one by one. I stayed in my room, praying I would see Rawyia again. She had promised she would not leave me behind. This assurance pacified me but did not loosen the fear tightening around my heart.

Shortly after the last guest left, I heard Mama speaking on the phone. When she asked Gamal to bring Rawyia home, I relaxed, though I was fearful of my father's reaction when Rawyia showed up.

Half an hour later, Gamal brought my sister back. He left immediately, and Rawyia walked into our bedroom. Her face was tight, and I could tell she had not lost her fire.

Mama, looking pale and shaky, followed Rawyia in. She closed the door and took Rawyia firmly by the shoulder. "Tell me you are still a virgin." Mama's voice broke.

"Papa called me a slut, Mama," Rawyia said nonchalantly. "I had to tell him I learned about sex here in this house, where he's kept us like prisoners and put Reda and Ahmed in charge. Ha! To protect our virtues, he said." Rawyia stared at the floor.

Mama widened her eyes in disbelief.

"Papa didn't believe me. Instead, my father told me to leave and never come back," she said, in a calm and assured voice, as she shrugged.

Mama turned her face away from Rawyia's pleading eyes. "Rawyia, you cannot go around ridiculing and undermining the protective role of Reda and Ahmed." She held Rawyia by the shoulders and shook her. "You will destroy our family's reputation. And you should not have left the house. Your father did not mean to throw you out."

"May God strike me with blindness if I lied." Tears welled in Rawyia's eyes. Still, no one believed Rawyia's insinuation— not my father, not my mother. Our parents thought they had secured our home from male temptations, so they dismissed Rawyia's statement.

Rawyia, Mama, and I, in silence, remained in the room for a while, each lost in her own reaction, especially Mama. The smile lines that had once crinkled around her eyes when she looked at us had turned to wrinkles that made her look old. Mama could not deal with the scandal, the ceremony, Rawyia's virginity, and Papa all at once. The load broke her happy spirit. I felt sorry for ruining her evening and hugged her tight.

"Mama, I assure you," Rawyia murmured, breaking the silence in a voice strained by despair, "I am a virgin still."

Mama lit up. We showered her face with kisses, drying her tears.

But I doubted Rawyia's words of reassurance.

CHAPTER 20

Rawyia and I stayed up late the night of my betrothal. We had a lot to talk about. Somehow, I knew Rawyia had lied to our mother. I could barely contain my anxiety and wanted to hear every detail.

"I have something to tell you, La, but remember, you promised never to judge me."

"Yes, I remember."

"Do you remember Anwar, Papa's accountant at work?"

"Yes."

"You must also remember his handsome son, Fouad."

I didn't understand. What did they have to do with anything?

Rawyia stepped over to the door and peeked outside to make sure no one was eavesdropping. "Last year during the celebration that ends the Muslims' yearly pilgrimage to Mecca, Fouad and I kissed."

"How and where did you meet Fouad? And when did this happen?" My mind raced with questions.

"Remember each year on the first day of the Eid el Kabeer, when our parents slaughter a lamb on the roof following the hajj pilgrimage?" Rawyia smiled knowingly. "I didn't share this secret with you then because you were younger and you might have wanted to imitate me."

I shook my head, rejecting how she undermined my maturity. But this was Rawyia. She protected me and knew I was not ready for her risky and wilder conduct.

Rawyia crossed the room to the balcony. "You remember when Papa and the older boys left for the Eid prayer early in the morning and the rest of the family went up to the roof to watch the lamb being sacrificed?"

"Yes, I remember."

Rawyia turned back to face me. "La, you won't think I am a loose girl like Papa does, will you?"

I shook my head. I could never see Rawyia as a loose girl. Still, she struggled with her confession and danced around the subject while I grew more and more impatient.

"How many times have you heard Papa accuse me of being an unruly girl? *You* know I'm not, but when Papa kept calling me one, I thought, *why not?* And became one."

"Are you telling me you've lost your virginity?"

"No, that's not what I'm saying. I'm trying to make you understand why I let Fouad kiss me."

I released a breath of relief.

"Well, while you were all feasting your eyes on the sacrificial slaughter of the lamb, I stayed alone in the apartment with Fouad. We hugged and kissed."

"Did Fouad force you into sex?" My mouth dropped open.

"No, of course not."

"I thought that when you kiss a boy, he forces you to have sex and you lose your virginity and bleed."

"I didn't have sex, or blood," Rawyia scoffed.

"But how did the encounter start?" I could hardly believe what she had just told me, and I felt a need to hear it again, from the beginning.

Rawyia took a deep breath. "I always watched television while the rest of the family was up on the roof for the lamb slaughter. When the doorbell rang, a handsome young man I had never seen before stood before me, asking for Papa. I asked who he was, and he said he was Fouad, that he was here to pick up the share of meat for the workers on-site, and that the slaughter of a lamb was always shared with the underprivileged. His eyes met mine, and I found it hard to speak. I mumbled something, and he said that if his father had told him that Mr. Kamel had such a beautiful daughter, he would not have given his father a hard time when he asked Fouad to come by our house. I enjoyed his smile and made sure to let him know I was attracted to him, through the inviting way I talked to him."

I could not imagine Rawyia engaging in such behavior with a young man. Nevertheless, I was impressed with her courage.

"I told him that the rest of my family was on the roof. He asked me to show him the way, so I led Fouad through the kitchen to the servants' stairway. He asked if I was alone in the house and why I wasn't watching the lamb being slaughtered. I told him I don't like violence, and he asked if I like love. I gave Fouad a lustful look. It just happened, and it made me want to abandon everything I'd been taught about right and wrong. I liked the look of passion Fouad gave me. He pulled me deep into his eyes. It felt like hypnosis. I found myself standing close to him, completely mesmerized. Fouad tried to take my hand in his, and I gave in. He pulled me closer and wrapped his arms around me. We both trembled, but it felt good. Then Fouad started unbuttoning his shirt, and . . ."

Although I was enjoying hearing about her adventure with Fouad, I shook my head in disbelief.

Rawyia shook me and tapped me on the head. "Hello, romantic. Wait till you hear the rest. You remember the movie *Duaa Alkarawan*, with Faten Hamama and Ahmed Mazhar?"

I nodded.

"Remember the scene where Faten fought Ahmed as he tried to kiss her by force?"

"Yes," I whispered.

"Well, that's what happened with us that day."

"Fouad forced you?" I screamed.

"How could Fouad have forced me, when I wanted him to kiss me?" She sounded frustrated. "I didn't want to resist him."

"Oh my God." I sighed. "I hope this was all that happened between you. What will Gamal do when he finds out? I hope you are being honest with me and that you are still a virgin. I'm scared for you, Rawyia."

I had trouble understanding Rawyia's risky behavior. While I wanted to believe her, my sister had plenty of courage in her for adventure.

"Don't be. Eleonor, my classmate, told me girls don't bleed the first time they kiss. Eleonor learned that from her father. He's a gynecologist."

I doubted Rawyia's claim.

"Tell me, in plain words, are you or are you not a virgin?" I demanded, just as our mother had asked earlier in the evening.

"While Fouad held me tight in his arms, I felt his thing become hard and it touched my body."

Egyptians used the word "thing" to refer to anything they chose not to name. It was a part of the culture. Rawyia assumed I knew what she meant, and I did.

"We both had our clothes on. Then I lost all power to resist, and I don't remember what happened after that." Rawyia spoke with an air of carelessness. I did not like the perpetual smile she had on her face the whole time she recounted her shameful interlude, but I did not know what to think.

"Where were you doing all this? Weren't you afraid someone would come and see you?"

"Oh, I forgot to tell you: I took him to our room and locked the door," she blurted without shame.

"Rawyia!" I took a deep breath to ease the impact of her image alone with him in our room.

"Don't worry, La—when he tried to have sex, I refused to let him take off my culottes. We were at war, but I won in the end." Rawyia's face tightened as she ended her story with a bitter laugh.

"Why did you do it, Rawyia?" I asked, still in shock.

"I did it to punish Papa." She cast her gaze to her portrait hanging on the wall, as if she were looking for approval from the young and innocent girl she had once been.

My sister's confession kept my head spinning all night. While Rawyia fell asleep and snored, I stayed up thinking about what my sister had told me and whether she had kept her virginity intact. For the first time, I saw her in a different light. She appeared old and experienced. My sister had done things my religion and culture forbade before marriage.

Rawyia had always expressed her hatred toward men and told me that the only thing they wanted from women was sex. So why had my sister succumbed to Fouad? Was Rawyia lying to me? These questions and many others crowded my mind and stole sleep. At one point, I tried to wake her, but she didn't respond.

I sat up when she finally awoke in the morning. "Aren't you worried what Gamal might think of you?"

Rawyia yawned, her face without expression.

"I bet if Gamal finds out, it will be the end of your life!" I shuddered. How could Rawyia not see the danger of what she had done?

"Don't worry about me." Rawyia stretched and sat up. "I've done it three times already," she whispered in my ear. "Every year, the same day at the same time."

My mouth formed a big O. "What about this year, now that you belong to another man?"

"Now Gamal will be the lucky one."

I searched her face and saw no shame. I wanted to believe my sister had morals and principles, but now I didn't know what to think.

"Rawyia, how can you give your body to someone you are not yet married to?"

"Remember when I fell in love with our neighbor? We were both young and innocent. Samy and I were satisfied just standing on the balcony, looking at each other and dreaming, like Romeo and Juliet." She was holding back tears. "Have you forgotten what Ahmed did? How he dragged me away and called me a loose girl?" Her voice broke. "Well, here I am, and I'm still loose in their eyes." She walked out onto the balcony. "So stop preaching to me about virginity, because as far as I'm concerned, it is mine to control and decide how to dispose of. Not theirs."

Her words confused me. I had never before thought of who "owned" my virginity. While I liked what Rawyia said, I was not ready even to entertain the idea of disposing of my virginity, Rawyia-style.

Rawyia walked back in and faced the vanity, checking her complexion in the mirror. "La," she said, smiling now, "today is the first day of your freedom! Do you want to go out with my legal husband and me tonight? Gamal promised to take me to an Arabic movie. I'm sure he won't mind if you tag along."

Rawyia's confession the night before had made me forget about my own new life. The promise of a night of freedom dangling before me helped me forget my sister's scandalous escapades.

"Let's call Ghassan, too!"

"Not so fast. Let's first go out once without any adventures, to test Gamal's cooperation. Then, next time, we'll see if Gamal is willing to leave us at Eleonor's home. I've already talked to Eleonor, and she says she will cover for us."

Eleonor's mother allowed Eleonor's boyfriend to see her

at home and allowed Eleonor to go out with him without a chaperone.

"Eleonor is very nice, and her mother is even nicer," Rawyia assured me.

I relaxed. "Does Eleonor have sex with her boyfriend?"

"No! Eleonor told me that because her mother trusts her, she will not break that trust."

"Maybe I could meet Ghassan in Eleonor's house."

"No, no, La, we don't want anyone to know what we're doing, not even Eleonor's mom. Remember, we are Muslims."

"You mean we should do everything in secret because we are Muslims?"

"No! Because Muslim girls are not supposed to interact with men."

"But I'm not a girl; I'm betrothed." I teased Rawyia.

"That's even worse," she snapped.

All these rules were getting too complicated, even though I took them with a grain of salt. I decided to let it rest.

Then something else occurred to me. "You won't have sex with Gamal when I'm with you, will you?"

"Of course not!" Rawyia rolled her eyes. Then, with a playful smile, she said, "But if Gamal and I do have sex in the car, just pretend you're not looking."

"Oh, no, please don't do it when I'm with you. Promise me, Rawyia?"

"Okay, I promise. Gamal and I will give you a sleeping pill first."

I screamed.

"Just kidding."

I couldn't believe my sister's bravado in making jokes about sex. I hoped Rawyia's bravery wouldn't lead to her demise.

CHAPTER 21

Early the next day, while Rawyia and I were still in bed, we heard Farook's voice in the house.

Kareema barged into our room. "Farook is in your father's bedroom," she said, opening the shutters.

Papa called me from his room, so I put on my robe and joined Farook and Papa.

"Laila, greet your husband," Papa said, "and get ready to join Farook's family for lunch."

"I can't go today, Papa. Rawyia asked me to see a movie with Gamal, and I agreed. Gamal already has tickets." I was lying for the first time and felt proud of myself for sounding assertive and in control of my life.

Papa did not object and invited Farook to join him for lunch instead. I figured Papa could not yet accept the fact that I would go out with a man, even Farook, and thought it would be safer that I go out with Rawyia and Gamal.

Over the next few weeks, Farook kept trying to take me out alone, but I thought that would be betraying Ghassan, so I turned down Farook's invitations for as long as I could. Farook accepted the rejections without objection. I set the pattern: Farook would come to our house, join Papa for lunch or dinner, and talk business with him until they got tired. Farook would leave, and my father would go to bed. I never joined them.

Farook took comfort in the fact that our wedding date had been set. In two years, when I turned seventeen, we would have a wedding ceremony, and then I would move in with him.

For Rawyia and me, it seemed as though the gates of heaven were open, and we couldn't wait to take off and fly through them. Equipped with innocence and a zest for adventure, we dreamed, ignoring the fact that each of us still belonged to a man.

Farook and Gamal could not be any different, but they were men from the same culture as our father and brothers. Farook and Gamal owned us, only under a different title: husbands.

Rawyia worked on getting Gamal to trust her fully so that we could implement our plan for me to see Ghassan, but Gamal would not cooperate. Nothing my sister offered satisfied him. He refused to take us to Eleonor's home and leave us there alone.

So we tried a different approach. I agreed to go out with Farook and take Rawyia as my chaperone. Farook accepted this proposition. When I pushed Farook further, he agreed to conditions that, unbeknownst to him, set up my first rendezvous with Ghassan.

First, Rawyia and I called Ghassan from our home, using Rawyia's tapping method, and arranged to be on a certain tram at a particular hour. When the time came, we told Farook the tram was a luxury for us. He agreed to leave his car parked in the street and ride the tram instead.

As I searched the tram, looking for Ghassan's familiar frame, our gazes met. We exchanged glances and smiles every now and then. That was enough for both of us.

A few months later, we upgraded our rendezvous spot to Brazilian Coffee, a coffeehouse downtown. Then I saw Ghassan in movie theaters; I called him ahead of time and gave him the name of the movie theater and the seat numbers we had reserved.

Ghassan would purchase a seat right next to us and then sneak in when the lights went off. Sometimes Ghassan bought the seats on both sides of Farook and me to make sure he sat next to me. He would rub his arm against mine.

At the movie theater, I was unable to act upon my desires and only dreamed of feeling his love with my whole body. I settled for the hair on his arm touching my skin and sending a current of ecstatic but agonizing lust.

Farook never noticed, and I never thought of the consequences of my actions. Sitting between the man I belonged to legally and the man I loved was risky and scary, but I dived in with a clean conscience and a shameless soul—just like Rawyia did with Fouad.

Farook was always engrossed in the movie and never tried to hold my hand. He respected my father's trust even though I was his wife. The little freedom I experienced blinded me to morality and ethics, and I was unwilling to give up the feelings and emotions I experienced when sitting next to Ghassan.

Closing my eyes, I sank in my chair, drifting away from my surroundings and into an imaginary dream where Ghassan took me in his arms and kissed me. But all the while, our arms only touched. I did not sense any guilt for committing a sin; rather, I burned with passion and pleasure.

A year passed before Farook decided to claim ownership of his betrothed wife. One evening, he called and asked Papa if he could take me to lunch at his family's home without Rawyia. It did not come as a surprise to me. I knew I had to confront Farook's father on his own territory sooner or later. Besides, I needed to keep Farook's trust and had run out of excuses for not visiting his family.

That Friday, I spent the entire morning in anguish. I didn't know how I would face Farook's family. After taking a bath, I returned to our bedroom to see Rawyia had my brown jersey skirt and checkered beige-and-white top ready for me to wear. My dark brown patent-leather shoes were on the floor beside the bed. Rawyia did my hair up in a chignon, drew eyeliner around my eyes, and colored my lips with a soft red lipstick.

The doorbell rang, and seconds later, I heard Mama and Papa greeting Farook. My body shook.

Rawyia took my hands in hers. "La, you are not going to war. Just relax. It's only a short visit." She smiled.

I did not.

When Farook saw me, he excused himself from the intimate chat he was having with my parents. He extended his right hand, admiring me with his salacious eyes.

"*Ahlan bil Aroussa,*" Farook said with a lover's smile. "Greetings to the bride."

I did not reply, my face void of emotion.

He wore a light blue short-sleeved shirt and navy gabardines. His Old Spice cologne pervaded the foyer, and his smile stretched from east to west, exposing his freshly brushed yellow teeth.

Numbness overcame me from the crown of my head to the bottoms of my feet. I searched Mama's expressionless face for a word to save me.

She took me in her arms and whispered in my ear, "Smile."

I remained in her embrace until Papa took my hand and walked me into the dining room.

"Resign yourself to your fate," he said in a voice only I could hear. "I know what's good for you. And do not allow Farook to treat you like a wife. You are not in his home yet."

"This is not fate, Papa. This is your doing."

I marched slowly back to the foyer, my vision blurry with tears. Farook offered me his hand. As I placed mine in his, I shot Mama a look of blame before Farook closed the door behind us.

On our way down to the ground level, silence hung between

us, the screeching of the elevator cables the only sound. I stood as far away from him as the small space allowed.

Has anyone ever told you how beautiful you are?" Farook asked me once we were outside.

I wanted to tell him yes, Ghassan did every time I saw him, but I kept my mouth shut.

Farook opened the passenger door to his car. I took my seat and rested my hands in my lap. He climbed behind the steering wheel and turned the car radio on. "What would you like to listen to?" he asked in a cheerful voice. Did he believe he was in synch with me emotionally?

"Anything." I gazed out the window to my right.

Farook turned the radio off and touched my chin. Squirming, I pushed his hand away, still facing my window. He placed his hand on both of mine in my lap and pressed gently. I pulled my hands away, crossed my arms, and under them hid my hands.

He started the engine and drove. "I promise to be patient and do my best to win your love," he said in a soft voice.

Why couldn't he be quiet and give me a chance to enjoy the freedom of my first trip without guardians? I wanted to jump out of the car, and run. I envied everyone walking in the street, even the beggars approaching the car at stoplights to ask for money.

"You are still too young to understand," Farook said, "but in time you will."

"Why did you choose a young girl who doesn't understand anything about love?" I said.

Farook turned on the radio again. The Friday noon prayer came from the speaker and forced both of us to be silent until we reached his building.

Farook's parents occupied an apartment in the Cleopatra district, overlooking the sea. There, they were less affected by the hot and humid summer weather than those of us who lived in the heart of the city.

The once-elegant building had not been adequately kept up, and the Mediterranean dampness had left rust on the iron frame of the entrance door and on the hinges of the old wooden shutters. The porter who greeted us looked like the structure he guarded. His face was wrinkled like an old piece of leather, and he had difficulty standing up to pay his respects. Farook put his hand on the old man's shoulder and pushed him down gently to remain seated.

Despite the blinding afternoon sun and the intense heat outside, the building appeared dark and cold inside. The smell of mold permeated the air coming out through the open door and caused me to shiver with disgust.

The porter noticed the look on my face. "Tenants don't pay their rent on time, and sometimes they don't pay at all. We don't like to evict them, but we stopped taking care of the building."

I didn't answer; I was too anxious and nervous about meeting Farook's father in his home.

As we entered the darkness, I struggled to find my steps.

"I should have brought a flashlight for you," Farook said as he took my hand.

I exhaled a breath of frustration.

"Your eyes will adjust before we reach the fourth floor," he said. When we reached the apartment, Farook rang the bell. I stood a few feet away from the door. A smiling young woman opened it. Inside, the balcony's French doors were wide open, and the sea breeze welcomed me with force. The young woman tried unsuccessfully to keep her hair in place.

The sea was so close that I could feel droplets of its waves on my face. My hair must've looked like the mane of a running horse, and my skirt flew in every direction, resisting my efforts to keep it from exposing my legs.

"This is Mona, my sister." Farook rested his arm around her shoulders.

I smiled as Mona helped me keep my dress in place.

She shut the door with difficulty. "If we keep the window shut, the heat is unbearable."

I maintained my pretense of a happy look but kept my distance when Mona attempted to greet me with a hug. As she guided me to the salon, I noticed her walking with a noticeable limp. When she turned around, she had an unusual stare permanently imprinted on her face. It didn't take me long to realize her constant grin masked a mental handicap.

Before I could take a seat, Farook's mother approached me with open arms. I surrendered my body to her overwhelming squeeze. She was of medium build, with a fair complexion. A white scarf loosely covered her head, exposing her gray hair. Every time the breeze wafted with force, her scarf loosened and she struggled to pull it back into place.

A peaceful smile masked sadness in Farook's mother's eyes. Everything about the old woman seemed to hunger for pity, and I embraced her with a warm and gentle squeeze. She cupped my face with her hands, guided me to bend down, and placed a kiss on my forehead. I began to feel comfortable and sat in an armchair.

Soon, Farook's brothers appeared. I remained seated as they introduced themselves. Except for Kenawi's obvious height and bold approach, the rest of them left no memorable impression. Kenawi had a penetrating, sharp gaze, like a hawk's hunting eyes. He had an imposing nose as well.

"Welcome to our family." He smiled and put his hand on Farook's shoulder. "My brother is lucky."

"Thank you," I said.

Their father, Haytham, appeared. He exuded an undeniable force I had not felt before. It frightened me to again face the Haytham *Tante* Akeela had told me about: the man who killed, the man whose sons feared him.

Within seconds, everyone disappeared, leaving me alone with Haytham and Farook's mother. I felt safe having her in the room, but I shivered thinking how terrified she must be, having a murderer as a husband. I felt sorry for her.

My father-in-law looked as if he had just awakened from a nap. His salt-and-pepper hair appeared uncombed. He wore a white galabia. The long cotton costume draped loosely over his protruding belly, and made him appear twice as big as the first time I'd met him. Haytham plastered an artificial smile on his face and asked me with a gruff voice to follow him into the dining room.

From the hallway, I could see that no one was in the dining room. What was happening? Where was the rest of the family? Out of fear, I trailed behind, trying to appear calm and unafraid.

In the dining room, a young man rushed back and forth, placing serving plates of veal fillets, and rice and a tureen of green peas in tomato sauce on the table. My father-in-law's presence in the room gave me an eerie feeling. I was stressed and uneasy, but did my best to maintain my composure while keeping my distance.

We sat on opposite sides of the table. Haytham began eating like a hungry lion, shoving the veal fillets into his mouth, taking no rest in between pieces. He seemed to be in a world of his own until he noticed me looking at him in revulsion. Haytham stacked three pieces of veal on his fork and reached across toward me, releasing them with his fingers. Any last vestige of appetite left me as they fell, one by one, onto my plate.

"Ah, my dear, why aren't you eating?" he asked, seemingly concerned.

"I'm waiting for everyone to join us," I muttered, hoping he wouldn't address me again.

"No, no. Go ahead and start. No need to wait."

But I kept waiting until the rest of the family appeared and quietly took their seats, Farook on my right, Kenawi to my left.

"Don't be afraid of my father," Kenawi whispered in my ear.

"He's always like this, but he's harmless."

A creepy silence reigned over the table. Farook's father continued to eat, apparently unaware of the tension in the room.

Suddenly, Kenawi began to spasm. Farook jumped up and escorted him from the table, but before they were out of the dining area, Kenawi collapsed. The other brothers rushed to help Farook lift the contorted Kenawi and took him out of our sight.

Haytham continued eating as though nothing had happened. "Oh, he's epileptic," he offered by way of explanation, "but it's nothing to be concerned about."

I wondered if Mona's and Kenawi's handicaps resulted from the terror their father must have exposed them to and hoped my visit would be cut short because of this situation.

Instead, Farook's father got up and approached me. He cuffed my wrist with his hand and headed us to the front door, asking Farook to follow.

My heart pounded in my chest. Where were we going?

We took the stairs two flights up. My father-in-law unlocked an apartment and stepped inside, still choking off the veins in my wrist, the cuffs tightening a click at a time.

"This is your apartment," Haytham said brusquely. "Your father promised to furnish it. You won't spend much time here, though; our apartment downstairs will be your base for eating and entertaining."

I almost passed out, unwilling to believe he already had plans for where and how I would live.

"This apartment will be used only to produce a grandchild for us."

The thought of giving this man a grandchild made me sick to my stomach.

My imprisoned hand felt numb and pained me. I glanced at it but did not dare complain. Like a drowning person begging for something to hold on to, I looked at Farook, desperate for help. He followed us with a big smile, savoring his father's words—practically drooling over the thought of impregnating me, I imagined.

The prospect of a life trapped in that dismal apartment, expected to manufacture grandchildren for that terrible old man, filled me with dread.

On the way home, Farook asked if he could pick me up the next day.

"Only if you let me visit my friend Eleonor, and without Papa's knowledge," I stressed.

Farook agreed without asking why, or who Eleonor might be. I was relieved.

When I got home, I hugged and kissed Rawyia repeatedly.

"So, he agreed to release you?" she asked.

"Yes, tomorrow is my big day." I did the cha-cha. "Would you arrange for my rendezvous with Ghassan, like you promised?"

"Of course. Just wait until Papa falls asleep."

Laughing, we threw ourselves on the bed, stared at the ceiling, and waited until we heard our father's snoring resonate through the wall.

My mother was still awake. We asked her to bring the phone to our room. Mama always showed a willingness to help when we wanted to call our school friends. She couldn't have guessed what we were up to when she brought in the phone and left.

Rawyia locked the door and dialed Ghassan's number. Within minutes, I received confirmation of my first date ever.

That evening, Rawyia fell into a deep sleep. I struggled with my emotions, and sleep never found me. I was too excited for my date, the first time I would actively sneak behind my lawful husband's back to see the man I loved. The thought was also frightening. I closed my eyes and saw Ghassan's chocolate skin and his thick black eyelashes. When I felt his breath on my face, I touched my cheek and smiled.

PART III: PROMISES

CHAPTER 22

Farook worked two periods, one from nine until two and the other from six until eight. Like most working Egyptians, he took a nap after lunch. Rawyia arranged my rendezvous with Ghassan during the evening shift and coached Farook to tell our father, if he should ask where we were, that we were going to his parents' house. Farook cooperated, hoping to win my love and also because he trusted that our father had raised us to be honest.

He believed, as he had once told my mother, that sheltered girls were hard to find and that any man should consider himself lucky to have found one. My father, on the other hand, trusted we would be safe in Farook's home.

Farook picked us up at five thirty in the afternoon and drove to Eleonor's house. He glanced at me adoringly while driving. I smiled but could not control the nervous shaking of my legs.

"Something wrong?" he asked.

I tried to tighten my muscles, but they didn't respond. From the backseat, Rawyia poked me between my shoulders. That didn't help, either. When we arrived, I did not follow the advice of my mother, who always told us to act like ladies and remain seated until the man opened the door and helped us out of the car by the hand. Instead, I jumped out the minute Farook stopped the car.

"See you in two hours." I dashed out, Rawyia behind me.

"Have fun!" Farook called out.

Smiling, I turned around and waved.

We skipped the elevator and flew up the stairway. Eleonor answered the door and told us her mother had gone shopping.

Rawyia removed her makeup bag from her purse and painted my lips a light pink. She traced the perimeter of my eyes with black liner, teased my hair, and soaked it with Eleonor's hair spray. I could hardly contain my excitement, and my gut churned relentlessly.

My sister kissed me on the forehead. "Relax, La." She turned to Eleonor. "Maybe I should go with Laila to make sure she is safe."

"Don't be silly, Rawyia. Laila has to learn to depend on herself."

Eleonor ran to her mother's bedroom and returned with a dark-blue spray bottle. She and Rawyia took turns spritzing me with the perfume.

Rawyia gave me a few last words of sisterly advice. "Do everything except penetration," she lectured, pointing her finger to my face. "And remember, you have to be back here before eight."

I gave Rawyia an annoyed look and shook my head, wanting to tell her that Ghassan loved me and that he wasn't after sex, but the time was not right to engage in an argument.

I hurried down the stairs, jumping two steps at a time. When I reached the concierge area, I looked back up toward the balcony. Rawyia appeared and threw me a kiss.

Ghassan waited at the door for me, his hands extended. I froze for a couple of seconds, glancing left and then right, before I ran to him. I surrendered my hand to his, letting it snuggle in his warmth.

We crossed over to a black Fiat parked across the street, its engine still running. Ghassan looked at me, and I let him read what my heart had written in it. He opened the passenger door, helped me inside, and then rushed around to his seat. Every movement, every glance, was mine forever.

Ghassan drove in euphoric silence. Like a magnet, love pulled our hands into a much-anticipated squeeze. My fingers tingled at his touch. I didn't know where Ghassan planned to take me, and I didn't care.

He drove to San Stefano beach, where we had met for the first time. I could not have thought of a more romantic place for our first date.

Ghassan had rented one of the cabins on the beach and took me inside, the safest possible place for our first meeting. People rented the cabins by days, weeks, or months, mainly to change clothes and wash if they swam. The cabin had no windows and was not much bigger than my family's pantry. It was furnished only with a bench and a chair, a toilet, and a shower, but with Ghassan alongside me, I felt as if I were in a palace.

I sat next to him on the wooden bench. The waves broke the silence around us. Love permeated my senses, taking me higher than heaven. Ghassan looked at me passionately. His eyes were twinkling, strikingly radiant, and his presence filled me with tranquility. He ran the back of his right hand across my cheek. I surrendered completely to his touches, from the tips of my toes to the part of me that had awakened for only a second time.

My entire being throbbed with ecstasy. In spite of my good sense, I shut my eyes, stopped resisting, and succumbed to his overwhelming presence. Ghassan guided my head to rest on his shoulder. We remained in the cabin for an hour, during which Ghassan touched and caressed every inch of my body. While we kissed and hugged, my innocence and virginity kept him from probing deeper.

When I gently pushed Ghassan away, he apologized and assured me that he had not brought me to the cabin for sex and that we could leave if I wanted to. But I trusted him, and so we remained there.

"Laila," Ghassan said as we lay together, "what are we going to do about your marriage?"

"What do you mean?" My eyes widened.

"It's very dangerous to meet this way. You are betrothed to someone else."

Ghassan's words threw me into a pit of uncertainty, and I wrung my hands and rocked back and forth. I could not face the situation alone. Even though I wanted Ghassan to think for me, I also knew that the time had come for me to grow up and take charge of my future.

"I don't know, I don't know," I said.

Ghassan took my hands in his and rubbed them softly until I stopped rocking. "Calm down." He pressed my hands gently, giving my tremulous heart a reason to quiet. "Let's talk about the future."

Smiling, I nodded.

"What are you going to do to complete your schooling?"

"I can't go to school anymore." I lowered my gaze to the ground.

"You don't have to feel ashamed, Laila." He held up my chin. "I will help you."

"How?"

"You can study at home, can't you?"

"Of course I can, but how will I get textbooks and take tests?"

"It will be difficult but possible. When is your wedding date?"

"It will take Papa two years to prepare my furniture and trousseau."

"Okay, so you have two years. Can you do it?"

"Yes," I said with enthusiasm and a desire to please him.

"My parents would like it better if I introduced them to an educated girl." He winked.

No one before Ghassan had supported my education. He made me feel as if not all men were like my father and brothers, and I loved him even more for it.

When Ghassan and I parted that evening, he committed himself to buying all of my textbooks and to helping me with any lessons I might find difficult.

Ghassan dropped me off at Eleonor's before Farook came to pick us up. Rawyia and Eleonor bombarded me with questions. I didn't respond but savored the sweetness with which Ghassan had bathed my lips.

As we went to bed that night, I told Rawyia about my plans to continue my education in secret with Ghassan's help.

"This is not what we have planned, La," she snapped. "Studying will tie you down in the house for a long time."

Her reaction surprised me.

"We need to concentrate on our future away from this city," she scolded. "Besides, what is this blind submission to a man you hardly know?"

I did not understand why Rawyia wanted to deprive me of the love I craved and rob me of the joy that had already begun to run in my veins. She would not ruin my happiness.

"I don't tell you what to do with your life, and from now on, I expect you to do the same with mine."

Rawyia looked at me, astonished, and shook her head. "We will talk later, when you cool off from your hot date."

That night, I did not care what she thought.

Soon, I spent night after night studying in secret, hiding my books under the mattress during the day. I tried enticing Rawyia to join me, while she pressured me to abandon this crazy idea. Even though my desire for education conflicted with the goals Rawyia envisioned for us, she never turned me down when I needed her to cover up for my rendezvous or my studies. She grunted and moaned when I asked her to quiz me, but she never denied me her help, and never complained about the flashlight I used under the covers while she slept.

With her eyes half-open, Rawyia would mumble, every time she turned over during her sleep, "Are you still up?"

"Yes," I would whisper.

Then she would pat me gently on the thigh and fall asleep again.

As time passed, my love for Ghassan grew even deeper. We met almost every week, thanks to our lies and schemes. When Farook showed signs of suspicion, we stopped our meetings for a few weeks, before resuming again. After each separation, Ghassan and I got closer, rejuvenating our love and keeping it strong.

The most trying times came when Ghassan spent the summer break with his family in Lebanon. I pined for Ghassan; his letters, sent to Eleanor's address, were my only comfort. Over and over I read them, and whenever my suffering intensified, my heart recited his words to me.

During Ghassan's absence, Farook got only the cold shoulder from me. A variety of excuses kept Farook away, except on Fridays, when Papa forced me to go out. I could not believe a man as old and as experienced as Farook failed to read the infidelity written on my face and in my behavior.

I was a betrothed girl, with in-laws and a new family, but my love for Ghassan was my world, my future, and my power.

Ghassan represented the sole rift that had ever existed between Rawyia and me. Rawyia implored me to think logically and focus on her dreams of independence, but I couldn't follow her in all things. This stubborn side of me was new to Rawyia. Getting a high school diploma became my obsession, a way to make Ghassan proud of me when he introduced me to his parents.

Rawyia taunted me by saying that going to Lebanon with Ghassan was just a dream, but it was a wish I would not allow even my beloved sister to steal from me. I did not know how I would realize my goal of getting a divorce, but I made the dream a reality in my mind.

CHAPTER 23

Right before my seventeenth birthday, I was ready to take the exam that would earn me a high school diploma, but to take the exam, I had to go to a nearby school. Rawyia and I rehearsed how, what, and when to tell Papa. I needed my father's permission to get out of the house, but facing Papa with a decision I had made without his involvement and approval was a nightmare.

"What if Papa locks me in the pantry?" I asked Rawyia. "Should I ask Mama first?"

"Mama won't help," Rawyia cautioned. "Tell Papa yourself and take your chance; otherwise, wait till we have left our husbands and then reapply."

"But by the time you and I divorce our husbands, I'll have forgotten everything I've learned in two years."

Rawyia sighed. "La, I don't have a magic solution."

"What if I just leave, don't tell Papa where I'm going, and never come back?" I was desperate enough to consider this.

"Where would you go, smart-head?"

"To *Tante* Hameeda's," I said hesitantly, meaning Mama's sister whom Papa hated.

"Did you forget that we are still under Papa's control? And what Papa thinks of our 'sinful' *Tante* Hameeda? Papa would drag you by the hair from our aunt's house, and no one would come to your rescue."

I decided to take my chances and inform my father.

The day of the high school exam, I woke up before the sunlight traced the horizon. Rawyia still sleeping, I removed my nightgown and slipped into a white cotton blouse with long sleeves. I put on a brown skirt that covered my knees, hoping modest attire would win Papa's approval. Then I jumped back in bed and lay next to Rawyia.

Trying to calm myself down, I recited the opening verse from the Quran seven times. Fareeda had told us that seven was a magic number, that God had created the universe in seven days. But, try as I might, my mind remained too unsettled to focus on my devotions.

I shook Rawyia gently. "Rawyia, wake up. I'm scared," I whispered.

"La, you are betrothed and you can do what you want to now," she whispered, and slipped back into sleep.

Taking a deep breath to steady myself, I prepared to ask my father's permission alone. I had no doubt that he would appreciate the two years I had spent studying and the efforts I had made to pursue my education. He would be proud of me and would appreciate the perseverance and determination I had inherited from him. My father, too, had studied at home in secrecy and faced many obstacles but had remained faithful to his goal and dream. He would see that in me.

Empowered with my pen, pencils, ruler, and compass in hand, I knocked softly on his bedroom door. Papa didn't answer. I opened the door, tiptoed in, and stood in front of my father's bed. He appeared to be sleeping. Mama often told us Papa slept with one eye closed and the other one open all night so as not to lose his control, and we believed her. Now both of his eyes were shut.

I don't remember how long I remained standing next to his bed before he turned to me with two fully awakened, icy eyes. My tongue froze.

"What are you doing here so early?"

"I'm looking for Mama," I said, hesitating to face him alone.

"She's not here."

I wanted to get out of his room and forget about my exam, but my feet were glued to the floor. The chirping birds outside the window reminded me of freedom and helped to thaw out my tongue.

"Papa, do you love me?" I asked, hoping to soften his heart.

Puzzled, he asked, "What do you want?"

"First, answer me," I said playfully.

"I will miss my dawn prayer," he said, even though the *Adhan* call to prayer had not yet come from the nearby mosque.

Papa didn't use the word "love." Mama told us he believed expressing love in words or actions stripped men of their control.

He got up, reached for his towel, and headed to the door. My moment would soon be gone.

"Papa, would you allow me to go take my high school exam this morning?" My lips felt stiff, and I could hardly believe the words had come through them.

Papa froze. "What do you mean?" he asked, without facing me.

"I've been studying for two years. I wanted to surprise you," I said in one breath.

Papa turned, his face masked in anger. "Does your husband know?" he snapped.

"No," I said defiantly.

"Does your mother know?" His upper lip twitched, and his lower lip fell victim to his grinding teeth.

I took two steps back. "No, Mama doesn't know either," I whispered.

"So you made the decision. I assume the other one helped you execute your secret plan."

"I am the one who studied," I answered with irritation. "Not Rawyia. Whether she helped me or not would not have changed my determination to educate myself."

My father stared at me in silence. As the seconds ticked away, I shivered with fear. I knew better than to interpret his muteness as a favorable response.

"Go to your room. I will give you my answer once I'm finished with my dawn prayer," Papa said through thin lips.

I nodded dumbly, hardly believing he had allowed me to escape his wrath even for a moment. My anxiety mounted as I waited for him to summon me.

Rawyia had not awakened yet, so I had no one with whom to share my fears. I could barely contain my nervousness. Even though I asked no more than what any human being deserved—the right to an education—I could only imagine what punishment Papa would mete out if my simple request displeased him.

Soon, Papa pounded his fist on the bedroom door. He burst into the room, dragged me out, and led me struggling to the tiny pantry down the hall. "You'll stay in here until I'm back from work," he snarled.

"Papa, no!"

The lock clicked. He'd left me there with no blanket, food, or water. The room was stiflingly close and dark, as if I had entered a tomb. I slumped to the floor, sobbing.

Sometime later, I heard Rawyia's voice. "Damn the day we were born!" she shouted.

Yes. I want to die.

"Why were men granted unlimited control over women?" Rawyia said for the thousandth time.

I could do nothing but weep.

Remembering how much I feared darkness, Rawyia turned

on the pantry light, using the switch on the outside. "La, I'm here. Why are you quiet? Are you crying?"

"No," I said, my cracking voice betraying me.

"La, Papa is gone and left the key with Mama. I'll get you out."

Rawyia's footsteps moved away. A moment later, I heard them hurrying back, along with Mama's heavier tread. When the door opened, I threw myself into Mama's arms.

"I wouldn't keep you inside." Mama kissed me on the forehead.

"May God take our souls!" Rawyia bellowed. "We've had enough of this sick life! Why won't Papa let Laila take the exam? Our father doesn't have the right to deprive my sister of an education. We are not under his control anymore. Laila could leave now and go to her husband if she wanted to."

Rawyia went on with her threats, though we both knew we had no recourse. Fear held us in its grip. It surprised me to hear Rawyia defend my pursuit of an education, but it did not shock me. She had always been supportive and never let me down.

I desperately needed someone to give me hope. It came a half hour later, when the telephone rang once and stopped—a prearranged signal from Ghassan. Rawyia and I sneaked the telephone into our room and called him.

"Laila, you must compose yourself," Ghassan said in a calm and understanding manner. "Don't do anything you might regret later. He is your father, and you must listen to him. Otherwise, you will be blamed and judged harshly by everyone around you. As for your exam, no one, not even your father, can prevent you from obtaining the diploma. You just have to wait for the right time." He paused for a moment. "When you and I get married, things will be different."

I sobbed as I listened to his loving words.

Rawyia made sure to sneak me back into the pantry before Papa returned from work. We couldn't afford to ignite our father's rage with a new offense.

When Papa came back in the evening, he released me from the pantry and took me to his room. "If you had come to me before you made your decision to study, I wouldn't have objected," he said, avoiding my cold stare.

I refused to be fooled. Speaking with Ghassan had emboldened me, and an ember of righteous anger grew within me.

"You have killed me twice," I said, "and I will never forgive you."

I left my father's room depressed and disappointed but also determined to fulfill my dream of getting an education, no matter how long it took.

CHAPTER 24

My parents' tirades were becoming more frequent and serious. Mama would come to us in the aftermath, and she soon became a friend, as well as a mother. She won our absolute trust.

One day, I felt confident enough to tell Mama about my love, every little detail.

Mama gave me a look of sympathy and concern. "Does Ghassan really care about you, Laila? Is he willing to marry you?"

Her response did not surprise me. She had supported me during my ordeal, within her limitations.

"Yes, Mama," I said with confidence.

"Can I talk to him?"

"Of course! I will call Ghassan for you." I kissed her on the cheek.

Mama brought the phone into our room. I was jittery, so I let Rawyia dial. Mama widened her eyes, trying to capture how many taps Rawyia made for each number. She couldn't focus. Still, Mama insisted on playing the detective by guessing

Ghassan's location. "Does he live in Gleem?"

"No, Mama, you've got the numbers wrong," I said playfully.

Mama gave us a pretend-to-agree grin and reached for the receiver before Rawyia could speak with Ghassan. Rawyia and I giggled. She wanted to catch Ghassan by surprise and tried to prevent us from warning him, but the line was busy.

Mama rubbed her knee in a circular motion.

"Calm down, Mama," I said.

"Are you sure of Ghassan's intentions?"

"Positive." I glanced at Rawyia for support.

"Well, we will soon know if Ghassan is serious. And that includes you, too, La."

"Ghassan *is* serious." I was annoyed at Rawyia's skepticism.

Kareema knocked and brought in a tray with a teapot, Mama's favorite glass—the one with a gold rim—and a tiny matching bowl containing four sugar cubes. The maid left. After pouring Mama's tea, Rawyia dialed the number again and handed the receiver to Mama.

Mama held the cup of tea in one hand and the receiver in the other. She squinted, the way she always did when concentrating. She took a sip and placed the glass on the tray.

Rawyia and I knelt on our bed, anxious to hear the first word that popped out of her mouth. Mama pointed her finger to the door and signaled Rawyia to lock it.

"I already locked it," Rawyia confirmed.

Mama's face lit up. She smiled, signaling someone had picked up on the other end. *"Allo,* is this Ghassan?"

No one seemed to speak from the other end.

"I am Laila's mother."

Silence. My mother's eyebrows arched in a question.

I tried to squeeze my ear between the receiver and Mama's ear to hear what Ghassan said, but I couldn't.

Mama smiled. "I am sure Laila loves you, too."

I let go, satisfied with how the conversation was proceeding.

Mama took another sip of tea. "Yes, I know, son. It is impossible to broach the subject with Laila's father, and this is why I suggest it should be done after the wedding."

Apparently, more silence.

"Is Ghassan trying to find excuses or what?" Rawyia couldn't keep herself from commenting.

Anxiety burdened my heart. I feared she might be right.

"Yes, I trust you, son." Mama's words lifted me up. "I do feel better now. You seem to be nice and sincere. I would like to meet with you. Let's arrange that as soon as possible."

Mama's cooperation lifted the burden from my heart, and I relaxed. She hung up.

After I took her cup of tea and set it on the tray, I threw myself into her arms. "Thank you, Mama. Thank you, thank you, and thank you."

"Laila, my dear, your father will never accept this arrangement. Why don't you wait until you get married and then ask your husband for a divorce?"

"How can I be sure Farook will divorce me?"

"You just have to take your chances," she said, looking hesitant. "But I will help you."

I had no choice but to accept Mama's advice. It was comforting to have her approval. From that point on, I accepted all of Farook's invitations to socialize, at least those that got me out of the house. Ghassan and I began planning for our future as if I were not legally betrothed. I had only a few more months before I'd be married and then, I hoped, divorced.

Shortly after our betrothals, Rawyia and I began to receive invitations to our *Tante* Hameeda's lavish Thursday evening soirees celebrating the beginning of the weekend. Though Hameeda was my mother's only living sister, our father forbade Mama to socialize with her.

Tante Hameeda lived differently from us. Her late husband had already had a wife when he married Hameeda, and, according to *Tante* Akeela, both women were content with the arrangement.

After *Tante* Hameeda's husband's death, she lived with her two daughters, Halima and Soraya, and their families in a large residential compound that consisted of two elegant villas. *Tante* Hameeda became diabetic in the aftermath of her husband's death, but that didn't put an end to her social life.

My parents were never invited to visit and would not have attended in any case, because of *Tante* Hameeda's flamboyantly secular lifestyle and decidedly nontraditional soirées.

The first time Rawyia and I attended, we arrived with Farook. The entry hall was more elegant than any I had ever seen in a private residence, with crystal chandeliers larger than ours at home. Formally dressed servants stood on either side of the hallway, greeting people. We passed through into a guest room the size of three ordinary salons. *Tante* Hameeda was sitting on a grand sofa and talking with our cousins Halima and Soraya.

Tante Hameeda walked up to welcome Rawyia, Farook, and me. Gamal had come to *Tante* Hameeda's earlier.

"Hello, my dears. Please make yourselves at home," she said, and took off to greet another group of guests.

We were left alone in the middle of the salon as dozens of people mingled around us. Across the room, I caught sight of Gamal, *Tante* Hameeda's nephew and a frequent visitor in her home. Gamal still refused to have anything to do with Farook and kept his distance throughout the evening.

The whole family accepted his detached behavior and that cemented my suspicion about my father-in-law's crime. I suggested to Rawyia that she ask Gamal if he knew anything about the charges.

"We don't need to know, La. You are divorcing Farook soon."

Many prominent people in politics and entertainment attended this party. *Tante* Hameeda regularly kept company with these local celebrities, some of whom we recognized.

A singer named Ahmed frequented *Tante* Hameeda's fun evenings. Some said that Ahmed was a "half man"—a castrato singer who was castrated before puberty to preserve his vocal range. When Ahmed sang, he sounded very much like the popular Egyptian diva Umm Kulthum.

After the late dinner, the guests gathered around Ahmed and listened to his imitations of Umm Kulthum's songs of love and longing while they sipped their Johnnie Walker on ice.

Tante Hameeda's lifestyle was new and exhilarating to Rawyia and me. Before long, we were socializing on our mother's side of the family on an almost-weekly basis. For the first time, we got to know our cousins, especially Soraya, who was in her thirties. Soraya had a son and a daughter. Halima, fifteen years Soraya's senior, had two boys and two girls. One of Halima's daughters, Shewekar, was a few years younger than Soraya, and the two of them spent a lot of time together.

Shewekar and Soraya were in arranged marriages as well. They were unhappy in their marriages, and both were actively unfaithful to their husbands. It surprised me to know that other women were forced into marriages like Rawyia and I had been. My cousins, too, accepted their fate, just as Mama had been relentlessly beseeching me to.

Rawyia and I became so close to Soraya and Shewekar that we shared our secret lives with them. Soraya and Shewekar were our chaperones and alibis; Rawyia and I played the same role for them.

Soraya and Shewekar introduced us to their boyfriends, and I introduced them to Ghassan. Meanwhile, Farook remained unaware. He often took us to *Tante* Hameeda's house and felt comfortable leaving us there because, as it happened, he, too, was related to our aunt Hameeda's late husband.

Shewekar had a brother named Sameh, a sophisticated young man. Sameh took an interest in Rawyia. He'd studied at Victoria College in Alexandria. Even though Rawyia still professed distrust for all men and the concept of love, I could see her falling for Sameh. He enticed her with a cosmopolitan lifestyle and offers of fun and inhibition-free evenings on the town.

Before long, the two of them began to slip away from the rest of us during our visits. Rawyia and Sameh would remove themselves to some other corner of the compound while Gamal sat in the salon and listened to music.

"La, cover for me. I will be in the garden with Sameh," Rawyia would whisper to me.

Afraid someone would notice, I would nod, then check my watch every second until Rawyia reappeared half an hour, or even an hour, later. She would saunter into the salon, flushed in the face, her hair out of place, and take her seat next to Gamal. It never crossed Gamal's mind that Rawyia might be cheating on him. I knew she was treading on thin ice, but I didn't know how to stop her.

CHAPTER 25

Two months before my wedding, Gamal's visits dwindled to once every three days, then once a week, and then even less. Rawyia didn't talk much about him. She gave me different excuses when I asked her why she wasn't going out with him anymore. It surprised me that she didn't seem to care.

One evening while Rawyia and I were in our bedroom, we heard Mama yelling in the hallway. "You scoundrel! You dog! You've ruined my daughter's life!" she fumed.

It surprised me to hear Mama use such words. The most she ever uttered when she got angry with my brother's misbehavior was *inta kalb*—"you are a dog."

"Who is Mama calling a scoundrel, and whose life is she referring to?" I asked Rawyia, puzzled by her disinterest in what was going on.

She sat in front of the mirror, calmly styling her hair. "I'm getting a divorce."

I knew Rawyia had lost interest in Gamal, but it shocked and disturbed me to hear about the divorce. How would that affect our plans? Although I felt lost and insecure, I kept my anxiety under control and focused on the situation Rawyia and I were facing.

We couldn't hear Gamal's voice, but our mother continued to yell. "You louse! When my sister gave birth to you, she didn't deliver a man! Get out! Get out of this house!"

My anxiety turned into panic.

Rawyia, unflinching, styled her hair and applied makeup. "Gamal knows about Sameh and me," Rawyia blurted. "One of the servants must have told him. I assured him nothing had happened between me and Sameh, but Gamal didn't believe me." She threw her hands up in the air and shrugged. "I didn't want Gamal anyway. I used him to get out of here."

"I thought you liked him!"

"No, La. I *pretended* to like him. The freedom that came with him was what I really liked."

"But you will lose it with the divorce, won't you?"

"Oh, no. Now I am a divorcee," Rawyia answered with exuberance. "I will have the right to do what I want."

Rawyia was maturing at such a speedy rate that I had to pose my next question even though I didn't want to. Her behavior was daring and rebellious. I had a difficult time understanding what she really wanted from the freedom she was pursuing. It scared me to see my sister dispose of her reputation without any regrets.

"Rawyia, did . . . did you sleep with Sameh?"

"What difference would that make now?" she retorted. "What's so special about virginity? Since the day you and I were born, we've heard nothing positive about being girls; we've just been bombarded with warnings about how important our virginity is to our family's honor."

My head spun in confusion and distress about my sister's future in this society, with its stigma surrounding women who were divorced and lost their virginity before moving to their matrimonial home.

"Don't worry about me, La. I'm still very desirable." She admired her figure in the mirror. "I know losing my virginity makes my chances for marriage slim, but I will use my charm to make every man pay for what the men I've known have done to me." Rawyia's words were confident and defiant, but her lower lip trembled.

I took Rawyia in my arms as she broke down and cried. "Tell me what happened," I said.

"Gamal did not appreciate my honesty. I tried to tell him no man before him had touched me, but he did not believe me." She looked at me for approval.

I nodded.

"I told Gamal about Sameh," she said, without any show of regret.

My sister was holding something back. The smile died on her face, and she frowned, staring at herself in the mirror, and bit her lower lip. She appeared immersed in reflection.

"Tell me, Rawyia. Who took your virginity?"

"I don't know. Maybe Sameh, and stop interrogating me, La." She shrugged.

I pretended to believe Rawyia. Even though she appeared too nonchalant, I sensed her anguish, so I stopped questioning her.

Rawyia had a different story for Mama and lied when she informed Mama she had sex with Gamal because they had a legal contract that bound them as husband and wife.

Papa didn't know for sure but assumed Rawyia might have allowed Gamal to have sex with her. Neither Papa nor Mama knew the whole story, though, and Gamal kept the reason for the divorce to himself.

In Egypt, it was bad enough when a man divorced a woman. It was even worse when they are cousins, for it meant a black mark on the girl and the entire family's reputation within the community.

After the disgraceful termination of Rawyia's marriage, the cold war between Papa and my mother's family escalated into open hostility. My father blamed *Tante* Hameeda and her children for corrupting Rawyia.

Rawyia, too, started her own war in the house, determined to take full control of her life. She knew her legal rights as a divorced woman and did not need the approval of any adult if she wanted to leave the house or travel somewhere.

But Rawyia felt like a pariah at home and had no one but me as a friend. Reda called her every dirty name, and Ahmed echoed the insults. Even Samir and Hady treated Rawyia with disrespect. Hala, too, urged me to stay away from Rawyia, but I did not listen.

The entire family saw Rawyia as a Jezebel who needed to be harnessed and tortured until she repented. Papa stopped speaking to Rawyia and spent much of his time moping in his room.

Two weeks before my wedding, I woke up and discovered Rawyia had not slept in our bed. Her spot felt cold when I inspected it with my hand. I panicked and went searching for my sister in every room except my parents', but I could not find her.

I waited in my bed for Mama to wake up. Feeling naked without Rawyia, I wanted to believe my sister would appear at our bedroom door any moment. As the minutes passed, I rocked back and forth in slow motion, thinking about how my life would be if Rawyia had finally left.

Mama walked into the room.

"Mama, where is Rawyia?" I whispered.

"Why?"

"I looked for her everywhere. She is not in the apartment."

"You don't know where your sister might be?" Her voice had a suspicious tone, and she paced the room frantically.

"I swear to you, Mama, I don't know." I had a sinking feeling in my stomach and began to imagine that Rawyia had left while

I slept to spare me the responsibility of her disappearance. She had taken care of me until her last moments in our house.

Thinking of my father's reaction had me trembling with fear. Deep inside, I knew Rawyia could not have gone far and that she would wait for me. It made my own escape seem possible.

By the end of the day, we learned Rawyia had taken refuge at *Tante* Hameeda's home. Mama asked her sister to order Rawyia back home, but Rawyia threatened to run away from both places and *Tante* Hameeda didn't force Rawyia to return to us.

When Papa got the news, all hell broke loose and he, again, blamed Mama for everything. He sentenced Mama to a life of misery and threatened to divorce her if she ever visited *Tante* Hameeda.

Mama stopped sleeping in the same room with our father. She sneaked out in the middle of the night to share my bed and carefully left again before I woke up. I always pretended to be asleep when she came and never once asked her about this separation.

Her health began to deteriorate, too. She was only in her early forties, but her eyesight weakened and her body shrank from rapid weight loss.

I knew Mama missed my sister and her intimate time with my father. Despite Papa's oppressiveness, Mama wanted to believe she loved him dearly. Knowing that I, too, planned to run away made me sick.

When I asked Mama what she would do if I went to live with *Tante* Hameeda, she replied, "I leave it to God Almighty. He will give me patience and strength."

As I'd suspected, Mama already knew I would follow Rawyia.

While I tried to reassure her that I loved her and that she had been a good mother, I couldn't erase Mama's feeling of failure. She seemed always to believe my father when he blamed her for everything.

One day, I persuaded Farook to take me to see my sister. Mama sent along some pocket money and lots of advice for Rawyia that I never bothered to relay. Rawyia had adjusted easily to her new life and couldn't have cared less about the problems in our house. She could finally go out and be with anyone, anytime she wished. She smoked now and had tried liquor. She dressed in sleeveless dresses with short skirts, wore makeup, and looked older. I envied Rawyia for the free style of life she chose and could not wait to join her.

"Just wait till your wedding," Rawyia told me. "Look at me. Everyone thinks I am a loose girl. I don't want anyone to think of you that way."

In most modern societies, Rawyia's desires would have seemed perfectly normal, the life choices of a healthy, intelligent young woman, but not in Egypt and definitely not in our family. Despite all the dirty names people hurled at my sister, Rawyia remained that young girl seeking her freedom and was not as loose as my father perceived her to be.

Days before my own wedding, Rawyia and I stood on the terrace outside *Tante* Hameeda's dining room so my sister could smoke. I asked if she had a boyfriend. She gave me a big smile.

"Of course. His name is Marwan. Marwan and I plan to get married. He is going to take me to Lebanon."

She told me all of this as if it were the most ordinary thing, but I could see that she was working hard to keep from appearing too excited.

"Rawyia, that's where I plan to live with Ghassan when we get married!"

Rawyia shook her head, always wanting to discourage me from my dreams of happiness with Ghassan. "You understand, don't you, that once you divorce you have to wait three months before you can get married again?"

"Three months?" I gasped. "That's too long. Why do I have to wait?"

"Don't ask me why. It's the law. It came from the Quran."

"We don't have to tell the sheikh when the divorce took place," I suggested innocently. The religious man of authority didn't need to know.

"It's not that easy," Rawyia said irritably. "The sheikh will know the date from your divorce document. If the woman is pregnant, a period of three months would be enough to determine the paternity claim. You understand now?" She raised her voice in frustration.

"Yes, I do, but I don't plan to get pregnant. I can swear to that."

"It doesn't matter. This is the law. Don't you know that all women's social and family laws come from the Quran? We have no choice but to abide by them." Rawyia turned away, mumbling, "I don't know how I can leave you, La. You don't know anything about legal matters."

"Are you leaving me?" I didn't understand. Soon, I would be with Rawyia at *Tante* Hameeda's, and then we could both move to Lebanon with our husbands.

"No, not yet! But if I leave before you are free, I will come back and help with your papers and passport. Then you can join me."

Rawyia's words were promising and soothing. They gave me confidence that soon I would be with her in Lebanon—Ghassan, too. In fact, he had already finished his university studies and returned to his homeland. It would all work out: I would be divorced, and Ghassan would marry me. For the next weeks, I lived with these dreams.

CHAPTER 26

My father chose the first Thursday of September for my wedding celebration and insisted on having it in our apartment. He limited the guest list to his family and Farook's, because the situation with Rawyia shamed him greatly and Papa didn't want to answer questions about her whereabouts. That meant about thirty people from his side and another twenty from Farook's. No one from my mother's family would attend.

Preparations for the event had started weeks earlier. My furniture and trousseau were shipped to my future home with Farook. The party plans were in order.

As the date approached, more and more dread filled me and I began to develop a plan. With Rawyia gone and Mama often depleted by her own sadness and illness, I turned to another member of our family, Samir, my youngest brother, who was now thirteen. Although timid and fearful because of his persecution by Reda and Ahmed, Samir could be very clever. I hoped I could count on him. In any case, with my wedding day upon me, I felt desperate and hoped Samir could find a way to help me escape. I knew he would try if I asked, because I had always been a comfort to him amid his troubles with Reda and Ahmed.

The night before my nuptial day, I snuck into Samir's room. Together, he and I made a plan involving his best friend, Tarek, whose father owned five taxis. I only hoped it would work out, or both of us would be in big trouble.

The next morning, on Thursday, I started to get ready for my wedding celebration. While Kareema painted my finger-nails red, my father materialized, looking for Mama. Kareema immediately left the room. Before I could hide them behind my back, he noticed my colored nails, charged across the room like a bull, and grabbed my arm, smashing my forefinger on the marble top of the commode until blood gushed from it.

"How many times have I told you not to color your nails?" he growled, and left the room.

Fear silenced me. My finger throbbed, and the pain was intense. With my unharmed hand, I grabbed a towel from the armoire and covered my finger. Blood soaked it. I removed the towel to examine my wound. My nail had broken below the quick and hung at the corner. I moaned and buried my finger in the towel again.

Mama came in and held my injured finger with tenderness. "May God be your judge, Kamel." She could not wish Papa any harm, but she told me often that God's punishment would be severe in the afterlife.

"Don't worry, Mama, it's just a minor cut."

Mama mended my broken nail with a Band-Aid before leaving. By myself, I put on my white satin wedding dress, covering my teary eyes with the white veil. No one assisted me or rejoiced at seeing me in my bridal regalia.

I had never understood the real meaning of loneliness until I wore my wedding dress. Part of me felt empty and sad. The other part had dreams of a future different from the one my father had arranged.

If only I had wings so I could fly away to Lebanon and stand next to Ghassan as we recited our wedding vows. I smiled and promised myself to end this charade as quickly as I could.

A somber cloud hovered over that day. It should have been a day of joy and celebration, but no one could avoid Papa's rage. Even Hala, usually so quiet and unobtrusive, got her share of abuse when she appeared with her lips painted a light pink. Papa slapped her, leaving a handprint on her cheek.

So angry was he, Papa couldn't bring himself to face his own relatives. He stayed in his room almost the entire time.

Even though the guests had normal conversations, a sullen atmosphere shrouded the room. Music played from our record player, but nobody danced. The family members who attended appeared to be busy talking and paid no attention to me. I had no friends at my own wedding.

When I walked in, no one commented on my dress or told me I looked pretty, but that did not bother me. I kept my appearance brief and returned to my room. After all, the legal ceremony had already taken place two years earlier.

Tante Akeela looked for Mama and went to my father's room. I heard Papa say he had sent Mama to her sister's home. By then, nothing could surprise me.

Egyptian weddings often last until late into the night and the early hours of dawn, but not mine. The absence of Papa, Mama, and Rawyia cast a gloom over the gathering and prompted the guests to leave early. The wedding party ended in two hours.

Seeing that part of the nightmare end could not make me any happier, and so I escaped to my private shelter and lay on my bed in the dark, needing time to reflect on my life. I had lost my adolescence before I had even experienced it, as did many girls of my age.

My hands ran over my white dress, and I recalled *Tante* Akeela's words: "A girl wears the white dress only once in her lifetime. If she remarries, she cannot wear a white wedding dress."

Tears welled in my eyes as I thought of Ghassan, but I consoled myself and vowed to fight until my dreams and hopes of a life with him were realized.

Papa asked me to take off my wedding dress before I left for my matrimonial home. I refused, wishing for Mama to see me in it. How could she have gone somewhere else?

When the time came for me to leave with my husband, I lifted the hem of my white gown and ran down the hall, stopping in front of my parents' room. There should have been a farewell, but Papa's door was closed.

I swore in silence never to set foot in the house again and entered my room for the final time. Passing through straight to the balcony, I filled my memory with one last glimpse of the neighborhood. Taking in all of the bittersweet memories that had been etched on these walls made me want to scream. Pain grew in my throat, and I walked back to the bed I had shared with Rawyia. Caressing her pillow, I lifted it to my face and filled my soul with her scent. I moaned in agony for leaving so much behind. Then I remembered the magazines I'd hidden behind the armoire and pulled them out.

To my surprise, *Tante* Akeela was standing by the door. She had a paper bag in her hand and a tender smile on her face. "I always knew about your secret magazines."

I gave *Tante* Akeela a quick hug. Then I opened the drawer of the bedside table, pulled out my schoolbook of autographs, and shoved it in the bag with my magazines. After I gave my aunt one last hug, I left the room.

"You have to come for a visit soon," my aunt murmured.

"I'll try, *Tante*," I said with dismay.

Farook waited to take me away, but I couldn't go yet. The house felt empty without Rawyia, and without Mama, whom I missed the most. Mama had wanted so much to see me in my wedding gown. I didn't want to leave without saying goodbye to her.

Tante Akeela saw me hesitate. "Is something wrong, dear?"

"I miss Mama." My voice broke.

"I'll take you to see her, but don't tell anyone." *Tante* Akeela took me by the hand to the kitchen and opened the door to the servants' stairways. "Your mother has been hiding up on the roof the whole evening. Go, my dear, and say your goodbyes. I will wait here and warn you if your father, Reda, or Ahmed comes looking for you."

I thanked her with a big hug, gathered the train of my wedding gown, and ran up the stairs to the roof.

Mama stood in the dark, her gaze glued to the sky. I had seen my mother before on the balcony late at night, talking intimately to God, but never before had she seemed so absorbed in prayer. She did not hear me approach.

"Mama," I whispered.

She turned around, startled, and sobbed. I took her in my arms, but she pushed me away gently. "My eyes longed to see one of you in a wedding gown," she said.

I despised our father for putting Mama in this situation. Although I felt sorry for her, I wished she had the courage to fight back, not only for herself but for Rawyia and me as well.

Slowly, I circled around her several times to satisfy her. Then I stopped and dried her tears with my kisses. "I couldn't leave without saying goodbye, Mama."

"I knew God would answer my prayers," she said through her tears. Mama's soul and body merged with mine in a tight embrace.

I wanted her to stop believing that God listened to her prayers, but I could not question her faith. It helped ease her suffering.

"If you have such a good relationship with God, why didn't you ask him for a kind and liberal man before you married my father?"

"Your father is kind and is no different from any head of a family. All men follow the teaching of Islam. Women have no choice. You, too, my dear, will have to abide by the rules of our religion."

"But the prophet Mohamed treated his wives with respect and kindness, Mama. The prophet valued their opinions and consulted his wives even in matters of war."

"Your father is not a prophet, my dear."

"Okay, then if Papa is like all other fathers, maybe you should be like all the other mothers. Go back inside and ask his forgiveness," I said sarcastically.

"I will, my dear. I have no other place to go. You run to your new home with Farook. You cannot change your destiny, nor drift away from the culture."

"I can, Mama. And I will."

With trepidation, I walked away, watching her smile dissolve in a pool of tears. I threw her a kiss and left, determined to live a life different from hers and shape my own destiny.

The custom at the end of a wedding was for the newlyweds to go to downtown Alexandria and tour El-Mursi Abul Abbas Mosque as a final blessing. As part of the plan my brother Samir and I had made, Samir came along with Farook and me for this final part of the ceremony.

Since our talk the night before, Samir had reached out to Tarek, who had befriended his father's youngest driver, Saleem. The driver was twenty-six and didn't mind using his taxi to help me escape. Samir and Tarek had arranged it so Saleem would wait near Farook's apartment building in his taxi.

Meanwhile, Farook's brother Kenawi drove us from my parents' apartment to the mosque. Farook took the front passenger seat, and Samir sat in the backseat with me.

Anxiety and fear settled deep inside me. My throat felt dry. Cold perspiration slithered down my back, into my cleavage, and under my arms—long, thin trickles of sweat—yet my extremities felt cold. I trembled with fear. *Will our plan work? Can I rely on Tarek and Saleem?*

My legs shook, and my gaze darted between the streetlights and my brother. Samir took my hand to calm me. The thought of what might happen to Samir and the disgrace I would bring to my family terrified me; however, my desire to join Rawyia and Ghassan gave me enough strength to stick to the plan, no matter the outcome.

We drove around the mosque seven times, as custom demanded, before heading toward my new home. I did not recite any verses from the Quran or ask God for blessings, since I knew better than to believe that my prayers would make my escape any easier. I had neglected the fate He had chosen for me.

As we pulled up to the entrance of Farook's apartment building, Samir whispered in my ear, "Look back. You see the taxi behind us? When Kenawi turns off the engine, open the door, walk quietly to the taxi, and get in. I will deal with Farook and all of the people waiting for you."

I squeezed his hand.

Never for a moment did I question Samir's courage to carry out this plan. I was too desperate to escape to consider the ways in which it could backfire. When I saw Farook's family waiting for us, I worried, fearing what my in-laws would think of me, but there wasn't enough time to reconsider. I was so close to living my dream, and I refused to succumb to fear. Not many girls in my situation had this chance, or the support of women from their family that I had. I felt Mama's, Rawyia's, and *Tante* Akeela's presence and heard their voices urging me to keep going and never look back.

Our car stopped. Samir jumped out and signaled the taxi to approach. I did as my brother told me, and Samir quickly pushed me into the backseat of the taxi. Half of my veil dragged outside as Samir shut the door and banged on the hood, signaling the driver to take off. No one—neither Farook nor any of the other people waiting for me—had time to react.

The taxi's tires squealed as we drove away. I sat at the edge of my seat, looking left and right and shaking. My heart raced to catch up with what I had just done. After I took a deep breath, I ran my tongue over my dry lips and sank back into the seat.

"Forgive me, Mama," I whispered.

"I swear, this is better than any movie scene I've ever seen!" Saleem laughed, but I didn't find any part of the escape very funny.

Through the back window, I saw Samir in a fist fight with Farook, surrounded by many people.

"Stop!" I wanted to go back and save my brother.

"Nothing will happen to Samir. He has enough help." Saleem chuckled.

As we sped away, I trembled with relief and fear. I had committed a crime, but I didn't know what the punishment would be. *Oh, if only Rawyia were by my side!* I needed someone to assure me that everything would be all right. We were heading to *Tante* Hameeda's villa, but the way seemed too long.

Saleem glanced at me in the mirror and asked me several times if I would be all right. I only nodded and gazed out the window. What if Papa was waiting for me at *Tante* Hameeda's? "Stop!" I shouted. "Stop, now! Please!"

Saleem brought the car to a halt on the side of the street. "What's the matter?"

I gave Saleem my aunt's phone number and asked him to call to make sure no problems were waiting for me.

Saleem parked the car in an alley, locked it, and disappeared for few minutes. I quivered, unable to control my shaking body, until he came back, smiling.

"It's safe, and they are all waiting for you."

I squeezed my hands nervously and thanked God.

"Don't be afraid, beautiful young bride." He turned his head and gave me a salacious smile.

I ignored Saleem and remained silent until we reached my aunt's villa. Rawyia was waiting at the front door, along with *Tante* Hameeda and Soraya.

Rawyia welcomed me with a triumphant smile. I threw myself into her arms, sobbing. "Samir got word to us earlier that you would be coming. I can't believe it! We are finally free!" She winked. "Almost free, I might add."

I lifted my white dress and rushed inside, laughing and crying while trying to control the nervous shaking of my hands.

"I cannot believe I am free at last," I repeated.

Rawyia led me to the room where she was staying. I took off my dress and tossed it aside. She handed me one of her sleeveless dresses, in yellow and blue. It did not cover my knees. I loved it.

Mama spoke at length on the phone with *Tante* Hameeda, trying to persuade her to send me home. My aunt refused.

"Samir is safe at home," *Tante* reported, "and you and Rawyia can be assured that I will protect you, even if it means the end of my relationship with your mother."

I hugged my aunt hard. "At last someone is on our side."

"You must understand that you've created a very serious situation," *Tante* said. "We don't know what your father or your older brother will do."

I began to pace.

"Your father swore that if your mother ever comes to this house, she will no longer be his wife."

"Don't worry, *Tante*," Rawyia said, "we'll meet with our mother outside of your villa. Papa can't stop us from seeing her somewhere else."

Tante Hameeda asked me if I was sure of what I wanted.

"Yes! I don't want to be Farook's wife."

"What is your reason?" *Tante* Hameeda asked.

I knew from Mama that my aunt believed in love before marriage, and that knowledge gave me the courage to speak.

"I want to be the one to choose the man I will marry, and I have already made my choice. I'm in love with a young Lebanese man. His name is Ghassan."

"Is Ghassan willing to marry you?"

"Of course," I assured her. "He wants to meet with my father."

"Can you arrange for Ghassan to come over here?"

"When?" I asked joyfully.

"Anytime," my aunt replied.

My heart felt as though it might burst. I embraced my new world and savored the taste of freedom without worries, forgetting the reality of my status as a married woman and a runaway. But I feared the reaction of Farook, my father, and Reda. At my aunt's, I would be safe, but I was not sure for how long. All I was sure of was my love for Ghassan. He was my future, my happiness, and my anchor. I vowed to allow no one to take him away from me.

PART IV: SAFE SHELTER

CHAPTER 27

Rawyia and I were finally together again at *Tante* Hameeda's house. We had been apart for only two weeks, but it had seemed a lifetime. The thrill of being young and unencumbered by the demands of our father and our husbands finally hit me, and I wanted to savor it. Rawyia, however, continued to be her realistic self.

"La, remember, we have accomplished nothing yet," she cautioned.

I couldn't bear to listen to Rawyia's naysaying and instead focused on exploring my new home. Our aunt had given us one of the guest rooms in her villa. The bed had ample room for Rawyia and me. The pink lace coverlet embroidered like a carpet of flowers dared my hands to touch it. I bent down and kissed it softly.

A dresser and a round mirror stood to the right of the bed, next to a love seat upholstered with a needlepoint canvas of pink flowers scattered on a beige background. Two small Bokhara Persian rugs covered the parquet floor, one on each side of our bed, and a gilded off-white armoire with two compartments faced the bed. A door to the garden overlooked a stairway covered with white jasmine that infused our room with its relaxing fragrance. I opened the sheer drapes and faced the manicured garden. Inhaling deeply, I opened my arms and took in the sweet air of freedom.

"Are we really free, Rawyia, or am I dreaming?"

"La, sit down and listen to me." Rawyia motioned to a spot next to her on the love seat. "It's not over. Remember, you and I are both in deep trouble. Farook might refuse to divorce you."

Rawyia's statement struck me in the heart like a dagger, cutting into my moment of happiness and bringing me back to the ugly reality that I had been so focused on my escape, I hadn't thought about what might happen next.

"But if Farook is an honorable man and has enough self-respect, he will divorce you," Rawyia continued, though she sounded doubtful. She and I knew that Farook didn't make any decision before consulting Papa.

"Could Farook be that stupid to listen to our father after my escape?" I asked.

"We'll have to wait. See what happens in the next few days." Rawyia seemed to be talking to herself.

A deep dread about Papa's reaction filled me. I had never thought of what my actions would do to our family's reputation. What I had done was serious enough to push my father or brother to kill me.

"Maybe I should go back." I shook with fear and doubt.

"No! Don't fall apart if you want me to help you. Don't show me this weak side again." She pointed her finger to my face. "I will ship you back and let Papa, Reda, and Ahmed shred you to pieces!"

"Okay." I paused and took a couple of breaths. Without Rawyia's support and empowerment, I would have caved to my father's threats. "So tell me, Rawyia," I finally said, "what have you been doing with your freedom?"

Rawyia smiled and made me promise not to interrupt her with "oohs" and "aahs." She lay down on the bed with her arms wide open. "I'm in love, La."

I couldn't believe what I heard. Love for Rawyia came in bursts like her temper.

"Is it the man you told me about before? Marwan?" I asked, curious to know if she had fallen for someone else. "Where did you meet him?"

"I met him downtown, at Santa Lucia. I went there with Soraya and Shewekar," she said calmly.

Santa Lucia impressed me. I had heard of the restaurant from my parents. Only the elite of Alexandria frequented the place. Many famous guests—like King Farouk, Egypt's last monarch; the late President Nasser; and a number of actors and singers—dined there.

"Rawyia, would you take me there?"

"Sure, La. From now on, you will be with me everywhere I go."

I listened to Rawyia with pleasurable anticipation, and my appetite for the life my sister had been living grew, yet I could not let go of my fear.

Rawyia read the worries on my face. "Don't look so scared. Everything will be fine. You're safe here. Papa doesn't like *Tante* Hameeda, and he doesn't visit. Besides, you have to understand that whatever men have, we have it, too—except, of course, for this." She pointed to her private parts. "Learn to trust yourself, La."

I nodded, even though I was skeptical.

"You and I have a brain—just like men—but we are smarter." Rawyia pointed to her triceps. "Men just have more muscles. Farook will not hand you a divorce without a fight. Just stay strong and hold on to what you have gained." She patted me on the shoulder. "Promise me you won't give up."

I put on a smile and pretended to go along with Rawyia,

although I still feared our father's reaction.

"I promise, Rawyia."

Rawyia informed me about the plan she had been devising since she'd left our parents' home. She and Marwan would marry and then move to Lebanon.

In fact, Rawyia would be traveling soon, and she and Marwan would arrange for me to join them in Beirut. She told me Marwan had money, and he loved her very much and would maintain my sister's lifestyle. Rawyia stressed Marwan's good looks but downplayed his old age. "Marwan is mature," she muttered.

Concerned, I asked, "Marwan doesn't look like Papa, does he?"

"No, no, not at all. Marwan looks much younger, and he is much nicer. You will like him."

Rawyia was about to tell me more, when we heard a commotion coming from outside our room.

She opened the door a crack and listened. "La," she whispered, "it's *mon chapeau*. Papa must have sent him over."

Mon chapeau. My hat. That's what Rawyia and I called Reda in his presence. Reda hadn't learned French, though he had long ago caught on to our calling him *mon frère*, my brother.

I joined Rawyia at the door and shivered with fear when I heard Reda asking *Tante* Hameeda to let him into our room. Rawyia and I pushed the door shut again, and I cried as Reda shouted at *Tante* Hameeda.

"If Reda is coming here to flex his muscles, maybe he should flex them on Ahmed," Rawyia blustered, as she paced. "Why are we hiding? I'm going out to face him!"

I was not sure what Rawyia meant about Ahmed and did not bother to ask; I was too emotionally immersed in Reda's invasion and threats.

"Oh, no, Rawyia, please don't. You are divorced, but I am not," I pleaded. "Reda might take me back home by force. Doesn't our brother have that right?"

"No, he doesn't," she snapped. "Now you are under Farook's control, and only Farook has power over you."

"You mean Farook can come here and take me?"

"Farook could get a court order and drag you back to his home in shackles. You are legally *nashez*—a disobedient wife. But I won't let that happen."

Rawyia's assurance to stand by me put a hopeful smile back on my face.

When the noise outside subsided, *Tante* Hameeda knocked lightly and entered our room. "Laila, my dear, your situation is serious. I don't know how to handle it." My aunt sounded worried. "Your father gave Reda permission to take your life if you don't go back to your husband's home."

"You mean kill me?"

She nodded.

Sick to my stomach, I tried to scream, but my voice died in my throat.

No one could help me, not even Rawyia. I had to make a decision. Whichever path I chose, my future would be turbulent. Rawyia encouraged me to stick to my plans, but, like Mama, I understood my limitations. Unlike Rawyia, I was not free and had deserted my husband. I was *nashez*, with no legal recourse.

I felt constrained by the contract my father had signed on my behalf. According to the law, that contract gave all men in my family the power to limit my freedom. My anger at God for favoring men, and for having created me as a woman, left me boiling.

How had women accepted, for such a long time, a life under men's superiority? Ancient Egyptian history told us that Egyptian women, unlike Greco-Roman or the Mesopotamian women, were the equals of men under the law. Ancient Egyptian women could own land, manage their own property, and represent themselves in court. They could sit on juries and testify in trials and were also subjected to the same legal penalties as men. They could divorce, even initiate a lawsuit to recover the assets of their household and win their case, and none of that prevented them from remarrying. So how and when had modern Egyptian women lost this freedom? My religion told me that Islam had come to liberate women—why had that idea not been enforced?

The time had come for women to regain their lost autonomy, and I would be the one to start. I felt empowered and decided to keep fighting for my divorce, no matter how big my losses might be. The repercussions could not be worse than losing my freedom.

Tante Hameeda retired to her room. Rawyia's escape, my upended wedding, Reda's threats—these all contributed to my aunt's already fragile health. It frightened me to think I would not be able to rely on her whenever I needed her support.

As I lay down in bed next to Rawyia, I longed for the comforting presence of my mother. "I want to call Mama," I said, ashamed that I couldn't put up a more mature front.

"You can't. Look, La, all hell has broken loose and you are the cause of it." Rawyia dropped the blame like a boulder, crushing my fighting spirit. "Mama can't come here. Do you want to be the reason for Mama's divorce?"

Her comment made me feel worse. "No, but I can meet with her elsewhere."

"We'll talk about it tomorrow. Let's sleep now."

All night, I thought of my father's anger and my brother's threat. I wondered if my actions had caused more harm than I had anticipated.

Should I call Ghassan in Lebanon? No. I wanted him to think of me as brave and able to handle these problems on my own.

Early the next morning, *Tante* Hameeda came to our room and announced that Farook had arrived and was waiting in the salon. "Farook wants to take you home and is refusing to divorce you."

"Didn't you tell him, 'Laila doesn't love you'?" I asked, my voice breaking.

"Farook is not here for love, my dear," she said. "You hurt his pride and honor. No man can live through that without a fight." *Tante* Hameeda's voice echoed sympathy for Farook.

Tears gathered in my eyes. I looked at my aunt, pleading, but she only sighed with frustration and walked out.

I began to entertain the thought of accepting my fate, in the sense in which my mother had meant it, and even felt guilty for what I had done to my family and in particular to my father's reputation. For a while, I paced around the room and then faced Rawyia, who watched me in silence.

"I will . . ." My voice immediately faltered.

"No, you won't, La," Rawyia said firmly. "You must learn to harden your heart, to ignore your feelings, so you can achieve your goals. Don't feel sorry for anyone. Farook knew you didn't want him, but he chose to go ahead with the marriage."

I could not take Rawyia's advice with ease.

A few minutes later, *Tante* Hameeda rejoined us. "On his way out, Farook said he would never divorce you. He intends to limit your freedom and cripple your future with the marriage contract."

I did not know what my aunt meant, but I listened in silence.

"Farook also threatened to 'change the map of your face' so that no man could bear to look at you."

Rawyia explained that Farook's threat meant he would disfigure me with acid. I broke down sobbing. There were reports of men who had done exactly that to their wives, or sisters, who didn't obey them.

At seventeen years old, I didn't feel worldly enough to handle these problems alone. My sheltered life did not equip me to make decisions on my own. I was not fully informed of the legal implications of my action. Why couldn't I have the rebellious spirit of my sister, instead of being the docile and obedient daughter? Now, breaking so many rules, causing so much turmoil, I didn't know how to shoulder the burden.

CHAPTER 28

I woke up the next day feeling disoriented, and closed and opened my eyes several times. No wooden shutters separated me from the outside world, like those in my former bedroom. My eyes feasted on the blue sky through the sheer, lilac-colored drapes. Inhaling the fragrance of the jasmine, I smiled at its delicate branches dancing gently in the stir of the morning breeze.

No Quran recitation echoed in the air. Instead, the sparrows chirped out in chorus. The sun bathed my face in warmth. I stretched and then stepped out onto the balcony for the first time without fear.

My aunt invited me to join her for morning tea. She offered me a plate of lentil-flour biscuits. *Tante* Hameeda had sent us a tin of these biscuits each summer, an exotic treat from Luxor, in Upper Egypt, sent to her by her husband's family. Now she offered them along with a cup of tea with milk. As I savored the flavors of my childhood, I allowed myself to forget my troubles.

Happy spending this quiet time with *Tante* Hameeda, I hoped she would not ruin our morning by bringing up the subject of marriage.

"So, did you sleep well, my dear?"

"Yes." I relaxed about my past and thought about my future. "I have decided to get my high school diploma, and I need your help, *Tante*."

"You have it, dear. Whatever you need, I will provide." *Tante* Hameeda extended her arms and invited me into a warm embrace.

This moment, and many more like it to come, made me feel safe in my aunt's house. No men lived in the villa except for the gardener, the chauffeur, and the cook. The atmosphere felt peaceful. Within the walls of my aunt's house, away from my father, Reda, and Ahmed, I felt satisfied, for the time being.

Tante Hameeda made good on her promise. She hired two teachers for my home studies. Under their tutelage, I realized how much I'd missed while studying on my own in my parents' home.

In addition, I soon developed a close relationship with my cousin. Soraya occupied the upper level of the villa. She had married a gynecologist and had two children, a nine-year-old girl named Manal and a thirteen-year-old boy, Rashwan. Soraya never spoke of her husband's absence. Rawyia told me Soraya's husband traveled abroad, but soon Soraya confided that she and her husband were separated and in the process of divorcing.

As time went by and my relationship with Soraya grew, she invited me to share the upper level with her, and my cousin quickly became like another sister to me.

Mama once told me that when Soraya was born, *Tante* Hameeda could not breastfeed her, so my aunt asked Mama to provide her own breast milk. According to our religion, when a woman breastfeeds a baby that is not hers, the child becomes like her legitimate child. By that, I mean Soraya could not marry any of my brothers.

Rawyia's plans to marry Marwan were coming to fruition. She was busy preparing for her move to Lebanon and no longer had much time to spend on my problems. My closeness to Soraya and my aunt's love consoled me as I thought about losing my sister's constant support and friendship.

The night before Rawyia's departure to Lebanon, we stayed up late. I tried to carve her beautiful face deep into the alleys of my subconscious. Rawyia's mouth moved, but I did not hear what she said or hear her laughter. I was happy for my sister, yet I envied the freedom she had won without much of a struggle. Her exuberance annoyed me—I wanted Rawyia to see how cheerless and desolate I was—but she seemed exclusively involved and in her own new world. I watched her finish packing while I struggled with many mixed emotions that I did not share with her.

As Rawyia and I were finally preparing for bed, Soraya entered the room, holding a golden chain with a tiny lock in one hand and a Kodak camera in the other. She took a tiny Quran from the golden lock. "I want you to keep this as a souvenir. The holy book will keep you safe." Soraya placed the golden chain around Rawyia's neck.

"Thank you, Soraya. I will cherish your precious gift as long as I live."

I wasn't sure if Rawyia meant what she said or if she would wear the lock with the Quran. Rawyia had told me Muslim women would suffer forever because of the limitations the Quran imposed on them. Rawyia even refused to recite the Quran's verses or perform the mandatory prayers.

Soraya turned on her camera. "Come on, girls. Give me a good, sisterly pose."

All the emotions Rawyia and I had managed to control exploded and pulled us like a magnet into a tight embrace. Rawyia planted a kiss on my cheek. The camera captured that moment. Soraya asked me to do the same to Rawyia. I kissed Rawyia, and Soraya's flash went off again. I didn't know if the tears on my lips were Rawyia's or my own.

"Laila, I will always be here for you, and Rawyia's not leaving forever. Your sister will visit." Soraya grabbed my hand, an understanding smile on her face.

"Yes, I will, I promise," Rawyia said. "Once your divorce is final, you will find me in Alexandria in less than twenty-four hours."

I believed her. I had no other recourse but to fight the men who held the key to my freedom and force them to unlock the chains and set me free.

Soraya said good night to us and went off to bed. I stayed up late with Rawyia to spend as much time with her as I could before she left.

Rawyia finished packing and gave her suitcase, which sat open on the bed, a long, thoughtful look. "If you'd like any of my clothes," she said, choking with every word, "please take them."

She dug into her neatly packed clothes, pulled out her favorite red nightgown, and tossed it gently in my face.

"When you miss me, wear it."

She locked her suitcase, set it on the floor, and jumped into bed. Holding tight to Rawyia's red nylon gown, I soon fell asleep in her arms.

At eight, Ahlam, the housemaid, brought in two cups of tea, some milk, four eggs, feta cheese, and four small baguettes. The maid placed the tray on the side table and left. Neither of us had an appetite, but Rawyia handed me a cup of tea and then took hers.

"I'd better get ready," she said, before the cup touched her lips. "My flight is in four hours."

Rawyia looked excited. I was happy for her but envied her as well. When she came out of the shower, she whistled the tune to Abdel Haleem Hafez's song *"Sawah"*. As she bounced into the bedroom, Rawyia took off her towel and danced in front of the mirror. "La, you will soon be as happy as I am."

"I hope," I whispered.

"Don't ever fear men. They cannot force you to do anything you don't want to do. Did you ever believe we would actually be free?"

"*You* are free," I said, my voice breaking. "I'm not free yet."

"You will be. Just believe in yourself," she said. "You own your life. It is yours to do with as your heart desires."

I wanted so much to believe Rawyia. When I heard her talk, I felt enthusiastic and full of hope. But when alone, I felt uncertain, insecure, and fearful of what would happen when my sister was no longer here to remind me of these promises.

The phone rang outside our room.

"That must be Marwan." Rawyia wrapped the towel around her body and ran to the phone. I followed and stood next to her as she picked up the receiver. "*Allo*, darling."

I smiled but felt angry with Marwan for invading our last private moments.

"Yes, I'm ready. I will see you soon. *Shukran, habibi*. Thank you, my love."

Rawyia hung up and skipped back to the bedroom.

I sat quietly on the edge of our bed as she got dressed. She was already in a different world, far from the one we had shared growing up. Although I wouldn't be alone after Rawyia left—Soraya would be my solace—the pain in my heart as I watched her prepare to leave became unbearable. I sobbed quietly.

Rawyia glanced at me and threw a kiss across the space between us—a space that was growing.

The porter rang the doorbell and announced that the taxi had arrived. Rawyia asked the porter to carry her suitcase down, then went back to the bedroom and took a last look at herself. She turned around in front of the mirror and adjusted her brown turtleneck sweater and the waist of her light beige skirt. Rawyia had already painted her lips, but she took a lipstick out of her purse and ran it over them again. I stood in the doorway, admiring her as my heart bled.

"How do I look?" Rawyia asked playfully.

"Beautiful," I whispered, my eyes tearing up again.

Rawyia ran past me toward the front door but then stopped and turned around to hug me. Soraya was there, and Rawyia hugged her, too.

"Don't forget your aunt," Soraya reminded Rawyia.

Rawyia dashed to *Tante* Hameeda's bedroom for a quick hug and then ran back past us and out the door. "Give my love to your kids, Soraya," Rawyia threw over her shoulder.

Soraya and I closed the door behind her.

For two days, I stayed in the bedroom Rawyia and I had shared, wearing her red nylon nightgown, but eventually I came out and joined Soraya upstairs. The time had come to live on my own.

CHAPTER 29

I wanted nothing more than to reunite with Ghassan, but Farook still refused to grant me the divorce that would allow me to travel. Without either a divorce certificate or the signature of my husband or father, I could not leave the country.

In the meantime, I watched my cousin fall in love. Soraya was infatuated with a man named Rashad—so besotted, in fact, that she sacrificed everything for him.

Her husband pursued his medical career in Europe, and Soraya didn't need his financial support because she had a substantial inheritance from her father. She had a feeling her husband would not come back. He had been cheating on Soraya when they were living together, so it did not matter to her that she had not divorced her husband yet.

In our society, women did not go out of their homes alone, so Soraya needed my company. She took me everywhere she went, even when she met with Rashad in the apartment that she had bought him using some of her inheritance.

Whenever Soraya and Rashad disappeared into the bedroom, I sat on the only chair in the living room and stared at the walls, waiting for them to complete their lovemaking.

When I first met Rashad, I found his slender, muscular physique, his piercing hazel eyes, and his imposing voice very impressive. I thought Soraya had found a man worth making her sacrifice for.

Rashad's brother worked for the telephone company, as the story went. He allowed Rashad to eavesdrop on Soraya's telephone conversations. Her distinct feminine voice caught Rashad's attention and curiosity. He spied on Soraya for weeks before he made his first move.

When Rashad found out how wealthy Soraya was, he approached her. He counted on his looks to win Soraya's heart. Her soft and gentle character enhanced her average beauty, and her financial wealth added enough charm to attract any man she wanted. Soraya had found in Rashad all she had ever desired in a man.

It disturbed me to see Soraya waste her fortune on a man who took advantage of her generosity and love, but I couldn't find the courage to tell her. Soraya was older than I, and divorced, with two children. I figured my cousin knew what she wanted.

Still, Soraya's infatuation with Rashad seemed to blind her to what soon came to be unusual behavior. In addition to the apartment, Soraya bought Rashad a car, clothes, anything he asked for. I had never seen such a relationship; it was usually the man who showered the woman with gifts.

"I am willing to do anything to have the protection and security Rashad provides." Soraya reminded me that I would soon need a man, even if I had an education and a job. I disagreed.

Several months after Rawyia's departure, Rashad pressured Soraya to sell the villa where we lived with her mother. Soraya had two half-brothers on her father's side, and Rashad convinced Soraya that those half brothers were conspiring to steal the last piece of her inheritance. Soraya believed Rashad had her best interests at heart.

My cousin explained the idea to her mother, arguing that the money from the sale would be more useful to them than holding on to the spacious house.

"Sell our home?" *Tante* Hameeda let out a shrill cry.

"Listen, Mama," Soraya said, "we don't need all this room. We would be better served by moving into an apartment."

Those were the exact words I had heard Rashad say to Soraya during their most recent rendezvous. That was when I had begun to suspect his motives. Rashad assured Soraya he loved her, and he promised to marry her. Soraya's powerful love for Rashad undermined her judgment. She never doubted his words and accepted his argument. She wouldn't listen to advice or criticism from her mother or me.

Tante Hameeda didn't have the strength to oppose both her daughter and Rashad. So, despite my aunt's protests, Soraya acquiesced to Rashad's wishes and sold the villa.

The preparations for the move weakened *Tante* Hameeda further. The closer we came to the moving date, the more my aunt lamented losing the lovely home where she had lived in harmony with her late husband. She reacted to this stress by becoming more frail and sickly.

Then one day, as I read a book in my bedroom while the servants packed up some of the colorful rugs to be taken to the new apartment, I heard someone scream for help.

I rushed into the next room, right into the chaos. Soraya and the servants were gathered around *Tante* Hameeda, who lay on the floor, her eyes open wide in panic. My aunt's mouth drooped toward one side. She could not speak. With the aid of the servants, we carried my aunt into her bedroom to rest.

Tante Hameeda was getting on in years, and we figured she had just taken a fall. She didn't appear to have broken any bones. But two weeks later, when *Tante* Hameeda had still not recovered, we called in her doctor. The doctor examined my aunt briefly and told us she had suffered a stroke. He prescribed some medicine, but the damage remained. Though *Tante* Hameeda made a partial recovery, she walked with a limp and her speech never returned to normal.

The building we moved into faced the seaside. Our apartment was an elegant residence in many ways, with a view of the Mediterranean. It had a foyer, a salon, a dining room, a kitchen, three bedrooms, and two bathrooms. We had to fit six people into it: *Tante* Hameeda, Soraya, her two kids, the maid, and me.

Soraya's family had a hard time adjusting to the move and living in an apartment, but I had no problem with it. As long as I was free, I could live in a wooden shack. But I soon began to feel as if the time had come for me to move on.

Because of all the lavish presents she had given Rashad, Soraya's cash had dwindled, and she would soon have no means of supporting herself, let alone her two children and her mother.

Soraya often told me we would be together in good times and bad, no matter what. I believed Soraya, but felt uneasy about the extra load I placed on her. She and I were both raised with wealth, and working had never crossed our minds. We both needed someone to take care of us.

"The shadow of a man is better than a roof over the head"— women in Egypt believed that proverb, but I never understood the meaning until I experienced it living with Soraya. While we had a roof over our heads, we lacked security. We had been raised to believe only men provided safety, and that in return we would spend the rest of our lives serving them. That also meant living with their abuse and hoping they wouldn't abandon us to take another wife.

My father, for example, sometimes threatened Mama that he would look for another wife if she continued to question the way he was raising us. One day, I even heard Papa say to my mother, "God has given me the right to marry four women."

"Only under special circumstances, and none applies to our situation!" Mama said, daring to challenge our father's knowledge of Islam.

"I don't need reasons to exercise my rights; however, disobedience is a legitimate reason for divorce."

"It would help you to understand your religion better, if you used the appropriate words. I am not disobedient. I am simply challenging your dogmatic beliefs."

Mama could not take Papa's arrogance, and sometimes she got the last word. Papa wouldn't answer when my mother spoke this way. Instead, he would order her to make him a cup of tea to remind her of her duties.

Even though Papa had threatened divorce many times throughout their marriage, Mama took seriously Papa's oath to divorce her if she ever set foot in *Tante* Hameeda's home. But that didn't stop Mama from staying in touch with me.

Soon after I moved into *Tante* Hameeda's villa, Mama began sending Kareema the maid on secret missions with money for me and various gifts for *Tante* Hameeda. Mama stayed connected from a distance, and we spoke by telephone from time to time. Eventually, her love for me prevailed and she found a way to see me.

Mama had a friend who lived within walking distance of Soraya's and *Tante* Hameeda's new apartment. It was neutral and safe from Papa's scrutiny. When my mother and I finally arranged to meet, we kissed and hugged in a rush to catch up on all the time we'd missed together over the last year. We sat on a love seat, wiped each other's tears, and laughed.

Finally, I had the confidence to ask the question I'd been longing to pose. Over the past year, Ghassan had made several short visits, during which he had assured me of his love and repeated his promise to marry me.

"Mama, what would you think if I called Ghassan to come over from Lebanon to meet Papa and propose that he marry me?"

"You *are* married, my dear—have you forgotten?" Mama asked in disbelief. "That would be not only haram by Islamic law but also illegal."

"I know it's forbidden, Mama, but what if Ghassan explains to Papa that he would marry me right after I get a divorce? This way, you, Papa, and the whole family would not be dishonored in the community."

"If you do that, you will sentence yourself to death. The thought of entertaining such action would be a crime for a married woman. Besides, your father has not recovered yet from Rawyia's shameful divorce."

My parents worried more about their reputation than about my feelings and choices.

"I am dead already, Mama," I snapped. "I would rather die than be Farook's wife."

Mama hesitated, cast her eyes downward for a moment, and then faced me again. "I can broach the subject with your father and tell him you have another man ready to marry you. I will try, my dear, but don't expect a miracle."

I felt comfortable having Mama's support, even though I doubted she would be successful.

The next day at *Tante* Hameeda's residence, around ten in the morning, the phone rang and I answered.

"Good morning, Laila." I heard the sadness in my mother's voice.

"Papa refused, right?"

"Because what you are asking is impossible," Mama said with frustration. "You must understand that."

"Yes, I do. Thank you for trying. I'll take care of my problem without my father's help."

"Listen to me, dear." Mama sounded worried. "Don't complicate the situation. Your father and brother will never forgive you. You must accept your fate."

"Help me choose my fate, Mama."

"May God protect you, my darling. I hope Ghassan is worth the sacrifices we are both making."

The next day, I woke from a restless sleep, feeling as though I faced the world alone. Turning the situation over in my mind, I decided on a desperate tactic. I would meet with my father-in-law, Haytham. Perhaps he could persuade his son to finally give me a divorce.

A taxi took me to Haytham's apartment that morning, at a time when Farook was at work. Worried he might ask my father to join us, I intentionally did not call him in advance. Once inside the building, I took the stairs because I didn't want to risk meeting anyone from the family in the elevator.

Outside their apartment door, I hesitated for a few moments, wondering what might happen, and if this was a good move. Would my father-in-law keep me there and force me to stay? Would Haytham call my father? Would he call Farook?

I waited until the ground under my feet stopped spinning and then rang the doorbell. Drops of perspiration oozed from my forehead like beads. My heart raced when I heard footsteps approaching. My blood jelled in my veins when I saw Haytham standing in front of me, as big as a giant and dressed in a white caftan. My father-in-law massaged his inflated stomach, then rubbed his eyes and looked at me. I stood before him, shaking.

"Thank God you've come to your senses. Come in, my daughter. Now that you are here, I forgive you." Haytham's voice reverberated down the stairway.

"I'm sorry, but I'm not here to stay," I said, before he could go any further.

Haytham clasped my hand and shut the door. Without resistance, I followed him. He sat on the sofa and forced me to sit next to him. I dropped onto the cushion and released my hand from his grip. Haytham closed his eyes and breathed loudly.

My mother-in-law entered the room, smiling, and I stood up to greet her. She joined us on the sofa.

"It's not what we expected." Haytham appeared disappointed. My mother-in-law's smile died on her face.

"I came here as a last resort," I said, my gaze on the floor. "I have nothing against Farook. I believe your son is a decent man and deserves the best, but I am not the one who will make him happy."

I waited a few seconds, hoping to hear an encouraging word, but nothing came from their mouths.

Still afraid to look at my in-laws, I said, "I hope you will help me get a divorce so I can get on with my life."

My father-in-law finally opened his eyes. "I understand your position," he said coldly, "and admire you for your honesty, but I would be lying if I told you that what you have done to my son is acceptable." He paused for few seconds, then said, "I'm disappointed in your aunt, a woman to whom I owe respect and gratitude. Her late husband helped me during my trial, when no one else believed in my innocence, and I won't engage in any confrontation with her. Therefore, I wash my hands of your problem. The only two people who can help you are Farook and your father."

"My dear daughter," my mother-in-law said, "where did my son go wrong? What is it you don't like about him? Farook is kind, polite, and very responsible. My son will give you a good life, filled with love, respect, and affection."

She had spoken with compassion, and I didn't want to hurt her.

"It's not about Farook. I'm sure your son is everything you say. It's me." I took a breath. "I don't love Farook."

The bluntness of my statement silenced them. Without waiting to hear their response, I excused myself and left without shaking their hands.

Once outside, I crossed the street and headed straight toward the sea. There, I felt comfortable and safe. The place seemed deserted, unlike in the summertime, when vacationers packed the shoreline. The raging waves exploded under my feet in solidarity with the anger simmering inside me. I don't know how long I stayed, or how many times I turned my life over in my mind, searching in every direction for a solution. I felt as if I were in chains. My anger turned to outrage as I watched the waves and the seabirds flying freely above them. I hated my father, and I hated the power my religion had given him. While I could not hate my mother, I hated her passivity.

Finally, I returned to the street and took a taxi back home. Soraya and my aunt waited anxiously for me, but I walked past them, straight to my room, and shut the door. Feeling impotent, I started to weep again. Although I wanted to relieve my aunt and my cousin of their financial responsibility for me, I could not. I had nowhere else to turn.

After a short time, Soraya came in and took me in her arms. "Your problems are mine, Laila." She stroked my head. "You can count on me. I will never abandon you to tears of despair."

I felt even more helpless. I couldn't tell Soraya I had thought many times of leaving, that I felt uncomfortable sharing the little money she had left. So I just thanked Soraya for making me feel welcome.

My father and Farook were still in control of my life. These men were my owners, legally, and religiously. Without their consent, I could not live my life the way I chose. If I wanted to be free, I would need to reach out to one of them.

I decided on Farook.

The next morning, I prepared to go see Farook, but on my way out, I heard my aunt talking to my father on the phone.

"Kamel, you must respect your daughter's wish and give her the right to choose a husband. The prophet forbade this kind of marriage." *Tante* Hameeda raised her voice, and it surprised me to hear her speak so coherently. Since the stroke, my aunt had spent most of the time in silence. I sat next to *Tante* Hameeda and glued my ear to the phone.

"Farook will remain her husband," Papa said, "and nothing, not even you, can change that."

The phone went dead.

I started with fear and sudden disappointment. *Tante* Hameeda said nothing. From the expression on my face, she knew I had heard what Papa had said.

"Please don't send me back," I said in a broken voice.

"That man is stubborn," *Tante* Hameeda mumbled, "but I thought the welfare of his children would soften him. I guess not. Don't worry, Laila—I will never force you to do anything you don't want to do."

My aunt's words were comforting, but they didn't help me out of my trap.

CHAPTER 30

Despite all my setbacks, I still had hope that one day I would get out of Egypt and marry Ghassan. He made several trips from Lebanon to Alexandria during this time, and seeing Ghassan gave me the patience to sustain me. Every moment of suffering vanished the minute I saw his face.

Tante Hameeda and Soraya accepted Ghassan as the man I would marry one day. They received him warmly when he came to the apartment to pick me up.

I never knew when Ghassan would come. He didn't want to get my hopes up and then disappoint me if he couldn't make it for some reason. He wanted so much for me to see him as a man who kept his promises—as someone who was different from the men in my family.

One time, when I insisted he tell me before showing up, he said, "I like to see the joy of surprise in your sparkling eyes."

Ahlam, the maid, got into the habit of announcing Ghassan's arrival by knocking on my bedroom door three times, followed by one hard bang. So when I heard the special knock on my door, I knew Ghassan had come.

"Is it Ghassan? Is he really here?" I always cracked the door open and asked her.

"Yes," she would reply with a smile and a wink, just as she did this time.

I shut the door, opened the armoire, sat on the dressing chair, and ran my fingers through my hair. Back at the armoire, I rummaged through my clothes and picked a red knit top, Ghassan's favorite, and tossed it onto my bed. Off came my white cotton blouse and black capri pants. I sat down again before the mirror. I removed the hairpins out of my chignon, and let my hair fall loose across my shoulders and brushed it with a part on the right side, just the way Ghassan liked it. Then I slipped into a black wool skirt and the knit top, rushed into the bathroom, washed my face, and returned to my mirror to make sure no mascara remained on my lashes. Ghassan had told me he liked me without makeup. It seemed to take forever, but it was only a few minutes. As I left my bedroom, I heard him talking with *Tante* Hameeda and Soraya.

My heart greeted his voice before our eyes met. Ghassan stood when I entered the salon, and my hands melted in the warmth of his. We didn't say much and dared not hug each other in *Tante* Hameeda's presence, but our souls merged in a tight embrace.

"You are both excused," *Tante* Hameeda said with a smile.

When we were alone in the elevator, Ghassan pulled me close and warmed my forehead with a kiss that lasted until the elevator stopped.

In his car, we headed for Marsa Matrouh beach, famous for its white sand and turquoise water, a four-hour drive west of Alexandria. We didn't speak much during the drive. He squeezed my hand gently, sending sparks through my body. Ecstasy and longing kept the silence between us alive all the way.

I wore the red bikini Ghassan had brought me from Beirut, and, despite my fear of swimming, he coaxed me into the water with him. I felt safe with him. Ghassan hugged me and kissed me in the water, but when he became aroused, he gently pushed me away.

Eventually, we got out of the water and walked along the white sand, holding hands. We stopped at a small grocery store. Ghassan bought cheese, baguettes, and Coca-Cola, and we ate sitting on a blanket he had brought.

"I can't wait to take you back to Lebanon with me," he said. "I want you to meet my parents."

I knew in my heart Ghassan meant every word. My mother had explained to me once that when a man preserved the virginity of the girl he intended to marry, it was proof of his honorable intentions.

I was betrothed, and a runaway. Would my circumstances diminish Ghassan's respect for me? "Are you sure your parents will accept me?"

"My parents love you already. They know how much I adore you. Besides, we in Lebanon love Egyptians, their dialect and accent. My mother especially loves the olive skin of Egyptian women. Egyptians are famous in Lebanon for their accents. They are different from those of other Arabic speakers."

I knew *Tante* Hameeda and Soraya enjoyed listening to Ghassan speak because of his accent. Ghassan referred to tomatoes as *banadoras*. We in Alexandria called them *tamatem*. In Cairo, people called them *outa*, but we all understood each other's dialect.

"I promise to wait for you, no matter how long it takes you to get your divorce," Ghassan assured me.

Before sunset, Ghassan and I headed back to Alexandria with renewed hope for our future. When the time came to say goodbye, *Tante* Hameeda and Soraya gave us some moments of privacy in the salon. Ghassan took me in his arms and licked the tears off my face.

"Smile for me once more."

I managed a smile for him, but for days after he left, I felt as if I lived in a body without a soul.

Once, Ghassan came to Alexandria for an entire week. The days I spent with him were treasured moments but never long enough.

Ghassan and I always chose Marsa Matrouh beach, not only because it was far from any place where we might run into my father or Reda, but also because of its beauty.

We would sit on the shore, dreaming and entertaining ourselves, while the sound of the gentle waves caressed the sand. We built dreams for our future together there, designing an imaginary little house on that same beach and picturing our children running on the white sand and bathing in the clear waters. On the beach, nothing else mattered.

We ate, breathed, and lived for love, and I never needed to say the word "no" because Ghassan never tried to push me beyond our hugs and kisses. He never showed any sign of frustration about my complicated situation. We both waited and counted the days until Farook would give me my freedom.

I knew I would have to do something soon.

Following *Tante* Hameeda's conversation with Papa, my life had been put on hold for two years. Stripped of all legal recourse, I could neither divorce, nor live like a married woman. Farook and I remained at a stalemate. He would not grant me the divorce I desired, and I would not fulfill my role as his wife.

I came to realize that one of the reasons I didn't like Farook was that he followed Papa's orders. He didn't seem to have a will of his own.

So I continued living with *Tante* Hameeda and Soraya, spending most of the time in my room. Usually I kept the door open, but I still felt like a prisoner. Soraya and Rashad eventually broke up. Soraya kept the household going by selling her jewelry and other valuables piece by piece. This made me feel increasingly guilty because of my dependence on her. More and more, I withdrew from the family, inventing excuses to avoid sharing even a meal.

Every night, while *Tante* Hameeda and the rest of the family slept, I stayed up, searching for a way out of my dilemma, but all doors seemed shut. The phantom of death became a regular visitor in my moments of despondency, and I thought about how I might take my own life. But my fear of God's punishment always prevailed, and that fear kept me going and a glimmer of hope alive in me.

Rawyia called me most every day from Lebanon, just to make sure I didn't give up. She encouraged me to pursue my goal of getting my diploma. I kept wishing she would get hers, too. I still believed education would be Rawyia's best weapon in her struggle to become independent. But no matter how often I told her that, her reply never changed. My sister insisted she didn't need her education, that she was smart and beautiful.

Rawyia and Marwan got married. She said she had everything she needed.

I finally took the exam. A few days later, I sent the maid to find out the results, which were posted on a bulletin board in the school building. Ahlam reported I had passed. I was happy. Some things in my life were working out as planned after all.

Unlike my graduation from junior high at Besonçon, this event had no formal ceremony. That didn't keep Soraya from giving me a present. She sold the last Persian rug in the apartment and took me for a complete makeover at a salon in Roshdy that she had visited frequently before she lost her fortune.

Tears welled in my eyes when Soraya announced the gift, and I tried to refuse it. She refused to take no for an answer. "I want you to remember me."

"I will remember you without this. How could I ever forget you, Soraya?"

"Please accept the gift. I want this as something special between you and me."

I could not refuse. At the salon, the hairdresser and the manicurist pampered me for three hours while I allowed myself to forget my problems. They styled my hair with a new shoulder-length cut and colored it blue black. They painted my fingernails a daring red, the color Papa said was only for whores. My toes got the royal treatment, a pedicure done by a young man named Saiid who had my attention from the first minute I walked in.

Saiid worked on my feet slowly, with tenderness, and before he painted my toenails he lifted my feet to his lips and kissed them, first one and then the other, while looking at me. I would have resisted this brazen act if I had been the "proper" young woman my father wanted me to be, but Saiid was obviously confident I would not object, and I didn't.

When my makeover was complete, I inspected myself in the mirror. I smiled, bouncing my new hairdo, admiring my painted fingers, and whistling at my toes. Soraya waited for me, and I showed my appreciation by giving her a big hug.

We were not far from where my parents lived, and I worried that my brother or father might see me as we left. Despite the joyous occasion, Soraya and I quickly grabbed a taxi and went straight home.

When we arrived, we took the elevator up to our apartment, still laughing and enjoying our outing. As we stepped out onto our floor, a shape materialized at the edge of my vision and came dashing toward us.

"Reda!" I gasped.

Soraya threw up her hands.

Before I could move, Reda was upon me. My brother's face turned black with anger, and his fist was cocked. I felt myself falling backward. I felt an explosive pain in my face, and then, in the next moment, fuzzy nothingness, and the world went dark.

When I regained consciousness, I had no idea where I was, and it took a few moments for my vision to clear. My tongue touched the corner of a chipped tooth.

"Soraya?" I whispered.

Then I saw the familiar faces of my cousin, my aunt, and Ahlam, and I slowly realized I was in my bed, safe—or so I felt for that instant. Then I remembered what had happened, and I realized there could be no such thing as safety as long as I was at the mercy of my older brother. Embarrassed, I pulled the covers over my face.

"I'm sorry for putting you through this," I said.

"Don't you ever be sorry in this house," Soraya said. "You are my sister, and I will protect you."

I reached out, and Soraya leaned toward me so I could hug her. "How did you get rid of him?" I whispered.

"We called the police, but Reda told them you were *nashez* and your husband was looking for you. The police sided with Reda and wanted us to hand you back to your brother, but *Tante* Hameeda bribed the officer with money left over from the sale of the rug. The police took Reda and left."

My body broke out in chills. If Reda had meant to kill me, he could have done so. But he hadn't brought a knife or any other weapon. He'd attacked me with his bare hands and struck me only once.

Reda had meant to hurt me and frighten me, but not to kill me. Even so, I still believed my brother might actually take his anger to its ultimate end. If he did, no court would convict him of murder. Although *Tante* Hameeda and Soraya promised to protect me, I knew their limitations and felt sure that sooner or later, Reda would succeed.

The time had come to make a move, and move as fast as I could. I had to end this marriage by any means necessary.

Our Islamic teachings forbade fortune telling, but almost every Egyptian household had someone—like *Om* Zoubeida in my parents' home—who read the future from a coffee cup or cards.

At *Tante* Hameeda's, Ahlam enjoyed telling our fortune. In sad and desperate moments, I called on her to practice her skill on me. She would give me a cup of Turkish coffee, and, after drinking it, I would turn the cup upside down to let the dregs drain into the saucer. They would create an intricate design for Ahlam to decipher. We both enjoyed the time we spent together in this way. Now, once again, my despair drove me to seek Ahlam's predictions.

Ahlam entered my room, wearing a simple cotton dress, strutting and swaying like a belly dancer. She sat down on the floor and placed a round brass tray in front of her. A matching coffeemaker, called a *kanaka*, sat atop a *sebertaya*, a small alcohol-burning device that kept the coffee warm. Next to that sat a white porcelain cup, slightly larger than an espresso cup, and a saucer.

I lay on my bed, staring at the ceiling, but I sat up when Ahlam began to speak.

"Whoever has taken your mind, may he enjoy it," Ahlam started with a big smile. "Do you want to see if the image of the young man in your cup is also thinking of you?" She raised one eyebrow in a challenging, teasing way.

"Yes, I do. Hand me the cup."

I didn't like coffee, but for the sake of knowing my future, I would drink it. Ahlam's readings never changed: in one, someone loved me and would marry me; in the other, Ahlam saw an open road ahead for me. Her fortune findings always gave me hope, even though I lived in misery and never walked the open road she described.

"Tell me something new," I said to Ahlam now.

Ahlam inspected my cup. "The letter 'G'—I see it clearly. Take a look." She pointed with her pinky inside the cup.

"I don't see it." I never saw what Ahlam discovered in my cup.

"Here, under my finger," Ahlam insisted. "I can even see a

big sea, which you will cross, and there happiness is waiting for you."

"I see it," I lied.

Ahlam told me what I needed to hear to comfort me. Despite my skepticism, I felt hopeful after the reading.

I waited a few days until the swelling and bruises from Reda's attack cleared, during which I charged myself with courage to go straight to my father. That compassionate chord Papa had shown the day so many years earlier when Rawyia and I had our tonsillectomies was what I had to strike.

The next time Kareema came by with gifts for my aunt, I told her of my plan and asked when I might catch my father alone. She suggested that Friday, because Reda and Ahmed were going on a trip with some friends.

So I went over after Papa's return from the mosque where he participated in the weekly *Salat El Gomaa* prayer. If I approached Papa right after the humbling moment spent with his creator, there might be a chance of finding the kindness and mercy I believed existed within him somewhere.

When I arrived at our house in Roshdy, it took me a few minutes to gather the audacity to go inside and take the elevator to the fourth floor. Once I got there, I couldn't lift my hand to press the doorbell and thought of abandoning the idea, but I had no other recourse. Finally, I knocked twice on the door and took two steps back.

Kareema opened the door and greeted me with a big smile. She looked behind her before she grabbed my hand, closed the door softly, and whisked me into the kitchen. An index finger over her lips, she whispered, "Shhh" and asked me to hide behind the closed door until she announced my presence to Mama.

I asked Kareema also to inform Hala, Hady, and Samir. A few minutes later, my siblings came into the kitchen. We hugged, and I took Samir in my arms. I thanked him for helping me.

"I am sorry you have so much trouble," Samir whispered.

"I am sorry for causing you so much trouble with Reda and Papa."

The three said in chorus that Papa had forbidden them to talk to me. We hugged again; then they ran out of the kitchen before Papa could see them with me.

Mama was surprised to find me there. She held me tight while I cried quietly. After a moment, she asked why I had come.

"I want Papa's help to get my divorce," I whispered.

She shook her head, then pulled me hard into her arms. For a moment, I let go of my anxiety and enjoyed the comfort of her embrace. We did not say much, but each felt what the other had needed. I had learned from Mama the body language of love and how to express inner feelings with physical touch.

Mama expressed her support with a long kiss on my forehead. "Okay, I will talk to your father again. You stay here."

While I remained in the kitchen, Kareema came back and did her best to keep me occupied. She cursed Farook for tormenting me. "May God avenge you and punish him hard."

"Tell her to get out of here before I drag her back to where she came from!" Papa shouted, so loudly that the sound carried into the kitchen from his room. "This house is no longer open to either Rawyia or Laila. Your daughters made a choice and disobeyed me. They brought shame to this family. Tell her to stay away for as long as I am alive. She is no longer my daughter."

I heard Mama's voice but couldn't make out her words. She was fighting a losing battle. When Mama returned to the kitchen, her face was drawn and she was near tears. I didn't want her to feel any worse, so I smiled, took her in my arms, and thanked her for trying.

In the kitchen doorway, I gave her a message for my father. "Ask him why he started me in school if he planned to raise me like one of his dogs."

Mama extended her arms, and I collapsed on her chest. I

released a long breath of desolation and blotted my tears with the backs of my hands.

On my way through the apartment to the front door, I saw Papa standing in the hall, motionless. His eyes were cold and full of warning. With apprehension, I challenged his stare with one loaded with rage and hatred, even though I still feared him. I turned around, hastening away before he could destroy the will and confidence I had acquired.

I took the stairs, holding tightly to the rails to keep myself from collapsing. When I reached the last step, I rested for a moment, then walked back home under the evening darkness, which had obscured the night sky, as well as my soul.

Tante Hameeda, the kids, and Ahlam gathered around me, eager to hear what had happened, but I went straight to my room. I buried my head in the pillow. I turned to God even though He had not, so far, shown His love. I prayed for His help until I fell asleep, hoping tomorrow would be better.

CHAPTER 31

The next day, at noon, a violent knocking at the front door echoed through the walls of my room and shook me awake. I jumped out of bed and cracked my door open, then stepped out quietly.

Soraya cautiously opened the long, narrow glass aperture of the front door.

A rough male voice came through the opening. "Baraa Kamel. I am here for Baraa Kamel. Does she live here?"

Soraya signaled me to stay back, but I came up behind her and rested my chin on Soraya's shoulder to get a look at the man through the glass.

Of medium build, with a dark-brown complexion, the man looked younger than my father but older than my brothers. The summer humidity formed lines of condensation in the crevices of his wrinkles. He patted them with a white handkerchief but couldn't stop the sweat from soaking the bandanna wrapped around his forehead. In his hands, he held a thick, battered folder that matched his bandanna in color and filth. Its edges were torn.

We waited while the man swiped his cracked and dirty fingers on his tongue and flipped through the pages. He plucked a remnant of a pencil from the back of his ear, then slowly raised his head and squinted at us, back and forth between Soraya's eyes and mine.

The man spoke with the commanding voice of an interrogator. "Which one of you is Baraa?" Saliva shot out like bullets from between his broken teeth, spraying Soraya's face.

Soraya slammed the glass aperture shut. The man banged on the door again, so loudly the noise disrupted *Tante* Hameeda's noonday prayer. She appeared in the foyer and approached us, Ahlam following behind.

"Why aren't you answering the door?" my aunt asked.

"Who is that man?" Soraya asked her mother.

"Don't worry," said *Tante* Hameeda. "We will hire a lawyer if we need to. Let's first find out what he demands." She opened the glass aperture again.

The man shouted from between lips that hid behind a bushy mustache, "Which one of them is Baraa?"

"Who are you, and what is it you want from Baraa?" *Tante* asked with authority and courage.

The man thumped on the dossier he held in his hand. "I want her personally to sign here and receive this court order. I have no time to waste." He removed a sheet and held it to the opening for my aunt to see. "The court has ordered her to join her husband in *Beit al Taa.*"

I looked at Soraya and whispered, "What is he talking about?"

"The House of Submission, which they call *Beit al Taa—*"

"*They?* Who are 'they'?"

"The government," Soraya said.

Tante Hameeda opened the door.

Soraya lunged forward and slammed it shut. "Mother, tell him the person he's looking for doesn't live here," she whispered.

"I can't lie. Farook must have told him."

Now the man began ringing the doorbell nonstop. *Tante* Hameeda gave me a helpless look and pulled on the door, but I blocked the door with my hand.

"Can't you bribe him, Auntie?" I begged.

"Just sign it, my dear," my aunt said. "I will talk to Farook and his father." *Tante* Hameeda opened the door, and we saw the man fully for the first time.

"Listen to her advice, girl. God abhors divorce, even if it is halal." The man pulled a pen from his pocket, stuck the tip of it between his lips, and wet it. He flipped through a few pages in his folder and stopped at a yellow sheet. The man banged on it with the pen, then pointed to the bottom. "Sign your full name here!"

"Do I have to use your pen?" My face wrinkled in disgust.

"Yes."

Ahlam, who had been standing behind us, stepped forward and snatched the pen from the man. She wiped it on her dress and handed it to me. "Here you go, milady. It's clean now."

I scribbled my name with apprehension and held on to the folder for a few seconds, staring at the document, until I could no longer control my tears. My hands shook as I gave the folder back to the courier. He pulled out a handkerchief from the pocket of his black pants and carefully patted the paper dry. Again he fed the pen with his saliva and jotted something down. Then he tore a yellow copy from the bottom and handed it to me.

"You have three days—and I repeat, three days only—to comply with this order." He dressed his face with a smirk and warned me, "If you don't, the police will drag you in handcuffs to your husband."

I had no response. Shock silenced my voice.

My aunt slowly shut the door and led me to the terrace. She picked a shady spot to sit down, and I joined her. "My dear, this is *Beit al Taa*, and it is a law we unfortunately cannot fight. You know that all social laws in Egypt come from *Sharia*, which is based on the will of God. *Beit al Taa*, or House of Obedience or Submission, is a provision in Islam's law that gives husbands the right to demand obedience from their wives."

"Why would God give men this right?"

Tante Hameeda ignored the tone of contempt in my voice and continued, "If you leave your husband's home without his permission, he has the right to force you to come back."

"What would happen if I left the country?"

"You cannot leave without his written permission. He can claim *nashez*, disobedience, and require you with a court order to come back. Once you return, you stay either at his home or in another living area, House of Obedience, which provides you with essential necessities. Divorce is not allowed unless he decides that is what he wants."

My eyes welled with tears. "Why does God hate women?"

"God has nothing to do with these laws. Let me tell you the story of Jamila, who married Thabit Ibn Qays," she said with a soft expression on her face. "Thabit Ibn Qays was a chieftain during the Prophet Mohamed's time. He had been converted to Islam by the prophet himself and was therefore a close friend and ally of Mohamed. Jamila asked for an audience with the prophet and complained she could not live with her husband. She did not accuse him of lack of faith, nor of moral or marital virtues. Instead, she said she hated him simply for being ugly and expressed her fear that she would fall into infidelity if she spent one more day with her husband. The prophet tried to advise and admonish her, but she insisted. In the end, he called in her husband, who loved her dearly, convinced him to take back the marriage portion settled upon her, and give her a *khul*. A *khul* divorce is one in which the wife gives up her material rights in a marriage in return for her release."

Her story made me feel only more frustrated. "How can that help me? Does that mean I have the right to divorce?"

"No, it is too late now. He already won the court order for *Beit al Taa*. Besides, you have no legitimate reason for divorce. An age difference is not grounds for one."

I listened in silence, trying to digest all the unfair and complex legal information she was throwing in my face.

"A woman who deserts her husband and runs away has no rights in a court of law, because she is considered *nashez*. She is legally forced into the House of Submission as a punishment for disobeying her husband."

I sank into my seat.

Soraya joined us now. "Laila, do you know that even if the judge grants you a divorce, you must wait three months to marry Ghassan?"

Yet another unpleasant legal matter. "Yes, in case the woman is pregnant—Rawyia explained it to me. But I'm still a virgin."

"It doesn't matter, my dear. The law doesn't allow exceptions. The three months are not only for determining who the father is, in case of pregnancy, but also to give a couple enough time to reconcile."

Feeling overwhelmed, I dragged my feet to my room.

Three days passed, and I did not comply with the court order, but no one came to haul me back to my husband. A week passed, and still nothing happened. Farook took his time, perhaps out of respect to *Tante* Hameeda, a distant relative of his.

Meanwhile, Ghassan returned to Alexandria, eager to find a solution for us. Our household had grown more and more nervous. We wondered why Farook had not enforced his threat, and we feared that any minute he would act. Ghassan's arrival restored my hope. He said he would meet my father and try to win his approval.

The day before he planned to make his appeal, we sat in the salon together with *Tante* Hameeda and Soraya, talking about what he might do or say. Ghassan had qualities that my father would respect: gallantry, warmth, and intelligence; he spoke with authority and sincerity, without imposition. But I had my doubts that his eloquence and self-confidence would be enough to change Papa's mind.

"Kamel is a hard man," said *Tante* Hameeda. "His mind is rigid."

I wanted to ensure Ghassan's success, so I nervously rattled off every precaution and warning I could think of. "Never look him in the eye. Papa considers it a challenge and a provocation. When he enters the room, stand up and wait for him to greet you first. Don't elaborate unless he asks you to. He will, but only after exploiting every possible argument to prove you wrong. And finally, don't be discouraged. He will want you to give up."

The next day, at six o'clock in the evening, Ghassan called me. "I am going now. Pray for me."

"I will."

"I love you, Laila."

"I love you, too."

The confidence in his voice calmed my turbulent soul, though I still feared the worst. Ghassan had to do more than convince my father of his qualifications; he also somehow had to convince Papa to persuade Farook to end the marriage.

For three hours, I prayed my hopes would not be dashed one more time. Eventually, I stepped outside the apartment and waited in the hallway. When the elevator door finally opened and Ghassan emerged, the expression on his face squeezed all of the hope out of my heart. He took my hand and led me to the salon, where Soraya and *Tante* Hameeda joined us.

"At first he didn't let me speak and asked me to go away," Ghassan said, "but I was determined to accomplish my mission. I stayed, even though by then I was certain he would not cooperate." He lowered his head. "Your father admired my courage; however, he refused my request. He said his honor had been wounded and that it bled with shame." Ghassan whispered, "I don't know what to do."

"Are you giving up?"

Ghassan hesitated for a moment. Then he turned to *Tante* Hameeda. "When do you expect Rawyia?"

"Rawyia arrives from Beirut tomorrow afternoon," *Tante* Hameeda said. It would be her first visit back to Alexandria, and we couldn't wait for her arrival.

"Good. She might have a solution."

Ghassan had nothing more to say, and after a short time, he excused himself. I followed him to the door. Our hands clasped warmly, we walked in utter silence. He released a deep sigh of frustration and pulled me closer. Heat radiated from his trembling body. I quivered while his arms slowly enveloped me in a long and silent embrace, my lips in a pool of sweat gathering between the silky black hair on his chest. He cupped my face and guided my starving lips to his. My mouth surrendered to the soft bite of his teeth and the taste of his tongue.

"Don't leave yet," I whispered.

Ghassan answered with a shower of kisses all over my face and neck. I rested my head on his chest and wrapped my arms around his waist. He tried to dislodge himself, but our bodies remained connected. I couldn't let go of him.

"I have to go," Ghassan said, pulling me closer. He raised my face to his lips and licked my tears dry. "I am leaving, but you will always be here." He placed my hand over his racing heart, then placed his hand on my heart. "Promise to keep me here forever."

"Forever," I replied, but I still could not let go. Every time he pulled away, I pulled him back. I wanted the world to stop right now. I trusted the present reality, but the mystery of our future frightened me.

Finally, I released Ghassan from my grip, but part of me left with him as he returned to Lebanon. The rest of me was alone.

CHAPTER 32

When Soraya and I went to the airport to pick up Rawyia, I didn't recognize her as she passed through the gate into the arrival area. She wore square sunglasses and a big yellow hat that matched her purse and high-heeled shoes. When she approached, her hips bounced left and right. She looked chic and different. The makeup on her face made her look older than her twenty years, and, as if she were singing a melody, she said, "Hello, Laaa."

I almost screamed when I saw the transformation, but I limited myself to a smile of admiration. "Rawyia, you're beautiful."

"I know, I know! And you will be as glamorous soon."

While we waited in the baggage area, Rawyia opened her purse, pulled out a pack of Kent cigarettes, and lit one with a golden lighter. She offered me one.

Embarrassed, I looked around and gently pushed my sister's hand away. "You know I don't like smoking, Rawyia."

"Good. I'm glad, La. I've been coughing a lot, but I like to smoke."

The smile never left my face as I watched her pick up her

two pieces of green luggage. Rawyia followed me to where Soraya waited in a taxi.

Rawyia did not stop talking during the ride back home. "Don't worry. I'll find a way to end your marriage. I just want to warn you, it won't be easy. Farook can come with the police to exercise his rights at any moment. If my efforts fail, I will have no choice but to buy you a fake passport."

"Rawyia, that's insane!" Soraya said before I could. "I will not allow you to get Laila deeper into trouble with the law."

"Rawyia, you cannot be serious."

"I *am* serious, La!" Before she could continue, the taxi stopped in front of our building.

The driver glared at Rawyia, then turned to me. "Don't listen to her."

"Mind your own business," Soraya said back. As we got out of the car, she threw a ten-pound bill onto the front seat and slammed the door.

When my aunt and Soraya retired that evening, Rawyia joined me in bed, just like when we were little girls. We talked all night.

"La, I'm serious about the passport. Money will buy you one. I learned that from Marwan."

"Is that what he does for a living?"

"No, of course not. But we have the money, and with money you can buy conscience, dignity, morals, integrity, anything— you just name it. Men here in Egypt will do anything for money. They are hypocrites. They recite the Quran and pray five times a day, but their conscience is dead. They don't follow the teachings of Islam."

Rawyia's voice was shrill, and she frowned. I tried but could not summon enough cheer to get her out of her unpleasant mood. She sounded seriously angry and frustrated.

"Let's not talk about this subject now," I said. "You are free now, Rawyia."

"No, La, I have to talk about this problem. Why hide it? Why do we have to accept the blame? Why do we have to be part of the cover-up? How will this crime end if we don't talk about it? La, it's happening to too many girls, and from the men who are closest to them."

She spoke with such bitterness, I thought she had forgotten about the brutal beating she had received from Ahmed. In fact, Rawyia had made me promise to forget what had happened. I wanted her to stop her diatribe and be happy again.

"Rawyia, please, let's focus on our future. Tell me more about Lebanese men. Are they different?"

Rawyia paused for a moment, as if trying to dispose of her anger before she spoke. She forced a smile. "Oh, way different, and they don't mix religion with everything, like Egyptians, and they treat women with respect."

"Oh, Rawyia, I am glad I fell in love with one of them," I sighed.

Rawyia deliberately ignored my statement. "La, let me explain your legal situation. You have become a prisoner in this country. You need the signature of either your father or your husband to get a passport. It's the law, but for women only. So what choice do you have? Either you accept a fake passport, or you stay here and live with Farook."

"I can't do it, Rawyia. I'm in enough trouble already. Can't you find me a safer solution?"

"No, I can't, and I've thought about it, and so has Marwan. Do you have one?"

I paused for a moment, and then something occurred to me that I hadn't thought of before: we might be able to put Haytham's respect for our aunt to good use.

"We could ask Farook's father to come here. He respects *Tante* Hameeda because of what her husband did for him. He wouldn't turn down her request." As soon as I spoke those words, I realized that, once again, I was grasping in desperation for a solution. Certainly, Haytham would stand by his son.

To my surprise, Rawyia agreed. "Good idea. Let's get *Tante* Hameeda's approval before we put in a call."

The next day, we discussed the idea with our aunt. She agreed, but out of fear that Rawyia's aggressive manners would complicate the mission, she proposed to talk to Haytham herself. We agreed.

Tante Hameeda invited my father-in law over for tea, and at four in the afternoon, he arrived and sat in the salon.

Rawyia and I remained in my bedroom. She sat comfortably in front of the mirror, admiring her face, as usual, then opened her purse, pulled out her lipstick and a small container, and refreshed her already-perfect makeup. Not satisfied with her hair, she irrigated it with my hair spray and winked at herself.

"La, you don't know how much you're missing."

"Please keep quiet. I'm not divorced yet. Don't raise my hopes so high again. I've tasted enough disappointment."

"We will rise up above all setbacks together. I'm not leaving without you."

She sounded so confident that, deep in my heart, I believed she would find a solution for me before she left.

"I'll take you to my hairdresser, Joe. But you must not laugh when you see him. He's gay and swings his hips when he walks."

"How exciting! I've never met a gay man before."

"Well, you won't meet one here. In Egypt, gay men keep their sexual preference to themselves because Islam forbids homosexuality."

Despite Rawyia's attempts to take my mind off my troubles, I found myself pacing around our room like a caged animal and letting out frustrated sighs. All these months of waiting had eaten away my hopes and chipped away the very foundation of my trust in myself.

I craved Mama's comforting embrace, encouraging me, giving me the strength to go on.

"Don't worry," Rawyia said, her voice filled with an air of certitude. "I'm here with you. If I have to, I'll move back to Egypt and stay until I make sure you're free." She got up off her seat in front of the mirror and gave me a hug. "I'll talk Marwan into buying me an apartment in Cairo to accommodate both of us. I got him involved, you know, and I made it clear to him that I will never be happy unless you are with me in Lebanon."

I had no other choice but to believe Rawyia, and forced a smile.

Just then, Soraya opened the door and walked into our conversation. "So, Rawyia, what are you planning for Laila?" she asked sarcastically.

Even before Rawyia had left for Lebanon, she and Soraya had found it increasingly difficult to get along. Soraya treated me differently than Rawyia did. I expressed my opinions freely, and Soraya respected them. She encouraged me to trust myself and make decisions about matters that concerned my future. Soraya gave me advice but didn't force it upon me and helped me build some self-confidence.

In contrast, Rawyia was more forceful and made me feel immature, as if without her by my side, I would not be able to manage my life. Rawyia had always occupied the throne of my heart, but I had changed since she'd left.

And now, as Soraya seemed to challenge her over who was more entitled to be my caretaker, Rawyia put her hand around my shoulders—a gesture of ownership, I thought. "I appreciate your help, Soraya, and will forever be indebted to you and Auntie, but La is my sister—and my responsibility."

I remembered my mother's passive personality and how I criticized her for allowing my father to control her. It frightened me to see myself living her life. No one, my sister or my cousin, would ever decide for me what I should or should not do. I was angry with myself for not speaking up, for allowing both Soraya and Rawyia to think I needed their protection.

"If you really care about me, let *me* take charge of my life," I said.

The statement shocked them for a moment, but they continued with their war. Annoyed, I left them arguing and headed straight to the salon, where my aunt and my father-in-law were meeting. I pressed hard on the door handle and pushed the door wide open.

My father-in-law, dressed in a dark blue suit and light gray shirt, struggled to feel comfortable on the fauteuil in his formal attire. He used a white handkerchief to pat dry the sweat bathing his neck and face. *Tante* Hameeda sat on the sofa, facing him. My entrance surprised them, yet they both managed to smile.

I locked my gaze onto Haytham's eyes and cried out with all my might, "I want my divorce! I don't love your son and would rather die than live with him."

The announcement melted the waxy grins off their faces. My heart raced with anticipation.

"Come and join us, my daughter," *Tante* Hameeda said in a calm voice.

I froze, stunned and unable to understand.

My aunt gave me a warm smile and motioned me over. To my surprise, I saw a look of contentedness, almost peacefulness, on my father-in-law's face.

Their calm demeanor dampened my anxiety, and my heart stopped pounding. Still, I remained standing by the door, ready to hear something inviting that reflected the pleasant mood they demonstrated.

"I have good news for you, Laila," *Tante* Hameeda said. "Here, sit next to me."

Though I was wary, the warmth in my aunt's voice calmed me even more as I sat down next to her. Yet I suppressed the bells of hope that wanted to toll inside me, opening the gates to my tears and further pleas to my aunt and my father-in-law to set me free.

My father-in-law approached me. He took another fresh handkerchief out of his pocket and gently wiped my tears.

"Well, I hope divorce will make you happy," he said in a low voice, as if forcing the words to come out of his mouth.

Absolutely stunned, I looked at him hard and then faced my aunt for her confirmation. Before *Tante* Hameeda could say a word, I fainted onto the sofa.

Ahlam held an alcohol-drenched cotton ball to my now-conscious nose. I shoved her hand away and got up to a euphoric commotion in the salon. Soraya, Ahlam, the kids, and even our widowed neighbor, Ostaz Fayez, surrounded me. Everyone looked happy. Haytham sat by himself outside the circle of well-wishers and still had a look of serenity on his face.

One by one, the others shook my hand and congratulated me, crying, "*Alf Mabrook!* A thousand congratulations!"

The maid blew several resounding *zaghroutas*. The ululations sounded like my family's jubilation at the time of my engagement all over again, but this time I shared their happiness—at least until I saw Rawyia.

The look of dismay on her face alarmed me. She stood mute, shaking her head, and her demeanor infused the jubilant ambience in the room with tension.

I opened my arms, inviting her into an embrace, hoping to defuse the agitation written over her face. She grabbed my hand and whisked me off to the bathroom.

Rawyia locked the door, pinned me against the wall, and, with her index finger touching the tip of my nose, said, "It's too early to celebrate. You don't have the paper in your hands."

Offended at her interference, I hated her for stealing this happy moment from me, but I wanted us to remain on good terms before she went back to Lebanon. Plus, I needed her to help me get out of Egypt. I pushed her away, wanting to get back to the savoring taste of happiness, but deep down, I must have believed Rawyia, for my feet did not respond.

"Simply put," Rawyia continued, "your father-in-law is not your husband. Haytham cannot make the divorce decision. We need Farook to confirm the good news. So please, hold off on the festivities until the document is in your hands."

Disheartened, I returned to the salon. My father-in-law stood and headed toward the door.

I caught up with him and asked him to stay a little longer. "I'd like to talk with you," I said in a warm and polite voice.

Haytham followed me to the dining room for privacy. I closed the velvet curtain separating the dining room from the salon, and we stood a few feet inside it. He rested a hand on one of the dining room chairs.

"Does Farook know about—"

"No," my father-in-law interrupted.

"Do I understand that you have not consulted with Farook?"

"That is true."

Rawyia's warnings rushed through my head like thunderbolts threatening to obliterate my hopes and dreams. However, my father-in-law, whom I had previously feared, continued to hold on to an expression of calmness and fatherly demeanor that changed his ordinarily stern expression into one of a gentle, loving human being.

"I will make sure my son understands how much you despise him. Consider your divorce a done deal. I will meet with your father tonight and do my best to put an end to this impossible charade."

I did not believe my father-in-law and refused to be tormented again, so I decided to gamble with my reputation to escape the chains of our culture and expedite my divorce. As he was about to leave, I stopped him again. "I am in love with another man!" I blurted.

Haytham's face grew hard. His lips curled, as if he were struggling to rein in his outrage. He glanced at me with disgust, his eyes narrowing. Then he turned away abruptly and left me standing in the dining room.

Feeling proud of myself for taking control, I went straight to Rawyia.

"Are you out of your mind?" Rawyia asked with a deep look of concern on her face. "Where did you learn that honesty is the answer to problems? How many times do I have to tell you, men don't respect truth and honesty? Where do you think you're living? This is Egypt, the land God dedicated to men." Rawyia paused to take a breath. "You have sealed your future forever with Farook."

I read disbelief and frustration in her eyes. My sister had already given up on me, but I was not ready to give up on myself.

The next day, Rawyia packed her bags and returned to Lebanon. "You've taken the matter into your own hands. You handle it yourself. I'm getting out of it."

Eleven days passed, and Farook did not enforce his court order. Farook's father had said he would talk to my father, but my courage now failed me and I anticipated the worst. The possibility that after all this time I would have no choice but to live with the husband I had not selected horrified me. I worried Farook would not accept his own father's position unless my father agreed, and I regretted my outburst, for fear that Haytham might have changed his mind.

Once more, I had to try with Papa, even though he had already turned me down twice. I decided to call Mama early in the morning, the time when Papa usually performed his dawn prayer, so I could beg her to approach my father again and inform him that Farook's father had agreed to accept a divorce. I hated myself for having to beg for my rights. As Mademoiselle Nabila had told us in school, "Humans and animals were born free, and no one can take freedom away from them unless they allow it."

On the phone, Mama sounded fresh and happy.

"Louli, my dear daughter," she began, with a chuckle in her

voice. When she called me by that nickname, which only she used, I knew Mama had pleasant news.

My breath caught, and I couldn't answer.

"Are you there?"

"Yes, Mama, I'm listening."

"Your father-in-law surprised us with a visit last night. Your father stayed up all night and didn't even eat dinner."

"Just tell me what happened, Mama."

"Well, your father gave his word he wouldn't interfere if you and Farook decide to divorce."

I had been tossed back to Farook, but the game seemed to be coming to an end. My anxiety eased, and a new blood began running in my veins, invigorating me with a promising development. Without a goodbye, I put the receiver back in its cradle and ran to Soraya's room.

"Soraya, wake up! Mama just told me Papa won't interfere if Farook wants to divorce me!"

She jumped out of bed and took me in her arms. "Alhamdlellah!" she cried. "Thank God!"

Later that day, I called Mama back to apologize for hanging up on her. She told me about the agreement Papa had made with Farook's father, in which Papa promised to return the gifts: mahr, the dowry, and the shabka.

"I left the jewelry on the dresser inside their boxes, Mama."

"I know, dear. I found them." Her voice broke a little, but she continued, "Laila, your father put a lot of money into making your furniture and trousseau. Don't leave them behind. You will need them later, when you remarry."

Mama explained to me that, legally and according to our religion, Farook had no right to keep my furniture and trousseau. I assured her I would respect my father's request, although I had no desire to keep anything Papa had chosen for me. She seemed happy and, for once, able to celebrate with me. I savored this moment of progress in my pursuit of freedom.

CHAPTER 33

"Allo, Rawyia, it's me."

"Yes, La, what now? What new mess have you gotten yourself into?" My sister's frustration and lack of patience came through the telephone wires, and the coldness in her voice chilled me. "You know I can't help you anymore. It's hard for me to undo what you've done, especially when I am living miles away. I'm even tempted to tell you that maybe you should just start accepting your fate."

She spoke so quickly and harshly, it threw me off guard, and I couldn't get the good news out of my mouth.

"The only way for you is to go back and live with him," she continued. "Show him hell on Earth. Leave sex out of your marriage to avoid pregnancy. Only then, I'll bet, will he give you a divorce."

My heart raced with joy, and I smiled triumphantly for having accomplished the hardest task of my life without Rawyia's help. Invigorated, I pushed my shoulders back and cocked my head with pride and self-confidence.

"Are you there?" she asked.

"Yes, Rawyia, I'm with you." I chuckled.

"I don't mean to depress you, La."

"Rawyia, Papa has agreed to proceed with the divorce if Farook asks for it."

She breathed audibly into the phone.

"Did you hear what I said?" My calm voice surprised me.

"Yes, La, I heard you." Her voice was still ice-cold.

"Is something wrong?"

"No," she said quickly. "I'm happy for you, but I will be happier yet when you get the divorce papers in your hand. Have you contacted Farook yet?"

"No, that's my next move. I just wanted you to be the first to know."

"Don't celebrate yet! Call me back when Farook is ready to divorce you." She hung up before I had a chance to ask her about Ghassan. She'd always given me a brief report about the occasional phone calls they exchanged.

Ghassan, too, had not called since he'd left. I couldn't wait to share the good news. I refused to believe that he had given up on me and continued to call him despite his lack of response. He was probably busy.

After waiting for Farook's call for twenty-four hours, I decided to take matters into my own hands and phoned him early the next morning. He wasn't home, so I left a message. How could I convince him to release me from this purgatory?

I rehearsed my approach and what I would say, promising myself not to beg for, but to demand, a divorce. By then, I believed strongly that if I didn't fight for my rights, I wouldn't deserve to live a life better than the "fate" my father had imposed on me. I was determined to change my life, the life that my mother, Shewekar, Soraya, and *Tante* Akeela accepted. Fate didn't apply to my situation. I had the power to change it.

Finally, sometime in the afternoon, Farook came to the door and Ahlam ushered him into the salon. Before joining him, I quickly reviewed the strategies and arguments I had devised.

"Thank you for coming," I said, ignoring his extended hand as I sat on the wingback chair facing him. My hands were shaking, so I placed them under my thighs to keep from exposing my jumpiness. I got right to the point. "Have you spoken to your father yet?"

"You mean regarding the divorce?"

"Yes. Are you willing to give me a divorce tonight?"

He shot me an irate look with his black eyes. I bowed my head, hoping to defuse his anger. Silence filled the room, and I heard pain in every breath he took. Finally, he released an agonized sigh, stood up, and moved to the sofa next to me.

"What have I done wrong?" He sounded warm and friendly, but I repelled his desperate approach and gave him a penetrating look.

"You want to marry a girl more than twenty years younger than you," I said.

"Yes," he murmured. "But I'm ready to give you the divorce. When would you like it?" His reply came quickly, as if to dismiss the reality of which he needed no reminder.

"Now!" I said, with too much enthusiasm.

"All right, I agree, but on one condition."

"Name your price." I stood and leveled my eyes with his.

"I want the furniture, your trousseau, and the jewelry I gave you."

"Is that all?" I asked, stressing every syllable of my question and raising my eyebrows in surprise.

"Yes. I'll be back tomorrow with the sheikh and two witnesses." He got and proceeded to leave.

"If I provide the witnesses and the sheikh, will you give me the divorce today?" I didn't want to take the chance that he might change his mind in the meantime.

"I will if that's what you want." Farook shook his head and screwed up his face in disgust. He stared at me with stony eyes.

I had the impression he was waiting for an answer that would soothe his ego. Instead, I flew out of the room to announce the good news.

"*Tante*, he agreed to divorce me, now!" I went looking for Soraya and found her in the bedroom, immersed in her prayers.

She continued with her prostrations, but I noticed her smile through the white veil covering her head. I took a seat on the chaise lounge and waited for her to finish. When she spoke the last word of the salutation, I joined her on the prayer rug and we hugged.

"*Mabrook!*" she said in her musical voice, warming my heart with assurance and confirming the reality.

"I need two witnesses. Where can we find them?"

Soraya removed her veil and slowly folded the prayer rug. She paused for a moment. "It doesn't matter who the witnesses are, as long as they're men."

I followed her out to the terrace, where *Tante* Hameeda sat in her favorite bamboo chair. A cup of Turkish coffee sat on the small table beside her, untouched.

"*Tante*, would you please join me in the salon?"

To my disappointment, she declined to come with me. My aunt supported my choice, but Muslims in general did not like to be a part of divorce.

"I sent Ahlam to get Saed the building porter and Khamees the cook. They will be here soon," she said. "Ahlam will get her brother-in-law, the sheikh, to perform the divorce." She picked up her coffee.

As we waited for the sheikh and the witnesses, I became fretful once again. What if Farook changed his mind? I could hardly bear to imagine it, so I hurried to the salon and looked in from the door. The chair he had occupied was empty. I panicked until I glanced toward the far corner of the room. He was slumped over in one of the two fauteuils facing the balcony. His left foot, crossed over his right knee, was jiggling rapidly.

His gaze seemed fixed on the empty space beyond the walls of the salon.

Farook did not acknowledge my presence, not even with the twitch of an eye. I sat down quietly on the edge of the chair next to the door, with my hands resting on my lap, ready to block his way if he came out of his trance and decided to leave. He sat there, shaking his head, a look of dismay on his face.

Despite his obvious pain, I couldn't stop my imagination from wandering. It took me out of the house on wings of joy, all the way to Lebanon. Everything in the room seemed to share my happiness. The stems of the printed flowers on the sofa swayed gently with the rhythm of my heart, and the crystal hanging from the chandelier chimed with the breeze. I visualized the exciting world of an emancipated divorcee, a world so very close I could almost live it now.

Farook cleared his throat, and I landed in reality. He stood and fiddled with his wedding band.

"Why are you so anxious for this divorce?" His voice startled me.

I took a deep breath. Was he taking a step back? Although I wanted to tell him I couldn't wait to sever all ties with him, that he represented all the men who controlled me, I had to keep him calm and cooperative. Better not to respond.

"You do understand, if I wanted to, I could own you forever, even if you refuse to live with me," he said. "With the marriage contract, I have the law on my side. I could prevent you from marrying any other man as long as I live. I could imprison you in a place of my choice."

A chill traveled through my body as the words rolled off his tongue. The thought of going to my knees, bowing and begging, crossed my mind. At this moment, I was willing to demean myself to obtain my freedom.

He unnerved me by pacing with his hands clasped behind his back. Then he stopped and faced me. "But I will be a gentleman and leave you with a good memory that will forever remind you of me. I do love you, Laila, and divorce will not change my feelings."

His voice sounded soft, and his words confused me. What did he want?

I nodded to acknowledge his confession and to keep him from losing his temper. Hoping to catch sight of the sheikh and the witnesses, I peeked out the door.

"You are anxious, aren't you?" he said with a lifeless smile.

I didn't answer.

"I see you're not wearing your wedding band."

"I took it off a long time ago. Would you like to have it back now?" I started to leave the room.

"No. Stay where you are," he said, sounding like my father.

I sat down again.

"Have you decided which divorce you want?"

"It doesn't matter to me as long as it is a valid divorce." I tried to appear composed, though I didn't understand his question.

He gave me a disgusted look. "Let me explain to you the different options; that way, you won't waste any time before you start enjoying your new label as a divorcee."

Though I knew "divorcee" carried a social stigma, the word didn't scare me.

"You have two choices: a grand divorce or a minor one." He sat down now in the middle of the sofa and spread his arms over the length of the gilded frame, like an eagle hovering over his prey.

I felt ignorant about divorce procedures. I believed women were divorced when their husbands made a simple verbal declaration once, twice, or three times. People kept talking about the papers I would need that would prove my divorced status, but I didn't understand what he meant about there being two types of divorce.

He seemed to be savoring his control of the situation, and as he laid out the differences, I listened to him with hatred.

"Well, my dear wife, the law has given me several choices to use for divorce." He said it with relish.

"Just tell me which one you want." I said, sinking deep into my chair. I just wanted to get the divorce and be free.

"*Baynounah*—the grand, irrevocable divorce—is what happens when I repudiate you by stating I divorce you three times over. This is a final and most serious divorce. But God provided a chance for reconciliation."

I was confused but also curious to know more about the rules and conditions of my religion. "What is the chance?"

"We can hire a man to perform a marriage as a *mohalel*, or surrogate. He would marry you, consummate the marriage, and then divorce you."

My eyes widened in disbelief. "We? Hire a man to marry me? Why?"

"This is the only way I would remarry you legally."

I felt no need to hear another word about this type of divorce, since I planned never to come back, nor to ask him to remarry.

"But if you like your new husband," he continued, "and decide to remain his wife, then you have the right to do so."

"I have a right?" I said, my voice dripping with sarcasm.

"Yes, you can choose to stay with him if you want to."

I was surprised and confused by *sharia* law. It seemed strange that after the woman was married to someone else, she could choose whether to return to her first husband or not.

"Please go on," I said calmly.

"The grand divorce will certainly not be my choice, since I would not take you back if another man slept with you, even if he were your husband. I plan to use the revocable, minor divorce, since I know you will soon realize your mistake and will ask me to take you back, a request I might consider."

He spoke with lordliness, but I kept my patience and composure alive.

"I will go along with whatever choice you prefer," I repeated.

"For the revocable, minor divorce, I declare it either once or twice verbally, and if we desire to remarry, it will be like marrying you all over again, with two male witnesses, including a renewal of the dowry. This is my preference." He visibly forced himself to grin. "I hope my gesture will allow you to see my merciful side."

Smiling, I thanked him for his gallantry and drifted away, thinking about this unfair treatment. I hated this society, this culture, and the *sharia*. I was angry with God again; I blamed him for what the *sharia* imposed on my life.

"Since you are in a hurry, I will declare the divorce orally and there will be no need to wait for witnesses or the sheikh," he said.

I shook with tension and anxiety. To get a passport, I needed the divorce document. A verbal divorce would be useless. However, I remained calm to keep myself from saying anything that might trigger his anger and cause him to change his mind.

"Do you realize that you still have not given me a reason for the divorce?" he asked.

I knew I had to have a valid reason, according to the *sharia*, and that I had to give the sheikh an explanation. Except for our age difference, I had none, and that was irrelevant, since a man could take a wife as young as nine. Even though I wanted to tell Farook he did not follow the teachings of our prophet, who forbade forced marriage, I remained silent.

"You can simply say you don't love me, and I will divorce you instantly."

I didn't know if he was serious or if he was ridiculing me.

"I won't let you suffer any longer," he whispered. "I blame myself."

At long last, Ahlam charged into the salon and announced the arrival of the witnesses and the sheikh. Before I ran out to greet them, I gave Farook a quick look and saw, once again, the pain in his eyes. I suddenly felt sorry for him.

I helped Ahlam bring two side chairs in from the dining room and place them facing each other on opposite ends of the coffee table. When the sheikh entered, I extended my hand to greet him. He ignored it, turned to shake Farook's hand, and patted him on the shoulder.

I understood that some religious men considered touching any part of a woman's body, even a hand, *nagassa*, or unclean, and that they would have to perform extra ablutions before their prayers.

Sheikh Akram, a man in his late fifties, wore a brown caftan and a white turban and carried a white handkerchief in one hand. He addressed Farook kindly, in a soft, low-pitched voice. "Are you the one seeking the divorce?"

"No."

"Where is the woman?"

Farook pointed to me. The sheikh examined me from head to toe, his upper lip contorting with disgust. He gave Farook a sympathetic grin. I wanted to laugh but maintained my serious demeanor as the sheikh took his seat on the sofa. I sat down on the chair at the end.

The sheikh, who had a pen stuck behind one ear, carefully opened a green dossier, placed it on the coffee table, and whispered, "*Bismillah al-Rahman al-Rahim*." Then he wiped his face with both hands. He took his time patiently folding the long, wide sleeves of his caftan, before taking the pen from behind his ear.

I squirmed in my seat and sat on my hands to keep them still. I froze my face to stop a smile from exposing my joy. Soon, so soon, I would be liberated!

Farook held on to the last few minutes that connected us. He waited until the sheikh asked him to join us for the divorce procedure. Reluctantly, he sat down on the chair facing me and locked his eyes on my face. I lowered my head and listened impatiently to the sheikh's speech of reconciliation that preceded the divorce.

"God considers divorce the most undesirable, if lawful, right. Are you both aware of that?" he said, his voice suddenly booming out.

We both nodded.

"What is your reason for divorcing her?" He addressed Farook, assuming again that he was the one asking for divorce.

Farook's gaze met mine for a second. "Maybe you should ask her."

I dropped my gaze to the rug under my feet. "We don't like each other," I mumbled.

"Have you explored every possible means to restore the good feelings you once shared?" The sheikh's voice sounded cold, like that of a clerk in a government office.

We didn't reply. I pulled my fingers out from under me and fidgeted with them.

"How long have you been married?" the sheikh asked me with a blameful look.

"Two years," I said.

"Has the marriage been consummated?"

"No, never!" I said, not waiting for him to finish his question.

He gave Farook a look of pity and then asked him if he wished to divorce.

"Yes," he replied softly.

I expected the same question, but the sheikh ignored me. I wanted to exercise my right and tell him that I, too, wanted a divorce, but I sat motionless and waited for the verdict.

Farook and the sheikh conferred about the type of divorce. Farook told him he preferred the minor type that he had explained to me. I didn't want to anger the sheikh, so I kept my thoughts to myself.

When their conference ended, the sheikh finally addressed me. "I have a question for you, and I need to speak to you privately." He turned to Farook to get his approval. Farook stood and left the room.

"May I call my aunt in?" I asked timidly, forgetting that she didn't want to be involved.

"No." He moved closer and leaned his head toward me to whisper in my ear. His smelly breath hit me before his words did. "My daughter, I have a sensitive question to ask you, and I need an honest answer."

"I know," I said, wiping drops of his saliva off my cheek.

He reached for his notebook and nervously paged through it. I waited for him to find the question, but he didn't. His hands quivered.

"So, what is the question?" I asked, impatient to get on with it.

He ignored me and kept his eyes glued on the pages, turning them over slowly and deliberately.

"Is this about the X menstruation?" I asked.

He glanced at me, perplexed. I thought of what my aunt had told me about the questions that I could expect from him and realized he didn't understand what I meant by "X," the code Rawyia and I used for our menstrual periods. This thought made me want to laugh, but I suppressed it in the face of this serious man.

He slowly scribbled something on his paper and then asked me in a faint voice, "When was your last . . ." He cleared his throat and stopped.

"You mean *el ada el shahreya*?" I shot the slang phrase for "menstrual period" at him, in exactly the way Ahlam pronounced it, intending to shock him.

"Yes, yes." He took his handkerchief and wiped perspiration from his forehead.

"I told you before: we did not consummate the marriage."

He took a deep breath and shook his head. "It's the procedure," he replied in a low voice.

"Why does it matter, if the marriage was not consummated?" My voice rose with irritation. "I am menstruating now," I lied, just to surprise him and put an end to his intrusive examination. "Do you have any more questions?"

"*El Ostaz* Farook is a kind man, willing to give you a good life, and I don't see anything wrong with his physique. What is your reason for rejecting him?"

I didn't answer.

"You are immature," he mumbled, fiddling with his notebook.

"You're right," I shot back. "I still have a few more years to reach Farook's maturity."

He kept his head buried in his papers and ignored my sarcasm.

"Just write down that we have never consummated the marriage, and that should be enough," I said with exasperation.

"Enough for what?" he asked, raising his voice.

"To remarry without waiting three months," I replied.

"The three months are a mandatory period."

He called out to Farook to join us again, and Farook resumed his seat across from me. The sheikh then called on the two witnesses, Khamees and Sayed, who had been waiting in the hallway outside the apartment. They marched quietly into the salon and stood behind Farook like two secret-service agents on guard.

The sheikh asked them to state their names and professions.

"Khamees Abou el Gheit," Khamees said. "Chef." He patted Farook on the shoulder.

"Sayed Ahmed Nabawi, porter of the building."

I searched all eyes in the room for sympathy but got only looks of displeasure. I looked over my shoulder for Soraya, *Tante* Hameeda, or even Ahlam. The lights were off, and it grew dark. The silence was ghostly. I laid my hands in my lap and focused on them until the amazing words floated from the sheikh's mouth like musical notes, sending a thrill like an electrical jolt through my body.

"Please, *Ostaz* Farook, renounce your claim on her." The sheikh pointed at me.

Silence and more silence shrouded the room. The sheikh coughed. I raised my head. For a second, my anxious eyes met Farook's empty stare.

"You are divorced!" the sheikh said, pausing between words.

My heart became a volcano of happiness trying to erupt, and I wanted to fly around the room. I suppressed the impulse and began arranging in my head the life I had been planning for the past two years: first divorce paper, then passport, and lastly Ghassan. I felt as if I were close to touching the stars.

"I wish you all happiness. It is from my heart that you hear it, the heart that loved you and will always love you. I am deliberately divorcing you with a single declaration to leave the door open in case you change your mind. As for your trousseau and furniture, they are yours." Farook spoke quietly, between clenched teeth.

I kept my gaze lowered to the Persian carpet under my feet, counted the tiny flowers, and traced with my eyes the geometric line that surrounded them. I was in a different world and had no desire to listen to him talk about trousseaux and furniture. I was not planning to take them. All I wanted was my divorce document.

I watched Farook with impatience and joy as he signed the document in silence. When the sheikh asked me to do the same, I scribbled "Baraa Kamel," my eyes swimming in tears of happiness.

"You can take everything. I have no use for it," I said in a confident voice.

"They are yours," Farook whispered, "and will remain yours forever."

I shrugged but could not hide the smile reflecting the elation building in my heart.

Unaffected by his last words, I flew out of the room and found Soraya waiting with open arms in my aunt's bedroom.

"Congratulations," she whispered in my ear as we hugged.

Tante Hameeda, however, could not have expressed her uneasiness any better than she did through the look of worry she gave me.

"Is it true, *Tante*?" I asked. "Am I officially divorced?"

"Yes, my dear," she said, bitterness in her voice. "You are now a divorced woman. May you never regret it, and may God always protect you. Always remember that the world you are about to explore is a sea full of hungry sharks ready to devour a minnow like you."

"I won't forget, *Tante*," I said, smiling. "Don't worry about me. I know how to take care of myself."

I felt invigorated and confident and feared nothing and no one. I had changed my fate and was ready to live free of the domination of my father, brother, and Farook. It would be hard for me to sail safely in a world I knew very little about, but I believed that no matter how difficult my life would be, it would not be worse than being tied down to a marriage with a man I had not chosen and who was almost as old as my father.

When my brother called late that evening and vowed to cleanse the family name of my shameful act and restore its honor with my blood, I didn't care. Intoxicated with happiness, I could sing and dance. And when I lay down in my bed that night, I opened my arms to embrace my new world. Many dreams and hopes flashed in the darkness, dazzling me with promises of a new, incredible future. I was a free woman, and no one—not Farook, not my father, not my brother—could change that.

PART V: NEW BEGINNINGS

CHAPTER 34

Divorce did not give me the immediate freedom I expected. Our social laws restricted me from acting like a free woman, and *Tante* Hameeda warned me that my father might try to convince Farook to reclaim me with a court order before the end of the three-month waiting period. All of this made me feel insecure. I needed someone to empower me with positive thoughts, but Rawyia and Ghassan were far away, and I didn't want to burden Soraya and *Tante* Hameeda any more than I already had. Though I knew this divorce meant I could soon join Rawyia in Lebanon, the thought of leaving Mama behind cast a cloud over the joy of winning my divorce. Rawyia's departure had broken Mama's heart, and I didn't want to cause her even more pain. I found myself torn between the future I had been fighting for and her suffering. I wished I could imitate Rawyia, who always put her self-interest above all other considerations. My heart was exhausted from all these conflicting thoughts, and sleep was my antidote for disappointment.

The day after the divorce proceedings, I placed a call to Ghassan but again got no answer. I tried to sound calm when

I called my mother next, but a mixture of exhilaration and apprehension filled me.

"Good morning, dear." Her worried voice tormented me. "Farook called last night."

"Mama, I promise I will come back for you." I ignored her comments. Farook was gone from my life, and I wanted to talk about my future. "I have to go to Lebanon as soon as I get my passport. Ghassan is my future, Mama; please don't make it harder for me."

But the more I talked, the more deeply her weeping carved into my heart.

"As God is my witness, Mama, the minute I settle down away from this country, I will get you out, too. You can come live with me. You would come, wouldn't you?"

"Only God knows, my dear. If he keeps me alive, maybe." Her answer pacified me until she added, "Farook sounded very sad when he called."

"You know why I couldn't stay married to him."

"Yes, dear. I'm just worried that maybe you aren't being fair, and God's punishment will haunt you." I heard her breathe heavily.

"Then pray for me, Mama."

"Louli, my heart, promise me you will come back. Swear on the Quran." She fought to catch her breath.

"I promise that as soon as I settle down in Lebanon, I will send for you and you can live with us, as I said."

She sobbed. I kissed the receiver and slowly hung up before she could hear me break down and cry, too. All the while I had been pursuing my divorce, I had never thought of this moment. My gut tore apart as I thought about not seeing Mama ever again. I could not imagine her not being in my life anymore. *What have I done?* I thought, as I suddenly realized how much I was giving up for my freedom: Mama, my sister Hala, my brothers Hady and Samir. The pain of separation was unbearable, and I was not sure I could handle the suffering alone, or even with Rawyia. I would be severed from the only people I had known all my life, the people I had grown up with and shared childhood memories with. I thought of the world I was about to face, unsure it would be any different. Before I fell apart, I called Rawyia. She would pull me out of this desolation and comfort me.

"*Allo*, Rawyia, it's me, La," I greeted her, with pretend excitement. "I am divorced!"

"Congratulations, La." The coldness in her voice hit my heart like a rock.

"Have you heard from Ghassan lately?" I couldn't hold back on my primary interest.

"Now that you are finally free, the time has come to learn some lessons before you dive into a second marriage. I will see you soon in Alexandria." She hung up.

I froze. Why had Rawyia not answered my question? What had she meant by "learn some lessons"? Had Ghassan stopped loving me? Was she avoiding the subject to spare my feelings? Although I feared the worst, I kept my hopes and optimism alive.

Amid Soraya's financial problems and the high cost of international telephone calls, I could not afford to call Ghassan as often as I wished.

Six long weeks after my phone conversation with Rawyia, she surprised me with a visit. She was bossy and full of energy, as usual. I had not expected her so soon, but I welcomed her with the same enthusiasm I had always shown her. After she greeted our aunt and Soraya, we went to my room and cuddled in an endless embrace while we talked. She filled my heart with hopes about the future, telling me how wonderful it was to be free and living in Lebanon. Her enthusiasm appeased my worries and suspicions and helped me touch the future of my dream.

Finally, however, I couldn't help asking the question in my mind.

"Have you talked to Ghassan?"

She got up, faced the balcony, and took a deep breath. "That's the only thing I miss: the air of Alexandria!"

I knew Rawyia was not supportive of my attachment to Ghassan, but somehow I felt uncomfortable about the way she avoided my questions. My throat became dry when I repeated the question, and she still ignored me. I refused to assume the worst and convinced myself that she was excited and busy with planning my voyage to Lebanon. I'd wait until later to ask her again.

She turned around, opened the armoire, took out my favorite silver knit top, and tossed it playfully in my face. "La, you don't need to bring anything from here. I'll buy you new clothes in Lebanon."

I sat up and fixed my gaze on her, but she looked away. Rawyia picked up her suitcase from the floor and opened it on the bed. She pulled out her clothes, throwing them left, right, and over her shoulders, some onto the floor. Then she handed me a short-sleeved dress in red and blue, with matching underwear.

"You like red, don't you? See, I haven't forgotten. This is the fashion now in Lebanon: miniskirts."

Still avoiding my gaze and ignoring my silence, she turned to her messy pile and unearthed a pair of low-heeled red shoes.

"Here, these go with the dress. Try them on."

I did not move.

Finally, she returned my gaze. "La, how can I make you understand that life is not all romance? You think you love Ghassan, but when you meet other men, you will discover that what you feel now is not the real thing. I want you to get some experience and enjoy your freedom before you imprison yourself again. Listen to me, La: you are still young, not to mention inexperienced. Do you want to have to go through the divorce procedure all over again?"

"But I love Ghassan! Nothing you say will change my feelings for him."

"Well, if you won't listen to my advice, maybe you should stay in Alexandria."

She sounded angry, and I panicked. I couldn't imagine my future without her support. "Okay," I said, on the verge of tears again. "I won't marry him immediately, but don't ask me not to see him."

"Okay, okay. Just try on your dress."

During the rest of her visit, we avoided talking about Ghassan and focused on getting me out of Alexandria.

My brother, meanwhile, had never stopped stalking and threatening me. Many nights, he camped in front of our building for hours. To avoid another encounter like the time he had broken my tooth, Rawyia and I decided we would go to Cairo, on a preliminary exodus before the big trip to Lebanon, once I had obtained my passport.

Finally Rawyia and I were on the same page again, ready to face the challenges of a world I knew nothing about. With my sister by my side, I trusted the future would be much better.

When it came time to say farewell to Soraya and her family, I struggled to find the words. We cried and hugged.

After Soraya released me from her embrace, she handed me the striped leather purse Rawyia had bought me for our trip. "Go in peace, Laila, and remember, I will always be here if you ever need me."

"I love you, Soraya!" I waved goodbye.

Rawyia took her suitcase, and I followed her, holding my purse. I left all my clothes behind. According to Rawyia, they were too conservative and out of fashion. Downstairs, we waited in the lobby, holding hands until the porter flagged a taxi. Before I stepped inside the taxi, I looked up and saw

Soraya standing on the balcony. My heart was pounding, and I felt it rip in two. One part wanted to stay, and the other part pulled me away. I waved goodbye and then got in the backseat with Rawyia.

She took my hand in hers. "Once we reach Cairo, you don't have to fear anything."

I nodded and asked her if we could stop by San Stefano beach.

She ordered the driver to take us there. "Make it quick, though. We don't want to miss the train."

I nodded.

When we arrived, I took off my shoes and walked a few paces down the beach. The sand had not yet absorbed the heat of the afternoon sun, and it felt comfortable to walk on. When I reached the shoreline, my feet kissed the sea goodbye.

I didn't know how long my farewell lasted until I looked back and saw Rawyia leaning on the back fender of the taxi. She had her arms crossed over her chest, a familiar pose of impatience. I waved, but she didn't acknowledge me. Not heeding her frustration, I took a few steps into the deep blue water of the Mediterranean. Bending over, I gently swiped my hand over the surface and pensively watched the waves folding over my feet. I took in all the memories my heart could store for the years ahead of me away from home and turned back to the taxi.

The driver sped to the train station. I pinned my forehead to the window, and stored in my memory everything my eyes could capture. I realized it might be the last time I would see Alexandria and my mother. I cried in silence. I had never imagined it would be this hard to uproot myself. But leaving Alexandria as a free woman was my solace. When I got back to the taxi, I laid my head on Rawyia's shoulder.

"You have me, La. I will never leave you," she whispered.

I was sure Rawyia meant her promise, but her words did not ease my apprehension about the future. It was all still a mystery.

Rawyia spoke in French, but that did not deter the driver from turning his head around and staring at us. Like most drivers in Egypt, he assumed the taxi and its passengers were his.

"So, why is the mademoiselle crying?" he asked.

"We hired you to drive us, not to chat." Rawyia turned to me with annoyance. "Why *are* you crying now? Would you have preferred to live under their control forever? Think of all we can do now. We are free, La. In this country, women have no power. Men don't respect us. We are nothing but a body they use for their pleasure, whether it's for sex or to inflate their ego by giving them children."

"Don't you understand that we won't see Mama again?" I asked, hardly able to control my sobbing.

She removed a handkerchief from her purse and wiped my tears. "Watch the road!" she shouted to the driver in Arabic. Then she whispered to me, "Have I told you about the one year of alimony that divorced women are entitled to? They call it the 'alimony of pleasure.' It's a monthly installment for the good time a woman has given her husband." Rawyia laughed, trying to pull me out of the dejected mood I was in.

"What pleasure, Rawyia?" I asked.

"I know you haven't consummated your marriage, but that's not the point. I just wanted you to understand our place in this society. We are not, and never will be, treated with respect. So stop crying and grow up!"

I wiped my tears and forced a smile.

Rawyia mellowed a bit and wrapped her arms around my shoulders. "I know you miss Mama, and I miss her, too. But I promise you, once we settle down and become financially independent, I'll help her get out so she can come live with us."

The driver enjoyed the drama through the rearview mirror and could not keep his curiosity to himself. He tried to hand me his handkerchief, attempting one more time to get involved. Rawyia didn't acknowledge him.

"Please control yourself. He probably thinks we're runaways," she whispered, once again in French.

I smiled. "But we are."

"No, you are a divorced runaway. I am simply your accomplice."

We giggled. Her playfulness reminded me of all our good times together, and I felt calm by the time we reached the train station.

"Do you need my help to the train? I would gladly abandon my taxi to be at the service of you young girls." The driver smirked.

Rawyia dismissed him with her payment and then pulled my arm, drawing me close. "La, walk straight to the platform and pretend to be confident. Do not look back, left, or right. Don't acknowledge any comments men might make to us. If they smile at you, don't smile back. Understood?"

"Why?"

"Because the way you're behaving is attracting men's attention. They'll think we are loose girls."

"Okay. I'll do what you want."

"Follow me!" She took off into the station, leaving me, the taxi, and the driver behind.

I hurried after her but didn't catch up until she reached the ticket window. She turned and gave me a mischievous smile. The sweet taste of adventure began to sink in.

"Watch the luggage," she said.

I nodded and looked around. There were people everywhere, some standing with aimless gazes, some rushing toward the platform, even though the train hadn't yet arrived. A few chic, well-dressed women, but mostly men, crowded the platform. They looked tired, but their hungry eyes were ready to devour any female passing by. The women we saw were older, and most wore veils or wrapped their hair with a scarf. Rawyia and I, smartly dressed and with no head covering, were the target of looks that hinted at disgust, suspicion, or pity.

"Ignore them," Rawyia said. "Act normally, and wipe that guilty look off your face."

Heading for our platform, I realized I had never seen so many people before. We had always traveled by car, and had never been exposed to such a mélange of different classes. Anxiety had settled inside me. Rawyia's courage and assurance had calmed my fear, but that was not enough to ease the pain of separation still burning in my heart. I had uprooted myself from my family for a future shrouded in mystery. Ghassan had not called me for a while. Rawyia had evaded answering questions about him. My throat dried out, and tears swam in my eyes. Looking forward was as painful as looking back.

Rawyia pulled me out of my melancholic mood. "It's a different world. You'll get used to it," she whispered in my ear. When the train arrived, she took my hand. "I got us seats in first class. It's clean, and let's hope the men who can afford it are decent." But her tone was doubtful.

The train ride to Cairo took two and a half hours. The whole time, Rawyia strained my ears with talk about the good life in Lebanon, but none of her descriptions of our future included the man I longed for. I turned my head to the window and closed my eyes until the conductor came by and checked our tickets.

After he left us, I asked Rawyia where we would be staying. She told me we would live in an apartment that belonged to a friend of Marwan.

"Is he going to stay with us?" I asked.

"Oh, no. He's in Paris. We have the place to ourselves. It's very clean and in a very good neighborhood."

I smiled. The idea of living alone cheered me up, especially since we would be almost two hundred miles away from Alexandria.

Rawyia opened her purse and pulled out a pack of Kent cigarettes.

"Rawyia, please don't smoke. Men are staring."

"If you keep behaving like a thief," she snapped, "you will look like one and people will treat you as such."

"I just don't want passengers in the cabin to misjudge us," I said, and reminded her of what our father had told her when she was only nine years old and chewing gum: that he had seen whores during World War II who were more decent. "I don't want them to think we are whores. Look how they're staring at your thighs. Cover them, please, with your purse."

Instead, Rawyia crossed her legs—something our father had forbidden us to do in his presence.

"Do you think you will go to hell?" I whispered to Rawyia,

"No, La, they will." She nodded slightly toward the two men facing us and laughed.

The two men kept their eyes fastened on her thighs.

Though I had left home, I still had not left behind the warped ideas about morality my parents and my society had taught me. The cultural taboos ran fresh in my blood, and I blamed Rawyia for the lustful way men looked at her.

CHAPTER 35

The sun had already disappeared behind the horizon when we arrived in Cairo. The dry desert heat hit me in the face with a vengeance. The train station looked chaotic, with no apparent rules or regulations. In comparison, Alexandria was an orderly and civilized city.

Men stood under the No Smoking sign and lit cigarettes. People stampeded at the ticket window, hands waving, fighting to get served first. Sweat glued their shirts to their backs, and those wearing suits carried their jackets over their shoulders. Women stood behind the crowd and waited to be served last. Young children begged for money. Rawyia handed two of them some change.

"My good deed, La. It will take care of my sins." She laughed.

Outside the station, we were bombarded with offers for taxi service. Rawyia pointed to the cleanest cab and, with an authority I admired, asked the driver to open the door to the backseat. He complied with a big smile. I snuggled closely next to her. She ordered him to head for Zamalek.

"Where in Zamalek, *ya arusa*?" ("Doll.")

"Drive, and I'll guide you."

Rawyia looked relaxed, and I felt good, too. The web of cars zigzagging without any respect for traffic lights or pedestrians both frightened and entertained me. When traffic slowed down, young boys rushed to the taxi and offered us fresh jasmine necklaces and boxes of Kleenex. Rawyia grabbed two necklaces from a boy and handed him some change.

"May God protect you and send you a groom as generous as you," the child cried.

"I don't need one," Rawyia shouted after him. She placed one of the jasmine necklaces around my neck and the other around hers.

When we reached our destination, the driver got out and handed our suitcase to the *bawab*, the building porter, who had come to meet us at the curb. Rawyia, being her always-generous self, warmed the *bawab*'s hand with a healthy tip and whispered to me, "*Il va nous servir bien maintenant.*" ("He will serve us well from now on.")

The apartment had one bedroom and one bath—less space than our Alexandria apartment—but was comfortable and completely furnished. There were parquet floors throughout, and a balcony looked out onto a residential street lined with eucalyptus trees.

Rawyia opened all windows. "La, here in Cairo, you can sit on the balcony all day long. Papa, Ahmed, and *mon chapeau* are many miles away."

I melted comfortably onto the armchair in the salon and, feeling my freedom, crossed my legs.

Rawyia shut the windows because of the dusty desert wind that plagued Cairo now and then.

"No, please leave them open. I don't want any doors or windows shut again."

"It's late, La. Let's sleep." Her eyes sparkled through the lenses of her glasses.

Exhausted, we got into bed and snuggled together like puzzle pieces. I fell asleep, electrified with excitement. We woke up the next morning with our bodies still comfortably embracing, a silent promise never to let go of each other again.

The *bawab* could not wait to show his appreciation for Rawyia's generosity, and at dawn, he appeared at our door. "I came to check if you needed my services."

We were annoyed, but his kind demeanor saved him from my sister's stinging tongue. She handed him money.

"So, what is your name?" she asked in an authoritative voice.

"Your servant, Abdel Basit."

"Please don't show up here again unless we ask you," she said in a mellower tone. "But since you're here now, you might bring us some food. We need milk, tea, sugar, cheese, and croissants—and make sure the croissants are warm. I want *jambon*, mortadella, *saucisse*, and two French baguettes."

Abdel Basit jerked his head backward at her request for pork products—ham and two kinds of sausages—which Muslims considered haram, not kosher. But he recovered and asked her, with a grin, "Are the *hawanem* Christians?"

"I've given you an order." She raised her voice to a higher pitch. "Just bring it. And don't ever open your mouth unless I give you permission! And now show me the width of your shoulders—you are dismissed." She slammed the door.

I was speechless.

"If I don't do that, he'll forget his place and his limitations."

"But you asked him to bring food that is haram."

"La, everything we could not do at home, we will do now. Get used to it. Besides, Papa bought us ham—have you forgotten?"

"Are we going to drink alcohol, too?" I felt nervous about the sudden changes we were making to the ethics and morals of our heritage, but I had no choice but to follow Rawyia.

"Why not? If you like it, drink it. Almost all Lebanese drink. Why would Marwan and I be any different?"

Rawyia could not wait to get me on the wagon of change that she had been riding, but I wanted nothing to do with drinking beer or liquor. I still valued what I had been taught.

Now that we were settled in our new apartment, I wanted to hear more about Ghassan. All of my efforts to bring up the subject during our train ride had failed. I began to feel seriously nervous and angry around Rawyia, resenting her pompous attitude and determination to patronize me. Although the mystery that shrouded her behavior frightened me, I kept my annoyance under control, hoping she would satisfy my curiosity soon.

When I tried once again to steer the conversation in his direction, she frowned. "La, I want you to go out with different men and give yourself a chance to see if Ghassan is who you really want."

Just then, the *bawab* returned with Rawyia's order, and we proceeded to make a breakfast of the food he had brought. I wouldn't eat the sausages, because Mama had told us that sausages contained ears and noses of pigs, but I had *jambon*, as I thought it had none of those parts. We drank the tea and ate some of the baguettes and a cheese croissant in utter silence. I felt Rawyia's annoyance, so I decided to be patient. After all, I was so close to meeting Ghassan in Lebanon.

"Is Marwan going to join us here in Cairo?" I asked.

"Of course he's coming." She smiled, seemingly relieved at the change of subject.

"Do you love him, Rawyia?" I searched her face for a sign of excitement.

"Love?" She chuckled. "Marwan is our father's age, and impotent, too. He married me for show-and-tell. I make him look normal to his community and family. He gives me this comfortable life."

"You don't have sex with him?"

"He tries almost every night, hoping to satisfy me. He can't.

I told him I was not interested in sex, but he did not believe me. He wants me to get pregnant. I am not sure how long I can take this. But for now, I am happy. La, he's the only man I've ever met who wanted me for myself and not for sex."

Suddenly she fell apart, like the dry petals of a neglected rose. She sobbed uncontrollably. My stomach tightened. For years I had camouflaged my weaknesses with her strength. Seeing her crying like this, I felt naked.

"Rawyia, you're scaring me."

"I need to tell you something, La."

"I'm not ready to listen, and I don't like it when you cry."

"No, you need to hear this." She sobbed again for a moment but then composed herself. "You need to know why I hate men. For years I've kept from you what happened that day."

I felt shaken to the core of my being. I knew which day she referred to, when our cousin Ahmed caught her using her homemade telephone device to talk to the boy, Samy, on the balcony next door.

She looked up toward the ceiling. "Where were you, God? I had faith and trust in you."

A shiver passed through me. Ahmed's name awakened many horrible memories that I had tried to bury deep in my mind, but Rawyia's words revived them. I took her in my arms and stroked her hair until she calmed down. Then we sat on the sofa, facing each other, and she told me the piece of the story I had never known.

"I buried my butchered innocence in Ahmed's room, but I have been bleeding ever since." She paused and took a breath. "Do you remember the yellow dress I had on that day?"

I nodded and recalled the bloodstains on it, which she'd claimed were from the X, her menstrual blood. I saw again the bruises on her body from the beating Ahmed had given her. I remembered her rolling the yellow dress into a ball, wrapping it in the cover that she tore off a magazine, and asking me to hide the bundle in the lower drawer of our armoire.

"Do you remember that I told you I didn't want you to see the world through the dark glasses I wore?"

I remembered. And I remembered her saying she was a fallen girl because she had talked to Samy from a distance, through a paper cup.

"La," she said in a voice thickened by choked-back sobs, "he raped me. Ahmed raped me."

I covered my face with my hands, unsure if I could get through this horrendous confession. My hands shook violently. I could hardly believe her. I didn't want to believe her, but I knew she told the truth. She broke down again, and I scooted closer to envelop her in my arms. I cried and let her cry against me, and suddenly I felt like the older sister, the one looking after her more vulnerable sibling. I ran my fingers through her hair, held her tight, unable to control my sobbing, and waited until we cried it all out.

When we finally stopped crying, Rawyia took my hand and placed it over my heart. "Promise me, La, you will never bring up this subject again."

I choked up but managed to say, "I promise you, Rawyia. I will never talk about that subject again."

I wanted to forget what Rawyia had gone through. Pain squeezed my chest so hard I could hardly breathe. At that moment, I felt no regret about leaving Egypt. Now I understood Rawyia's anger and her cynicism toward men, why her eyes had lost their sparkle since that day. I had thought even then that there was more to the story but hadn't wanted to know the truth, so I had pushed the memory of that day deep inside me and forgotten it had ever happened until she'd brought it back to life.

"Have you told Mama?" I hoped she would tell me she hadn't. Instead, she hit me with another chilling truth that froze my body in disbelief.

"Yes, I told Mama, but she defended Ahmed and asked me to put the lid on my accusation to spare the family a scandalous rumor."

I covered my ears, not wanting to hear that Mama knew and had not protected my sister. I did not want to hate my mother or to leave Egypt carrying in me a treacherous memory about her. Moaning in pain, I rocked back and forth.

"La, don't be disappointed with Mama. It is Papa who should carry your anger. He terrorized our mother. I couldn't tell then if Mama believed me. Just remember, she helped you and me escape to keep us away from any more harm we might have faced at home."

I settled for what Rawyia had told me, to keep Mama's loving memories intact.

After Rawyia's confession, we both pushed ahead, pretending nothing had happened. The pain never healed, but it became invisible again. We continued to move forward in our new life, refusing to allow anyone or anything to keep us prisoners of the past.

CHAPTER 36

Marwan joined us in Cairo, and his old age shocked me. Rawyia had tried to prepare me, but seeing him that first time made his age real. To any teenager, a middle-aged man in his late fifties was old, the same age as our father. Rawyia defended him when we were alone, saying, "Marwan is not my father!"

His gray mustache blended well with his hair color, which gave him a distinguished appearance. He wore a light blue pin-striped suit and a white shirt open at the collar, without a necktie. I accepted him. All I cared about was the security he was providing.

He took us to the famous nightclubs along Pyramid Street, and people assumed we were his daughters. One afternoon, we met our neighbor in the elevator. He winked at Marwan and told him, "Two beautiful daughters will keep you busy."

"I feel sorry for Marwan," I whispered in Rawyia's ear.

"Don't be," she whispered back.

We were inexperienced and hungry for the exciting life we would never have known if we had remained behind the thorny gates of my father's house. Marwan guided us. He spoke with a soft tone, treated us with kindness, and genuine care—things our father failed to provide us. He lavished Rawyia with expensive gifts of jewelry and clothes and arranged for our apartment. In return, Rawyia boosted his ego in social gatherings with undivided attention and an occasional kiss on his lips.

Marwan had a number of acquaintances in town, but he did not come to Cairo for business reasons. He came to be with Rawyia.

Rawyia insisted on staying with me, rather than returning to Beirut with him, and he did not object. We were grateful for the comfortable life he provided us; nevertheless, Rawyia complained privately to me. "Do you see what kind of society we live in? I married a shell of a man to survive and gain respect. Men rule here—and in every other Arab country. Ghassan has been raised in one of those countries. It's the culture. We live in a world that sees women as the evil descendants of the original grand cobra that seduced Adam."

I resented Rawyia's inclusion of Ghassan in her conversation about Egyptian and Arab men. To me, Ghassan was different because of his support as I finished high school. He believed in women's freedom. I refused to join Rawyia in her intense hatred for all Arab men, but I kept my thoughts to myself.

Although I arrived in Cairo filled with excitement about this new adventure, I did not like the city. Huge and crowded, it had an unpleasant smell—unlike Alexandria, which had the fresh scent of the sea. At first, I found the Cairo traffic amusing, but it soon became an annoyance: horns constantly honking, drivers cursing each other, and traffic jams that never seemed to end. The heat and dust were oppressive, and so were the people. Cairo was a big city with big-city attitudes. People rushed around and didn't seem to care about others. Men in the streets always made comments as Rawyia and I passed them. "Where are you going, young beauties? Wouldn't you like the company of a man?" Women shot looks of disapproval at us.

I didn't enjoy going out very much, and I never ventured into the streets by myself. Crowded and difficult to navigate, they were not straight and regular, as in Alexandria, but crooked, jumbled, and complicated by many little alleys. But Rawyia was game for anything. She didn't seem to mind going about the city on her own. I went out only with her, or with her and Marwan.

As time marched on, I grew more and more disgusted by all the hypocrisy in my world, especially in the way people used their religion to justify bad behavior and their rigid ways of thinking. The more I thought about all of this, the more I wanted to get out—to leave Egypt and Egyptians behind.

We went to a restaurant one evening. Rawyia insisted I come along. Marwan took us to a place with gourmet meals and a long wine list. Not long after we were seated, another man joined us, a friend of Marwan, named Safwat. He shook my hand and smiled at me. I smiled back, although I did not find him attractive. Safwat kept trying to get me to talk, but I didn't have anything to say. He complimented my elegance and beauty. I did not feel elegant or beautiful and became suspicious, especially when he took me aside on our way out and asked if he could see me again. The bold request scared me. I didn't want to see anyone but Ghassan.

Another one of those obvious arrangements by Rawyia happened when we went to a dance club. A strange man approached me and asked if I would join him for a dance. While we danced, he said sweet words to me and asked if he could take me out sometime. This happened a number of times at various clubs with several different men. Always my answer was "No, no, no." But the more I resisted them, the more alluring I seemed to become in their eyes.

It became clear Rawyia was deliberately trying to make me forget about Ghassan. This made me angry, and I told her so.

"Look around you," she said. "See how many men are chasing you. Why Ghassan? Leave your past behind you. Start your new life without him."

"He loves me, but you want me to forget him and marry one of those drooling old men we keep meeting here?"

"Men are all after sex. Love is not in their genes. God did not mold them any differently in Lebanon." Then she tried another argument. "La, you need to be aware of the Arab mentality. It will never be acceptable to any family, whether here or in Lebanon, to wed their son to a runaway girl. You will never earn any respect in this society, no matter what you achieve. The sooner you accept that, the easier it will be to realize your dreams."

It didn't matter to her that Ghassan had assured me that his parents already loved me. Every time we talked about him, she got passionately angry. I didn't understand why, and I didn't believe what she tried to tell me about him. When she saw desperation written all over my face, she sighed with frustration. "What if he died? What would you do then?"

The ground under my feet caved in. I lost my balance and collapsed on the sofa.

"Just a question. Don't fall apart." She hugged me.

"Please, Rawyia, don't ever ask such questions again."

She nodded, then shook her head. "I just want you to believe that you can have a good, successful future without Ghassan or any other man."

Ghassan would not have just abandoned me for any reason. He was decent and kind, and he loved me. In spite of all the warnings I got from Rawyia, I believed he was waiting for me. The dream of a happy life with Ghassan never ceased to exist in my heart and my mind. It remained vivid and beautiful, and I refused to abandon it.

The most important step I had to take, now that we were safe in Cairo after my divorce was to apply for my passport. Rawyia, of course, already had hers and knew how to do the application. She helped me fill out the forms, and when we finished, I asked her if I shouldn't come along with her to file them.

"No, you don't have to come," she said. "I know my way around. It's so crowded, and I know you don't like being in crowds. You can stay here and wait for me."

The passport office was in an old building compound that housed hundreds of offices. Large numbers of people lined up to get their passport applications, and many returned the next day because they hadn't gotten served the first time. Rawyia warned me that processing the application would take some time, and we would just have to wait. When she came home, she told me she waited in line for hours but had not been served before closing time.

I trusted her to handle this chore for me and was grateful to her for taking the trouble. She eagerly visited the passport office to check if it had been issued but each day came back complaining.

"I had to wait in line for hours again," she reported. "And then the guy at the desk told me, 'It's not ready. Come back in two weeks.'"

The next time, the clerk told her they needed another form. She had to go to another office to get the form, fill it out, and return to the first office and wait in line yet again to present the new document. Her tales of the bureaucratic runaround repeated themselves in a variety of ways. A particular document needed to be stamped. Rawyia went to a different building for the stamp, only to learn it wasn't the right stamp and she had to go back and get another.

Time after time, she couldn't get my passport. The official who handled my application wasn't in that day, or the papers were hung up in this or that office. The matter dragged on for such a long time that Rawyia had nothing left to say, and I stopped asking. Egyptians were accustomed to bureaucratic delays and complications in their lives, and there was nothing to be done about it except to wait and hope the problem would be resolved the next time Rawyia went back and stood in line.

In the meantime, I tried to reach Ghassan. From the first day after our arrival in Cairo, I sat down on the corner sofa in the entry and picked up the phone. A woman operator answered, and I gave her Ghassan's number in Lebanon.

"Please call this number for me," I said.

"Okay, I'll call you back when I make the connection," she said.

I sat beside the phone and waited. A half-hour later it rang, and the operator said, "I have reached the number, but there is no answer." In the background, there was a repeated buzzing sound. "You see, it keeps ringing but nobody is answering."

I thanked her. That evening, I tried again, with the same result. I tried a few days later and again had no success. I called Soraya back in Alexandria and asked her if Ghassan had tried to call me there. She said he had not.

"Please," I said, "if he calls you, tell him I am in Cairo and give him our number here." Soraya assured me she would.

At least once a week, I attempted to call, but each time I got no reply. Sometimes the operator didn't even call me back. I became more and more frustrated, but I kept on trying. Many times I refused to leave the apartment when Rawyia wanted me to go somewhere with her. I had to stay and wait for my call to go through. As time went by, I called less frequently, about twice a month. I decided there might be something wrong with his telephone and that I'd wait until I got to Lebanon to find out.

Meanwhile, Rawyia was in no hurry to leave for Lebanon, and she gave me little encouragement in my attempts to phone him. She seemed determined to force me to forget Ghassan. But the more she tried, the more unwavering my resolve became. Ghassan loved me. I was sure of that. There was some valid reason why he and I were not able to reach each other. This blind certainty enabled me to keep my hopes and dreams alive through two very long, trying years in Cairo.

During that time, I tried diligently to register at one of the universities in Cairo but failed for lack of ID, which Mama couldn't provide, even though we were two hundred kilometers from Alexandria. I still felt the need to hide and be cautious, so we limited our activities outside our apartment during the daytime.

CHAPTER 37

Two months after my nineteenth birthday, I woke up to the bells announcing Mass at St. Joseph's Catholic Church down the street. The strong smell of a Cleopatra cigarette filled the space around me. Rawyia sat cross-legged at the foot of the bed in her red-and-white mini-dress, holding a cigarette and releasing a stream of smoke through her nose.

I sat up and rubbed my eyes. "What's wrong? Why are you up so early?"

She took a deep puff from her cigarette. I couldn't read anything in her eyes, hidden behind the glare of her glasses. Her silence made my heart beat faster.

"Rawyia, please say something."

My sister took a deep breath and extinguished her cigarette in the silver ashtray she held in her other hand. She stood up, left the room, and returned a moment later, carrying her purse. She sat down again, pulled out a small green book, and reached across the space between us, handing it to me. A bright gold eagle decorated the cover.

"Your passport, La."

Surprise paralyzed my tongue. I held the passport close to my heart and got out of bed. Rawyia stood and hugged me while I kept the book in one hand, close between our hearts.

"Why are you crying?" she asked.

"These are tears of joy. You've given me the wings that will take me to Ghassan."

"Give it to me. I'll keep it with mine in my purse."

I pulled back from her and sat down on the edge of our bed. "No, Rawyia, I'll keep it with me for now. I want to read it."

"Our flight is next Thursday."

I opened the book and read the first page. My eyes stopped on the date of issuance, and I stared at it for a moment as it registered in my head. The passport had been issued a year earlier.

"I am sorry, La."

I stood, lost in thoughts, helpless and confused. Rawyia and I looked at each other in silence, two pairs of wide, unblinking eyes locked in an indefinite stare. As I inhaled deeply, my lungs filled with disappointment. My gaze lowered onto the passport still in my hands, and I saw Ghassan's smiling face hovering over the open page. My heart fluttered with joyful anticipation.

Rawyia's eyes begged me for forgiveness. I had no choice but to shrug off the pain before it left a scar in my relationship with Rawyia. My sister must have had a good reason for hiding the passport so long. She was the only person from my family whom I trusted. Still, I could not ignore the ominous feeling developing inside me. I sensed her action had to do with Ghassan's unresponsive behavior.

Instead of a convincing excuse, she murmured sympathetically, "Please forgive me."

"Rawyia, why did you?" I asked with trepidation.

"Don't ask me now. When we get to Lebanon, you will know why."

I froze. My heart beat violently, but I refused to anticipate the worst. "I want to know now why you don't want me to be with Ghassan."

She looked me in the eyes and shook her head. Then she turned away. "La, in spite of all we went through, you still live in your own world, fantasizing about a man to make you happy. Men don't know what love means. Ghassan is no exception."

"I know he loves me," I said, stressing every word with a high pitch. It had been more than two years since I had seen him or even heard his voice. Five years since I'd first met him on San Stefano beach, and my love for him had kept me going all that time. I refused to give up on him now, or to allow anyone to talk me into forgetting him. I paced in the room, frustrated and annoyed at her patronizing words.

"What do you think he wants from you?" Her frustration exploded. "Sex, and nothing but sex! Not love, not romance."

My throat thickened. "What do you mean?"

Rawyia retreated to the kitchen. I followed her and stood at the door, waiting for her to say something. She filled the kettle with water and fretfully searched for matches.

"Look in front of you. They're on the stove," I said.

She lit the stove and remained standing with her back to me.

"La, your heavy breathing is not helping me tell you any-thing." Her voice quavered slightly, trained to hide something. My stomach tightened. She was keeping something important from me.

"Did you see him in Lebanon?" I asked.

"Yes." She gazed at the water in the kettle.

I was not surprised by her response. By this time, I'd been expecting to hear something unpleasant.

It had to have been at least two years earlier, because she hadn't been back to Lebanon since she'd brought me to Cairo. A moment or two passed, during which we read each other's minds. I assumed the worst, and she knew I was open now to listen to her.

She took my hand and guided me to the sofa. I sat facing her, but her gaze wandered away and only our breathing broke the deafening silence in the room.

"Let me tell you what happened," she whispered. "Sometimes when something goes wrong in our lives, it devastates us, but we should not let it destroy us. Life experiences will help you grow stronger. Take me, for example. If I hadn't been abused, I would never have had enough courage to win my independence, nor been confidant enough to advise you. Tell me, La, can you think of anything worse than being raped?"

A foreboding feeling welled inside me, ready to erupt into a long and agonizing cry, but I remained silent. I refused to allow what I heard from Rawyia to extinguish the flame of hope still flickering in my heart.

She stood and touched her head, chest, and legs. "I survived in one piece. What happened didn't stop me from living happily. Are you willing to destroy what you have achieved so far for a man?"

Tears welled in my eyes. Rawyia tenderly cupped my face in her hands and then pulled me into her arms. She took a deep breath.

"Ghassan has married another girl."

The walls closed in on me, and I stopped breathing. Rawyia's words seemed to be coming from a different universe, and her face became its big, round mouth.

I parted my lips to say something but then shut them tightly and took a long and agonizing breath. There was nothing to say. I moaned like a wounded animal.

She held me tight and patted me on the back. "I'm sorry, La. Please, forgive me."

"No, Rawyia," I said after another moment. "I'm sorry for not listening to you, and I promise I will never fall in love again. Ghassan is out of my life."

I lied to show her how strong and mature I had become,

so she would not worry about me. But in reality, my dreams and hopes had crumbled like dead autumn leaves, leaving me destitute in the winds of uncertainty. Ghassan had been the safe shore of my journey for . . . how many years? Without him, I felt naked and aimless. I wanted to run as far away as my feet would take me. I wanted out of the entire Arab world. I could not accept what had happened, and I could not pretend, as my sister did, that it didn't affect me.

My eyes would not close that last night. The myriad conflicting emotions within me repelled any sleep. In the morning, before the sun traced the horizon, we were up, happy and anxious to leave—and a bit fearful as well, in my case. My passport had been issued with no questions asked. I had turned twenty, and the passport gave me the right to leave the country on my own—no need for the approval of parents or a husband.

We sat on the sofa in the salon, side by side, each contemplating our own thoughts, until daylight crept in through the shutters. Then Rawyia pulled a pack of cigarettes from her purse and very slowly placed one between lips that she had painted a fiery red.

I broke the silence. "Why don't we call Mama and let her know we are leaving?"

Rawyia took a deep puff from her cigarette and released the smoke from her nose. "It's better to call her from Lebanon. They're looking for us. Have you forgotten?"

I had not forgotten our brother's pledge to track me down and make me atone for the family's dishonor. But a long time had now passed, and we had never seen a hint of him in Cairo. The threat seemed remote.

After walking into the bedroom, I turned the radio on and sat at the edge of the bed. The room appeared lifeless, with the rug rolled up, the windows shut, and the curtains drawn. Closing my eyes, I lowered my back down onto the mattress. Samir Sabri, the radio host, announced the next song on his weekly *Special Requests* program.

"This song is for Alia, Shereen, Alice, Monique, Mimi . . ." He read a long list of names and then said, "Here, for all of you leaving Alexandria, '*Adieu Mon Pays*,' from Enrico Macias."

The music began, and Macias sang in a warm and melancholic voice.

With those soft strains running through my head, I thought of Mama, Ghassan, and Alexandria. I sobbed, realizing again I might never see my mother.

Rawyia returned to the room and ran her fingers gently through my hair. "If you want to call Mama, go ahead, but don't tell her we are leaving. She will be hurt."

She took me in her arms. We listened to the rest of the song and cried together.

When the singing ended, we went out to the entry to use the telephone. We had spoken with Mama four or five times from Cairo. Our conversations were always brief; we mainly wanted to say hello and assure her we were all right. She did not ask us about our life, and we did not volunteer information. We didn't have to ask her not to tell Papa or Reda where we were. We knew she wouldn't.

Rawyia dialed the number and handed me the receiver.

"*Allo*, Mama, how are you?"

On the other end, Mama was eerily silent.

"Mama, remember my promise. I will come back for you," I said.

She wept, and her voice broke when she replied, "*Insha'Allah*— if God is willing. My prayers will always hover over your heads to keep you safe. Take care of yourselves."

She seemed to sense we were leaving Egypt. I suppressed my weeping, but I couldn't speak.

Rawyia took the receiver. "Mama, we will be fine. I will take care of her," she said, pretending to be excited and in control. *Allo... Allo... Allo...*" she said after a short silence. "Mama hung up," she mumbled. "Papa must have been next to her." She shrugged and took me in her arms again. "Don't worry, La, we'll be fine."

At the airport, Rawyia constantly glanced behind us. She asked me to walk fast and not look back. I was nervous yet excited. The roar of airplane engines, the voice from the loudspeakers announcing flights and passengers' names, and the sights and sounds of people on their way to distant places overshadowed my anguish. I smiled and began to relax.

Rawyia grabbed my hand. "Don't rejoice yet, and keep walking quickly," she urged me.

"Why are you looking behind you, Rawyia?" I asked, speeding up but not understanding what she was warning me about.

"I want to make sure no one has followed us."

"Who would follow us?" I shouted as we moved quickly.

"*Mon chapeau*—who else?"

"How would our brother know where we are?"

"I'm not sure, but I'm worried, and until we're sitting inside the airplane and the doors are shut, I won't feel safe."

I looked around, and my heartbeat raced to keep up with my footsteps until we reached the Middle East Airlines counter.

Rawyia opened her purse in a hurry and retrieved two passports and two tickets. She handed them to a young man dressed in a white-and-blue uniform with a gold airline pin shining on his collar. Abruptly, she turned around and scanned all of the faces behind us before filling in the luggage stickers.

"Is something wrong, miss—I mean, madame?" The young man startled her.

I stood behind Rawyia, trembling, and we answered in one breath, "No."

He opened the passports and took a few seconds looking through them.

"They're not fake!" Rawyia blurted out.

I pinched her hand to calm her down.

She pulled away and addressed the young man with a firm

voice, "Are you finished with your inspection?"

He handed her the passports with a mischievous look, took our luggage, and circled the handles with the tags.

"Have a nice trip, feisty one," he said, with a last glance at Rawyia.

She ignored him. "Follow me, La. We're entering the security zone."

Grinning, I hurried behind her.

She turned around with a smile. "Are you happy now?"

I nodded, wanting to explode in one long scream of jubilation. No longer was I afraid. I trusted Rawyia and was certain she was in control, that nothing would go wrong.

"I'm happy, too, La. We're almost there. Freedom's shore is getting closer and closer."

We stood in line, holding hands and waiting impatiently while the first-class passengers, mothers with children, and older passengers boarded.

At the gate to the shuttle, the steward took a few minutes inspecting our passports. It was unusual for women to travel alone, and the steward glanced back and forth between our faces and our documents. I stood behind Rawyia, my body touching her back and my knees shaking, until he handed her the passports.

We hurried to the shuttle and took the backseat. Rawyia squeezed my perspiring hand, and we both released a deep breath. Soon, however, I felt my heart aching inside my ribs. In silence, I mourned for the people and places I was leaving behind. Then, in a moment of doubt, the idea of our new life scared me. But one look at Rawyia, and I relaxed. She was all I needed. She would help me through this.

Finally, we exited the shuttle and climbed the stairway into the airplane. We found our seats in the back and collapsed into them. I claimed the window seat. The bright Cairo sun shone upon us. The aroma of food warming up in the kitchen cabin behind us awakened my appetite.

The flight attendant, a young woman in a navy blue uniform, her short hair neatly coiffed under a beret, stopped and pleasantly asked me to fasten my seat belt. Rawyia, the experienced one, had already buckled hers. It reassured me that all other passengers calmly took their places without paying any attention to us.

Rawyia and I smiled triumphantly at each other. She guided my head to her shoulder. The airplane doors locked shut. The engines raced, and so did my heart. Beside me, I heard my sister's voice reciting the opening verse from the Quran. It reassured me, and I relaxed, drifting into sleep.

A voice announced our approach into the Beirut airport. Full of excitement, I peered through the small window. White clouds floated under the blue sky and above tall mountains dressed in veils of white. I looked at Rawyia in disbelief.

"That's snow," she said.

"I didn't know Lebanon had mountains."

"Yes, La, it has everything! There are mountains for skiing, the Mediterranean for swimming . . ."

She rattled off the attractions waiting for us in our new homeland. Full of joy, fear, and homesickness, I could barely comprehend what she said.

"It's all waiting for you to enjoy, without fear of Reda, Ahmed, or Papa." Rawyia's face was illuminated by the sunlight streaming through our tiny window.

We were truly free!

Though I still mourned the loss of Ghassan and ached with sadness at having left behind Mama and the rest of our beloved female relatives, my sense of liberty, so long denied me, and overpowered my other emotions. I had been in search of this freedom for what seemed like a lifetime. With Rawyia by my side, I had managed to find it.

I gazed down again at the snowcapped mountains below

us. So this would be our new home. Once more, I turned to my sister. It had been a tremendous journey, and she had guided me through it all. Without her, I would still be trapped in a loveless marriage, or worse. It was she who had opened doors and helped me develop into the person I would eventually become—confident, trusting, loving, and, most of all, assured that I could fulfill my dreams. I squeezed her hand and thanked God for the protection and aid my sister had always, without fail, given me.

"I love you, Rawyia," I whispered.

EPILOGUE

More than three decades have passed since the day
I landed in Lebanon with my sister, and much has
happened in the meantime. I lived in Lebanon for
a little more than two years and then immigrated
to Canada. After the death of Marwan, Rawyia returned to
Alexandria, pregnant and alone. I eventually moved to the
United States. I am now married, live in Fremont, California,
and have two grown children. Rawyia lost her only child, a son.
But that is for another story.

Now she is in the hospital. She is in her early fifties, too
young to die, but cancer has invaded her liver. I call her regularly to ask how she's doing.

"La, is this . . . you? I am fine . . . now," she says, but her
voice is weak and she pauses after each word to breathe. "It's
your voice that keeps me hanging onto this life, even though I
cannot wait to be with my son."

"Your words are scaring me, Rawyia. I will come to see you,"
I pledge.

She begs me not to come, to wait until she's out of the hospital.

Although I want to get on the next flight to Egypt, she makes me promise to wait.

"Listen carefully. I need to tell you something," she said to me during one of these calls.

I tried to suppress my sobbing but could not.

"Don't cry, La. I'll be fine. You're still the same, emotional as ever." Her voice softened to a whisper. "Do you remember Ghassan?"

My heart raced vigorously. Ghassan's name still had a profound emotional effect on me. I realized now, in this moment, that I still loved him. But I was unwilling to share Rawyia's telephone time with anyone, even if doing so would get me news about Ghassan.

"Yes, of course," I said, even though I was startled to hear that name after so many years and couldn't imagine why she had brought it up.

"He never married another girl. He lost his life in a car crash, with two of his friends, before I joined you in Cairo."

Shock overcame me and strangled my voice. My eyes flooded with tears. The receiver dropped to the floor. I picked it up and struggled to sound normal. Rawyia's suffering tormented me, and I didn't want her to stress herself over my emotional devastation. I tried to say something to assure her I was composed, but I felt weak in the knees. I leaned on the wall behind me to steady myself.

"Please forgive me," she said, and each word was a struggle for her. "Back then, you were young and starting a new life. I thought the truth would have devastated you, so I chose to tell you what I thought would be less painful. I only wanted to protect you, La. Please forgive me."

My heart fluttered and raced so much, I feared she might hear my troubled heartbeat. I stayed planted in my place like the stones of the Sphinx. I still could not speak. Her words were daggers plunging into my heart over and over. I attempted to smother my pain, but it was difficult. I had just learned Ghassan had died, and Rawyia was fighting the deadly cancer eating her liver.

The ground under my feet caved in. I lost my balance, all the time controlling my breathing to spare Rawyia any suffering. My head hurt. I attempted to suffocate the pain and squeeze my forehead hard. I was alone at home. My boys were in school, my husband at work. I needed a drink of water.

Rawyia's feeble voice echoed again in the receiver and grounded me in place. "I need to hear it now, before I die. I am dying, La. I have cancer in my liver."

I was choked up, but I somehow managed to get the words out. "I forgive you, Rawyia."

"One more request, La. Teach your sons to respect women." Her voice was weak but still had the big-sister advisory effect I was used to.

I heard her breathing on the other end of the line, and I tried to find the words to tell her how much I loved her, how I appreciated everything she had done for me, to tell her to say hello to our beloved mother, who had died before I had a chance to see her again, but suddenly I heard another voice on the line.

"Your sister has taken her last breath," the nurse said. "She had a smile on her lips."

I collapsed in tears, unable to bear the fact that my Rawyia was gone and still reeling from the truth about Ghassan. For a moment, I wished she had not told me about Ghassan. Grief tore at my heart. I had lost Mama, Rawyia, and now Ghassan. Each took a part of me to his or her grave.

Rawyia wanted me to forget about Ghassan. She urged me not to mourn him for the rest of my life. She didn't want me to feel tied forever to the memory of a perfect lover. If I believed he had betrayed me and gotten married to someone else, I would hate him and would never think of him again—that was her thinking, her way of protecting me. But she couldn't go to her death without telling me the truth. On her deathbed, she thought of me, as always.

I share my story with trepidation, for fear of what these revelations will do to my family. And yet I can no longer keep silent about what it was like forty years ago. Women must be free to live out from the shadow of men, to claim the rights that are theirs by their sheer existence.

Laila and her sister.